A Primer of Biblical Hebrew Poetry

An Essential Guide for Reading and Analysis

David Emanuel

ZONDERVAN ACADEMIC

A Primer of Biblical Hebrew Poetry
Copyright © 2025 by David Emanuel

Published by Zondervan, 3950 Sparks Drive SE, Suite 101, Grand Rapids, Michigan, 49546, USA. Zondervan is a registered trademark of The Zondervan Corporation, L.L.C., a wholly owned subsidiary of HarperCollins Christian Publishing, Inc.

Requests for information should be addressed to customercare@harpercollins.com.

Zondervan titles may be purchased in bulk for educational, business, fundraising, or sales promotional use. For information, please email SpecialMarkets@Zondervan.com.

Library of Congress Cataloging-in-Publication Data

Names: Emanuel, David, 1965- author.
Title: A primer of biblical Hebrew poetry : an essential guide for reading and analysis / David Mark Emanuel.
Description: Grand Rapids, Michigan : Zondervan, [2025] | Includes bibliographical references and index.
Identifiers: LCCN 2025004991 | ISBN 9780310165828 (paperback)
Subjects: LCSH: Bible. Old Testament--Poetical books--Criticism, interpretation, etc.
Classification: LCC BS1405.52 .E43 2025 | DDC 221.6--dc23/eng/20250416
LC record available at https://lccn.loc.gov/2025004991

All Scripture quotations unless otherwise noted are the author's own translation.

Scripture quotations marked ESV are taken from the ESV® Bible (The Holy Bible, English Standard Version®). Copyright © 2001 by Crossway, a publishing ministry of Good News Publishers. Used by permission. All rights reserved.

Scripture quotations marked NASB from the New American Standard Bible® (NASB). Copyright © 1960, 1962, 1963, 1968, 1971, 1972, 1973, 1975, 1977, 1995 by The Lockman Foundation. Used by permission. www.lockman.org

Any internet addresses (websites, blogs, etc.) and telephone numbers in this book are offered as a resource. They are not intended in any way to be or imply an endorsement by Zondervan, nor does Zondervan vouch for the content of these sites and numbers for the life of this book.

All rights reserved. No part of this publication may be reproduced, stored in a retrieval system, or transmitted in any form or by any means—electronic, mechanical, photocopy, recording, or any other—except for brief quotations in printed reviews, without the prior permission of the publisher.

Without limiting the exclusive rights of any author, contributor or the publisher of this publication, any unauthorized use of this publication to train generative artificial intelligence (AI) technologies is expressly prohibited. HarperCollins also exercise their rights under Article 4(3) of the Digital Single Market Directive 2019/790 and expressly reserve this publication from the text and data mining exception.

HarperCollins Publishers, Macken House, 39/40 Mayor Street Upper, Dublin 1, D01 C9W8, Ireland (https://www.harpercollins.com)

Cover design: Tammy Johnson
Cover photo: Courtesy of The Leon Levy Dead Sea Scrolls Digital Library; Israel Antiquities Authority, photo: Shai Halevi
Interior design: Kait Lamphere

David Emanuel has distilled a career's worth of inquiry into a single volume, masterfully pulling together the many threads of method and technique that inhabit the poetry of the Hebrew Bible. Emanuel asks not simply "what," but "how" and "why," offering young exegetes the tools they need to explore, analyze, and be amazed by the beauty that is biblical poetry. The student is left with an expert and compelling guide to the most difficult, most captivating, and most delightful genre to be found in the Old Testament.

—**Sandra L. Richter**, Robert H. Gundry Chair of Biblical Studies, Westmont College

In this comprehensive yet accessible volume, David Emanuel lays out the formal elements of ancient Hebrew verse and demonstrates how they help readers uncover meaning, notice crucial themes, and identify boundaries between literary units. He also provides a readable overview of the distinctive word-choice and grammar employed by ancient Israelite poets—something other volumes on biblical poetry neglect. This volume will be useful to serious readers of the Bible, to intermediate and advanced students of Hebrew, and (I can attest) even to scholars. Emanuel's attention to linguistic markers of biblical poetry and his emphasis on functions formal features play make this volume especially welcome.

—**Benjamin Sommer**, Professor of Bible and Ancient Semitic Languages, The Jewish Theological Seminary

This helpful overview of Hebrew poetry with worked examples will prove a useful guide to students learning their Hebraic ropes. It is the kind of "primer" to which I will be pointing my students.

—**Jonathan Gibson**, Professor of Biblical and Systematic Theology, Westminster Theological Seminary

This fine book will be beneficial for students looking to move on from basic grammar acquisition and as a resource on the shelf of more advanced readers of Hebrew. I commend it for being lucidly thorough yet without being exhaustive (or exhausting!).

—**Helen Paynter**, Founding Director, Centre for the Study of Bible and Violence, Bristol Baptist College

An ideal guide to learn the ins and outs of biblical Hebrew poetry, David Emanuel's book stands apart by its straightforward explanation of the array of poetic functions in Scripture. If you are a student or minister of the word, this book presents reliable insight that works. Instead of dry and strained theories, Emanuel offers an abundance of biblical examples. Emanuel's primer gives us what we need and makes Hebrew poetry fun again.

—**Gary Edward Schnittjer**, Distinguished Professor of Old Testament,
Cairn University

Teaching students how to interpret and find meaning in biblical Hebrew poetry is challenging. In this book, Dr. David Emanuel weaves poetic forms, techniques, functions, morphology, purposes, and interpretive methods together to help readers discover meaning within poetic literature. Both professors and students will benefit from engaging with his writing.

—**Alaine Buchanan**, Dean, Graduate School and
Associate Professor of Bible and Theology,
North Central University

A Primer of Biblical Hebrew Poetry is a most welcome volume in the field of Hebrew poetry. The intermediate Hebrew student will benefit greatly from Emanuel's clear explanations and ample examples, while the established scholar will appreciate Emanuel's consistent engagement with recent scholarship. Whether as an introduction in the classroom or a resource on the shelf, this volume deserves wide use.

—**W. Dennis Tucker, Jr.**, Professor of Christian Scriptures,
George W. Truett Theological Seminary, Baylor University

As a biblical Hebrew teacher, it is easy to focus on narrative at the expense of poetry. This book provides the interpreter with the analytical tools necessary for analyzing Hebrew poetry in its many forms and settings. It is a must-have for both beginners and experts alike, and I look forward to using it in the classroom.

—**David Moster**, Director of the Biblical Hebrew Certificate Program,
The Jewish Theological Seminary

With a sensitive eye to both architecture and interior design, David Emanuel takes readers on a tour of the foundations, structure, techniques, and furnishings of biblical Hebrew poetic texts. More than describing and illustrating morphological and syntactical features as well as poetic structures and techniques, Emanuel offers methodological guidelines and a worked example of poetic analysis. His clear discussions and numerous examples dispel the mystery of Hebrew poetics while retaining the wonder of Hebrew poetry. For anyone interested in the function of poetic forms and their contributions to meaning, this primer is an indispensable guide.

—**Christopher B. Ansberry**, Associate Professor of Biblical and Theological Studies, Grove City College

In this primer, David Emanuel masterfully guides readers on a journey to understand not only the foundational mechanics of Hebrew poetry—ranging from parallelism, to allusion, to morphology—but also the beautiful ways poetry contributes to the meaning of the biblical text.

—**Rebecca W. Poe Hays**, Associate Professor of Christian Scriptures, George W. Truett Theological Seminary, Baylor University

Countless Hebrew students have seen their growing aptitude in the language come to a sudden halt as they venture from narrative into poetry. With *A Primer of Biblical Hebrew Poetry*, David Emanuel offers an extraordinary resource for overcoming the challenges these texts present and for fully appreciating the intricate beauty of their poetic form. Students and scholars alike will benefit from this remarkable guide.

—**Jeffery Leonard**, Professor of Biblical Studies, Samford University

Contents

Abbreviations xi
Introduction xv

Part 1: Laying the Foundation

1. **Introductory Matters** 3
   - 1.1 Emphatic Structures 4
   - 1.2 Text Presentation 6
   - 1.3 Overall Organization 7
   - 1.4 What Is Poetry? 10
   - 1.5 Where Is Poetry? 12
   - 1.6 Poetic Units 13

Part 2: Lexical Building Blocks

2. **Masoretic, Syntactic, Lexical, and Morphological Features of Poetry** 21
   - 2.1 Masoretic Divisions 21
   - 2.2 Syntactic Features 25
   - 2.3 Lexical Features 28
   - 2.4 Morphological Features 31

Part 3: Structural Poetics

3. Parallelisms 39
   - 3.1 Word Pairs 41
   - 3.2 Synonymous Parallelism 44
   - 3.3 Internal Half-Line Parallelism 50
   - 3.4 Tricola Examples 52
   - 3.5 Distant Parallelism 54
   - 3.6 Grammatical Parallelism (Synonymous) 57
   - 3.7 Ballast Variants 59
   - 3.8 Phonological Parallelism 61
   - 3.9 Emblematic Parallelism 63

4. Pivoting Patterns 65
   - 4.1 Chiasmus 65
   - 4.2 Tricola Chiasmus 69
   - 4.3 Functions of Chiasmus 70
   - 4.4 Terraced Pattern 81
   - 4.5 Staircase Parallelism 83
   - 4.6 Janus Parallelism 85

5. Enveloping Structures 88
   - 5.1 Envelope Figure 88
   - 5.2 Refrain 90
   - 5.3 Chorus 93
   - 5.4 Inclusion 94

6. Additional Cola Relationships 100
   - 6.1 Antithetical Parallelism 100
   - 6.2 Other Relationships 102
   - 6.3 Acrostics 107
   - 6.4 Enjambment 112

Part 4: Poetic Technique

7. **Basic Imagery**... 117
   - 7.1 Imagery... 117
   - 7.2 Metaphor 119
   - 7.3 Simile.. 124
   - 7.4 Hypocatastasis..................................... 126
   - 7.5 Metonymy 127
   - 7.6 Synecdoche.. 129
   - 7.7 Personification.................................... 130
   - 7.8 Anthropomorphism................................ 133
   - 7.9 Anthropopathism 136
   - 7.10 Hyperbole... 137

8. **Playing with Words** 140
   - 8.1 Paronomasia....................................... 140
   - 8.2 Alliteration.. 144
   - 8.3 Rhyme... 146
   - 8.4 Anadiplosis.. 149
   - 8.5 Proper Noun Wordplays 150
   - 8.6 Irony 153

9. **Assorted Techniques** 159
   - 9.1 Merismus 159
   - 9.2 Delayed Identification 164
   - 9.3 Hendiadys... 166
   - 9.4 Rhetorical Question................................ 170
   - 9.5 Oxymoron 175
   - 9.6 Apostrophe.. 176
   - 9.7 Epanalepsis.. 178
   - 9.8 Repetition... 179
   - 9.9 Biblical Allusion 182

Part 5: Putting It All Together

10. Guidelines for Poetic Analysis 193
    10.1 Text Selection............................... 196
    10.2 Reading the Text............................ 197
    10.3 Initial Translation........................... 198
    10.4 Concordance Work..........................200
    10.5 Initial Stanza Division 201
    10.6 Structural Features 202
    10.7 Poetics......................................203
    10.8 Revision 203
    10.9 Big Picture 204
    10.10 Textual Associations..........................206
    10.11 Commentary Consultation....................207

11. A Worked Example..................................209
    11.1 Structure.................................... 211
    11.2 Poetic Analysis of Psalm 54................... 214
    11.3 Final Thoughts 230

Appendix 1: Meter.......................................233
Appendix 2: Wisdom Poetry 236
Bibliography... 241
Scripture Index 251
Subject Index 259
Author Index 265

Abbreviations

General

11QPs^a	Psalms scroll^a
AB	The Anchor Bible
ABD	*Anchor Bible Dictionary*. Edited by David Noel Freedman. 6 vols. New York: Doubleday, 1992
AJSL	*The American Journal of Semitic Languages and Literatures*
BASOR	*Bulletin of the American Schools of Oriental Research*
BDB	Brown, Francis, S. R. Driver, and Charles A. Briggs. *A Hebrew and English Lexicon of the Old Testament*. Peabody, MA: Hendrickson, 1994
BHS	*Biblia Hebraica Stuttgartensia*. Edited by Karl Elliger and Wilhelm Rudolph. Stuttgart: Deutsche Bibelgesellschaft, 1983
Bib	*Biblica*
BSOAS	*Bulletin of the School of Oriental and African Studies*
CBQ	*Catholic Biblical Quarterly*
ESV	English Standard Version
EV	English Version
GKC	*Gesenius' Hebrew Grammar*. Edited by Emil Kautzsch. Translated by Arther E. Cowley. 2nd ed. Oxford: Clarendon, 1910
HALOT	*The Hebrew and Aramaic Lexicon of the Old Testament*. Ludwig Koehler, Walter Baumgartner, and Johann J. Stamm. Translated and edited under the supervision of Mervyn E. J. Richardson. 4 vols. Leiden: Brill, 1994–1999

HS	*Hebrew Studies*
HUCA	*Hebrew Union College Annual*
JAOS	*Journal of the American Oriental Society*
JBL	*Journal of Biblical Literature*
JBQ	*Jewish Bible Quarterly*
JHS	*Journal of Hebrew Scriptures*
Joüon	Joüon, Paul. *A Grammar of Biblical Hebrew.* Translated and revised by T. Muraoka. 2 vols. Rome: Pontifical Biblical Institute, 1991
JQR	*Jewish Quarterly Review*
JQRSup	Jewish Quarterly Review Supplement
JR	*Journal of Religion*
JSOT	*Journal for the Study of the Old Testament*
JSOTSup	Journal for the Study of the Old Testament Supplement Series
JSQ	*Jewish Studies Quarterly*
JSS	*Journal of Semitic Studies*
KJV	King James Version
LHBOTS	The Library of Hebrew Bible/Old Testament Studies
LSAWS	Linguistic Studies in Ancient West Semitic
LXX	Septuagint (Translation of the Seventy)
MT	Masoretic Text
NASB	New American Standard Bible, 1995
NIDB	*New Interpreter's Dictionary of the Bible.* Edited by Katharine Doob Sakenfeld. 5 vols. Nashville: Abingdon 2006–2009
NIV	New International Version
Orient	*Orient: Report of the Society for Near Eastern Studies in Japan*
SBL	Society of Biblical Literature
ScrHier	*Scripta Hierosolymitana*
SJOT	*Scandanavian Journal of the Old Testament*
Tg	Targum
TynBul	*Tyndale Bulletin*
UF	*Ugarit-Forschungen*
VT	*Vetus Testamentum*
WBC	Word Biblical Commentary
ZAW	*Zeitschrift für die alttestamentliche Wissenschaft*

Grammar/Syntax[1]

acc.	accusative
adj.	adjective
conj.	conjunction
const.	construct form
def.	definite
impf.	imperfect
impv.	imperative
m.	masculine
n.	noun
neg.part.	negative particle
n.phr.	noun phrase
obj.	object
pf.	perfect
pl.	plural
poss.	possessive
prep.	preposition
prep.phr.	prepositional phrase
prop.n.	proper noun
ptc.	participle
sg.	singular
subj.	subject
suf.	suffix
v.	verb
1cp	first person, common, plural
1cs	first person, common, singular
3mp	third person, masculine, plural
2ms	second person, masculine, singular
3ms	third person, masculine, singular

---

1. These are predominantly reserved for schematic representations.

Introduction

The Purpose of the Book

In recent years, scholars from various disciplines have invested considerable time and effort into analyzing and describing Hebrew poetry. This has led to a more thorough discussion of key observations and the proposal of new theories addressing diverse aspects of biblical poetic forms and techniques. Notably, several scholars have focused on producing comprehensive and practical guides to Hebrew poetry.[1] Given this scholarly activity, one might question the necessity of *yet another* volume on Hebrew poetry and ask what distinguishes this, the present volume, from those currently available in academic circles. Despite the considerable body of literature that attempts to untangle the web of biblical poetry, certain lacunae persist within this vital area of biblical studies. The present volume endeavors to contribute modestly toward filling such apertures and enhancing the resources available for the study of biblical poetry.

---

1. Numerous excellent books have been written over the years covering various aspects of poetry. It is not practical at this stage to provide an exhaustive list and discussion of every book, monograph, and article on the topic. However, some of the more prominent and accessible books deserve mention: Goh, *Hebrew Poetry* (which offers another overview of poetry in the Bible, as its title suggests, although lacking slightly in its depth on verse structures and linguist features of the language); Lunn, *Word-Order Variation* (who provides a detailed analysis and discussion of Hebrew poetry's unique word order); and Schökel, *A Manual* (who provides an overall coverage of Hebrew poetry although devoting considerably less time and attention to structural features); Watson, *Classical Hebrew Poetry* (whose taxonomic approach constitutes the most comprehensive book on Hebrew poetry to date and, in many ways, has inspired me to write the present volume; though his inclusion of comparative material—Akkadian, and Ugaritic especially—although important for more advanced scholars, proves a hindrance for those students in the earlier stages of their studies); Watson also has a companion volume, *Traditional Techniques*. Other volumes that discuss selected aspects of poetry, without intending to be a broad description of the language include, Alter, *Biblical Poetry*; James, *Invitation to Biblical Poetry*; and Collins, *Line-Forms in Hebrew Poetry*.

In addition to presenting and discussing poetic techniques, the present volume extends the learning boundaries just a little bit further to force students and young exegetes to think about the *function* of the poetic forms that appear in the Hebrew Bible. One of the goals of the present volume is specifically to encourage readers to not only identify the various poetic techniques employed by Hebrew poets but also to begin understanding how the ancient poets employed these features to convey and develop meaning in the compositions in which they appear. This approach asserts that merely identifying poetic forms fails to satisfy the requirements of responsible exegesis, and an essential stage in the analytical process involves determining how and why specific forms were used and why they appear at specific junctures in a poetic unit. Currently, many of the important articles and books on Hebrew poetry remain dedicated to describing a limited range of poetic forms and aid in identifying the forms as they appear in the Bible. One of the crucial aspects lacking, however, relates to a deeper discussion concerning how the various poetic forms contribute to meaning. The discussion and description of basic parallelism between cola can serve as an example. Its identification and detailed description—is it syntactic or semantic, is it gender matched, is there ellipsis, etc.—are necessary for poetic analysis. However, this discussion only constitutes part of the exegetical process. Further analysis must be made to understand *how* that parallelism functions within the larger poetic segments. Is it creating a point of emphasis; does it continue a sequence of an already established rhythm; is it a vehicle for another poetic form; etc.? Merely identifying the form is not enough for responsible exegesis, and the need arises for further investigation into the function of poetic forms. Although the present volume does not claim to provide all the answers, it serves as a conduit leading students further into that crucial line of discovery.[2]

Another important aspect of Hebrew poetry that fails to receive adequate representation in the study of Hebrew poetics concerns the numerous variations found in the morphology and lexical forms of biblical poetic texts.

---

2. The emphasis on function has been neglected by scholars in the field of Hebrew poetry. However, writers such as Ernst Wendland serve as exceptions to the rule. Wendland emphasizes that "it is not enough simply to recognize their [i.e., the poetic features'] presence in the text, one must also look to see how these devices interact with one another to perform a given communicative purpose or set of purposes in the discourse" (*Analyzing the Psalms*, 171).

Typically, this information remains buried within the Hebrew grammars, such as Paul Joüon and T. Muraoka's *Grammar of Biblical Hebrew*; *Gesenius' Hebrew Grammar*; and Bruce Waltke and M. O'Connor's *Biblical Hebrew Syntax*. As a result, important attributes of Hebrew poetics remain hidden from many students because those aspects generally fail to appear in second-year Hebrew intermediate grammars. As an example, Robert Chisholm's practical work, *From Exegesis to Exposition*, lacks an entry in his section on Hebrew poetry that describes the unique morphology or vocabulary appearing within this genre. Even Wilfred G. E. Watson's excellent and detailed taxonomic *Classical Hebrew Poetry: A Guide to Its Techniques* omits, for the most part, discussions on the unusual poetic morphology that appears in the Hebrew Bible. The current volume attempts to address this unfortunate deficiency by presenting a discussion on the morphological variations that appear in and are associated with poetic texts.

Overall, it has become abundantly clear that a single volume drawing the strands of biblical Hebrew poetry's techniques and methods into a single thread is desperately needed by students and professors alike. Without such a resource, instructors and learners remain disadvantaged in the field of biblical studies. Students, particularly, remain condemned to plow through multiple volumes of dense and overly verbose literature to glean the gems of poetic technique. It is my hope that the present volume proffers a degree of relief for new students seeking to enter the world of Hebrew poetry.

The present volume additionally serves as an all-important bridge between foundational biblical Hebrew and interpreting Hebrew poetry. To date, an incredible range of introductory Hebrew grammars exists, escorting students on their journey from knowing nothing about the language to gaining a sound understanding of the fundamental elements of Hebrew. These grammars vary in length, method, and complexity. Turning to one of the more technical grammars, Thomas O. Lambdin's *Introduction to Biblical Hebrew*, we find that Lambdin engages in detailed and comprehensive discussions on various aspects of philology and morphology. He also supplements his introduction with numerous excellent examples and exercises for translation—both Hebrew to English and English to Hebrew. However, just about all the passages he employs to exemplify Hebrew texts originate from the corpus of biblical Hebrew narrative, focusing on varying levels of complexity within this genre. After completing a course using this textbook, students are well capable of reading and translating narrative texts from across the Old Testament. Having studied and mastered Lambdin's grammar, students will undoubtedly acquire all the necessary tools to dissect just about all the unusual verb and noun forms they are likely to encounter in their further exegetical work. My contention, however, is that introductory grammars like this, even the technical ones, fail to provide an adequate springboard to launch students firmly into the world of biblical poetry. A transitional resource is lacking, a bridge that students can traverse to ease them into the unique challenges they will face when trying to understand poetic texts in all their various guises. The present volume has been written to provide such a pathway that can help students bridge the gap between the knowledge they have acquired from an introductory Hebrew grammar and the knowledge they need to cope with the intricacies and nuances of Hebrew poetry.

Few things are more frustrating than waking up hungry in the middle of the night, walking downstairs, opening the fridge door, and finding nothing readily available to eat. Similarly, opening a written resource and not finding the information for which you hunger can generate insufferable levels of frustration and disappointment—as the proverb reminds us, "hope deferred makes the heart sick" (Prov 13:12a). Consequently, I am compelled to offer a few words concerning the limitations of the present primer.

Not every poetic feature known and applicable to English poetry, or even biblical Hebrew, has been included in the present volume; consequently, this current primer is not exhaustive. Those with a general familiarity with poetry—Greek, Latin, or English, for example—will notice the absence of techniques such as polyptoton and metalepsis from the present volume. The primary reasons for omitting such entries stem from a desire to limit the volume's size, and therefore manageability, and to reduce the level of the book's complexity, enabling it to constitute an accessible resource. This book is intended to be a primer, a place where students, and others who are interested, can secure a foothold into the world of Hebrew poetics. It fails to function as an exhaustive reference to every poetic feature in the Hebrew Bible.[3] The present volume was written under a looming cloud of fear that

---

3. For a more detailed reference, students are directed to Bullinger, *Figures of Speech*.

I would end up contributing toward a problem I had hoped to resolve; that is, instead of elucidating the beauty of Hebrew poetry, I would be bogging the reader down in a quagmire of nuanced, detailed, and obscure classifications that would ultimately hinder their initial grasp and analysis of a poetic text. Consequently, some readers may find certain discussions of some of the poetic features a little more succinct than desired. To help compensate for this, I have attempted via footnotes and bibliographic entries to point interested readers toward further information on specific topics.

Extended Metaphors

As I attempt to present and illustrate the various intricacies of Hebrew poetry, throughout this book I draw upon two extended metaphors to aid in the elucidation. The first is that of an extended journey, such as a road trip extending across the United States. The destination, where you are going to stay, represents the highlight or the most important part of the vacation. However, along the way, it is likely that you would stop at various locations to see certain sites and experience exquisite views. Some locations along the way are visited briefly. Other locations, however, require more time to appreciate, possibly necessitating an extended stay at a particular location for an extra night to appreciate fully all an area has to offer. Journeying through a psalm or a piece of poetry works in much the same way. There is a starting point and a destination—the end of the poetic unit—in addition to sub-destinations, such as the end of a stanza. As you traverse the text, certain literary markers indicate that the reader should slow down, dwelling briefly on a thought or an idea, and there are even places where poets almost seem to stop, and instead of moving forward they choose to dwell on an image or a theme. Noticing this journey-like movement through poetic texts is crucial to understanding the poet's mindset and how he has chosen to organize his composition.

The second metaphor is that of house construction, because Hebrew poetic texts are composed and created in a similar fashion to houses. First, land is cleared and a foundation is excavated and laid. The wooden framework of the overall house structure is then set on the foundation.

This framework is then modified to include doorframes, steps, individual rooms, and a roof. After this, walls are erected, and the electricity, water, and gas supplies are fitted. Then the house is decorated and furnished. Hebrew poetry reflects a similar constructional organization. Certain aspects of biblical poetry are foundational, essential, and without them poetry cannot exist. Other elements constitute more of a framework for a poetic piece, providing an overall structure built on top of the foundation. Then there are further elements that can be seen almost as accessories, nonessential elements that are inserted to add a degree of color and life to the overall composition. Hopefully, describing Hebrew poetic texts in terms of the metaphors outlined above will facilitate a more lucid explanation of how the various poetic categories dovetail to create engaging and reflective Hebrew poetry.

PART 1

Laying the Foundation

1

Introductory Matters

When it comes to interpreting and analyzing poetry, a few observations merit attention concerning the issue of subjectivity, or to put it another way, how many of the perceived poetic features uncovered in a poetic text were intended by an author? The question of authorial intent is important and deserves consideration even if it cannot be answered conclusively. To illustrate the point, we can adopt an example from the world of visual art, Rembrandt's famous painting *The Night Watch*. If a viewer claimed to see an image of a Boeing 747 in the top left quadrant of the painting, how much weight or credence can we place on such a claim, and is it worth mentioning in a critical report on the painting? How important or relevant would such an observation be to a critical analysis? Since the artwork was completed in 1642, it is highly unlikely that the artist inserted a jet plane into his visual composition. And yet, as this contemporary viewer gazes at the picture, for him or her at least, it is there, staring at them in the face, even to the point that they can trace its outline. In their analytical presentation of the painting, is it worth even mentioning, or is it totally irrelevant because the painter did not purposefully include it? The same dilemma surfaces regarding how Hebrew poetry is read, analyzed, and discussed. After reading and studying an excerpt of poetry, what features should be raised and discussed in a term paper, essay, or article? How valid is it for a reader to wander into the realms of reader-response criticism, where any interpretation or poetic feature seen by the reader is valid, even if it stems purely from their imagination and not as part of the deliberate composition process of the original author?

To present a more realistic case, as part of my assessment process while teaching a class on the Psalms, I requested that students write a psalm of their own, utilizing the same poetic techniques they had learned—many of the features discussed in the present volume. After writing their personal compositions, they had to present their psalm to the class, reading it aloud and explaining the thought processes that lay behind their personal psalms. This was an exercise to help students internalize, understand, and apply what they had learned in class that semester. One student presented a wonderful psalm that recorded the death of Jesus on the cross. As part of their presentation, they elaborated on one line that caught my attention. It stated that as Jesus gave up his spirit and passed from life to death, the son went down on the cross. When I heard this, my heart leapt, as I praised the student for an excellent rendition of paronomasia, playing on the idea that when Jesus died, both the son went down from life to death—her original and unfortunately sole intention—and the sun went down, because there was darkness over the face of the land at the same time Jesus died. Unfortunately, the student had no idea of the dual meaning that presented itself so obviously to me, playing on the homophones "son" and "sun." I had identified a poetic form in their work that they had no idea even existed! Was my revelation of this feature justified and valid, even though they had no knowledge of it at all?

Every student and scholar engaging in the analysis of Hebrew poetry will encounter this conundrum, and no singular or perfect method or system of analysis exists for resolving it. My personal hermeneutic is that as exegetes analyze poetry in the Bible, it is important to respect, where possible, the author's original intention. However, considering my personal experience teaching the Psalms, I know—and I am sure that most interpreters are also painfully aware—that this is not always possible to discern. Nevertheless, the fact that we cannot always determine and outline a biblical author's thought processes when he wrote a composition should not deter us from striving, with humility, to establish the intentions and mindset of the ancient poets.[1]

1.1 Emphatic Structures

In an ideal world, when a poet or storyteller recites a composed piece of poetry or a historic legend, at certain points during the recitation they may

---

1. See also Freedman, "Pottery, Poetry and Prophecy," 12, for his discussion on this issue.

raise their voice, or pause, or speak with a particular tone to emphasize a crucial part of the recited piece. They also have the luxury of including specific facial expressions—a smile, frown, or wink—to help convey to the audience a specific nuanced understanding. Such expressions and intonations may additionally reflect what Muraoka calls an "overflow and discharge of inner intensified emotion."[2] Biblical Hebrew poetry, as we have received it, remains on written media, consequently, the writers needed alternative ways to express important and emphatic parts of their compositions. Primarily, such emphasis surfaces in their variegated deployment of Hebrew poetics. That said, they failed to leave with us any fixed and indisputable rules concerning how they sought to achieve levels of emphasis. Consequently, determining whether a specific poetic feature equates to an emphatic form remains an elusive task.

One needs to exercise extreme caution when it comes to understanding how the various poetic features are used. Therefore, in the present volume, when certain poetic features are labeled as emphatic forms, it does not necessarily suggest that emphasis constitutes their only function, or that whenever the form appears, it serves to accentuate a particular part of the psalm or belabor a point. As an example, a poet may adopt a semantic chiasmus to generate a degree of emphasis, especially if he uses chiasmus sparingly in a composition. However, just because it appears with this function in one composition, we cannot automatically assume that every instance of chiasmus equates to an attempt by an author to achieve emphasis. When attempting to identify emphasis in a biblical text, therefore, it is important for the exegete to amass additional evidence to support the claim.[3] The assertion that certain poetic forms or features in biblical Hebrew are always emphatic is perhaps overstated in the literature. Consequently, careful thought must be applied before arriving at such a conclusion.[4]

---

2. *Emphatic Words*, 14.

3. Emphasis can, theoretically, be generated from phonetic, morphological, syntactic, prosaic, and lexical elements. However, the present discussion primarily focuses on stylistic instances. Even though Muraoka's work on emphatic words in Hebrew focuses on prose rather than poetry, he raises the probability of certain words bearing an emphatic nuance in poetry. Some of the more prominent elements he mentions are the emphatic use of לֹא (Job 8:12; 14:16; 16:7; 23:17; and 33:14); אַף (Pss 58:12; 62:2; 68:22; 73:1; 85:10; and 140:14); and the climactic use of גַּם (Job 21:7; Ps 107:5; and 137:1). See Muraoka, *Emphatic Words*, 123, 130, and 161 respectively. The important point to remember is that lexical elements may signal emphasis in poetic texts.

4. Muraoka expresses this sentiment well when he says, "A perusal of the literature . . . has made it quite clear that the term 'emphasis' is often too rashly called in, like the pinch-hitter in a baseball game, without much thought being given to precisely what is meant by the term" (*Emphatic Words*, 11).

1.2 Text Presentation

The primary means for presenting biblical verses in the present volume derives from the Masoretic disjunctive markers that divide texts into verses and cola.[5] For the most part, this means verses are divided into two lines according to the *atnakh* and are thus labeled accordingly—"A" refers to the first half of the verse, and "B" refers to the second. However, regarding Psalms, Proverbs, and Job, the verse may be divided into three sections on account of their alternate methods for primary division. Thus, cola may be labeled with an "A," "B," or "C." That said, it is also important to keep in mind that the original Hebrew texts, as written by authors from the biblical period, did not include the current, or any, written system of cantillation symbols. The biblical Hebrew poetry as discovered in the library at Qumran, such as the Psalms Scroll 11QPs[a] (see Fig. 1), demonstrates that poetry was originally unmarked and preserved the consonantal tradition only.

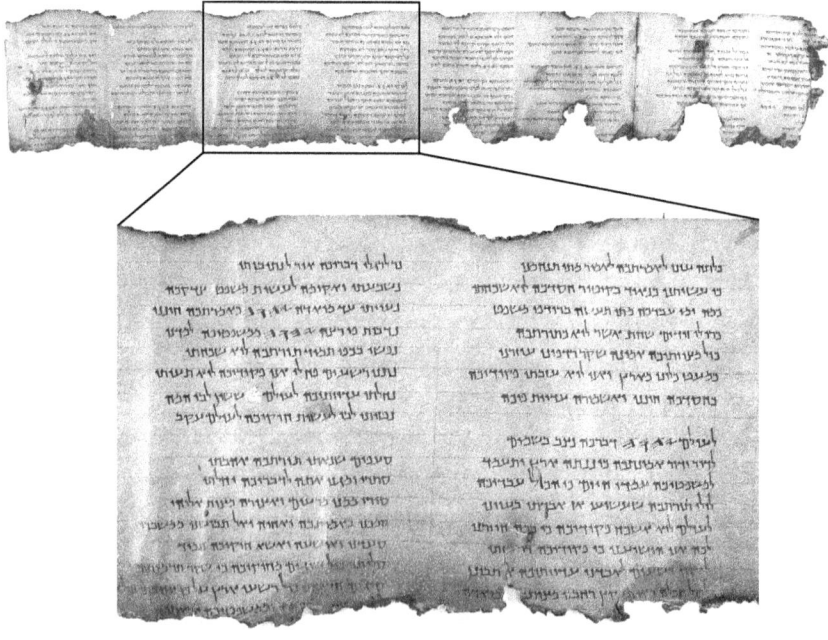

FIGURE 1: THE GREAT PSALMS SCROLL, 11Q5 (11QPs[a])
Courtesy of The Leon Levy Dead Sea Scrolls Digital Library;
Israel Antiquities Authority, photo: Shai Halevi

---

5. For a detailed discussion, see the explanation of the cola division system in the MT below.

Because the current volume serves as a primer for Hebrew poetry, the primary focus for presenting and discussing the examples is on the Hebrew text, as opposed to the English translations. Frequently, as one would expect, poetic forms employed by the ancient biblical poets are obscured and quite often removed entirely from the English translations. That said, due to the different levels of Hebrew language acquisition among the intended readership of the present volume, English translations are presented and discussed, with their differences to the Hebrew accentuated. For the most part, the English translated texts in the present volume are mine; however, in certain instances, standard English translations have been adopted.[6] To avoid confusion, readers are alerted each time this occurs. Furthermore, on those occasions where the Hebrew versification differs from the English translation, the Hebrew verse reference is placed in brackets after the English reference.

1.3 Overall Organization

The present volume is organized into five parts; after this introduction, part 1, are four parts followed by two appendices. Part 2 lays a foundation through a discussion of the morphological aspects of Hebrew poetry, perhaps the most neglected topic in recent studies on poetry and poetics. In this part, attention focuses on aspects of Hebrew language syntax, morphology, and orthography that surface in Hebrew poetry. Readers can expect to find, amongst other topics, descriptions of what many consider to be poetic suffixes, rare formations of certain prepositions, and the rarer vocabulary that frequently arises in poetry. Part 2 also includes an important discussion of the unique Masoretic cantillation marks responsible for dividing poetic texts into verses and cola. Being able to distinguish and divide verses into cola (also called lines) remains a crucial part of poetic analysis.

Part 3 addresses the structural framework of Hebrew poetic texts, similar to a superstructure or framework of a house, into which poetic "panels" are inserted. There are four chapters in part 3 that vary in length depending on

---

6. Primarily, I have adopted the NASB 1995 as my published EV because it remains one of the more literal and readable of the EVs.

the complexity and rarity of the features they cover. Chapter 3 discusses, with examples, the construction of cola and the relationships between cola within a textual unit. For the most part this relates to the phenomenon commonly known as parallelism, together with other types of repetition and contrast between cola. Additionally, chapter 3 discusses how Hebrew poets organize keywords in the formation of their compositions. Chapter 4 moves on to the topic of pivoting patterns, that is to say structural patterns such as chiasmus that exhibit a literary hinge of some description. The fifth chapter examines enveloping structures, techniques used to isolate individual textual units—verses, stanzas, and larger poetic texts. Finally, the sixth chapter, the last chapter in part 3, discusses various different kinds of poetic structures and cola relationships—the structural features that did not fall neatly into the previous classifications.

Part 4 addresses the higher levels of poetic techniques, the furnishings and trimmings of the overall construction. Like part 3, the subdivisions in this unit vary in length according to the complexity and rarity of each form. Chapter 7 opens part 4 with an examination of basic poetic imagery, such as metaphor and simile, together with the rarer features such as anthropopathism and apostrophe. Following this, chapter 8 explores a variety of techniques that exploit the sound and semantics of individual words. The final chapter in this part of the volume, chapter 9, elucidates a variety of miscellaneous poetic techniques—such as merismus, rhetorical question and oxymoron—that commonly appear in biblical poetry It is important to remember that the poetic features discussed in part 4 do not work independently of the structural features discussed in part 3. Rather, they coalesce with poetic structure to contribute toward the flow and fabric of poetic units.

Part 5 contains two chapters that attempt to draw together the concepts and principles discussed in the previous sections. Chapter 10 proposes a suggested method for synthesizing the information in the earlier parts of the volume into an analytical essay. The chapter's overall objective is to provide the framework for a method and process of how to tackle the analysis of a poetic text. Defining methodology such as this, unfortunately, can never consistently produce perfectly precise exegetical papers. In an ideal world, one could devise a procedure that any student could follow and finish with a perfectly analyzed text every time. Such a utopian methodological process, however, remains in the realms of unicorns and griffins. That said, the chapter still presents fundamental steps that competently guide students from reading a text to analyzing and appreciating its poetic forms and structure.

Chapter 11, the second chapter in part 5, presents an annotated worked example of a poetic analysis and discussion of a psalm. The discussion's purpose is to demonstrate how the method described in the previous section can be applied to a specific text. To focus on the poetic analysis, the worked example refrains from any in-depth engagement with contemporary scholarly views. The primary focus remains on the Hebrew poetry as presented in the Hebrew Bible and how the poet expresses meaning through the poetic techniques discussed in the present volume. Closing chapter 11 are a few final words drawing together the more salient points of the present volume. It is very easy to lose sight of the forest for the trees, and so the purpose of these final words is to remind the reader of the important principles and pitfalls of working with Hebrew poetry.

Two appendices appear at the end of the book, which address topics that readers should be aware of but are not viewed as being important enough to warrant a full discussion in the main sections of the book. The first appendix discusses the question of meter in Hebrew poetry. The present volume does not include the concept of meter in its main discussions, and the main reasons are provided in this appendix. The second appendix tackles the question of wisdom poetry, specifically proverbs and biblical aphorisms. For the most part, the present volume does not distinguish between substrata of Hebrew poetry; however, wisdom poetry possesses a few distinctive features that warrant a brief discussion because second-year grammars, overall, fail to address its unique characteristics. Although the appendices are brief, they alert readers to relevant topics surrounding poetic analysis.

At the end of chapters 3–9 I have included a few questions for consideration. Asking questions during the process of poetic analysis is likely more important than committing ourselves to unsubstantiated answers. The point of these questions is to prime the readers' thinking and provide additional assistance for the analysis of certain poetic techniques and structures. Naturally, the questions are not exhaustive, and the reader should not feel limited to only using these questions to interrogate the biblical texts. The questions are also designed to nudge the reader into the direction of identifying the function of poetic forms as opposed to settling solely for their identification. As mentioned earlier, a crucial motivational factor for the present volume is to remind readers that identification and recognition of poetic forms in the Bible—maintaining sight of the forest—is only the first stage of analysis, and perhaps the most vital (and neglected) stage of understanding a poetic text remains, uncovering how a poet expresses meaning and significance through his chosen poetic forms. Additionally, at the end of each of these chapters readers will find a short list of bibliographic entries that relate to the topics discussed in each chapter.

1.4 What Is Poetry?

An important question that warrants at least a brief discussion is whether Hebrew poetry truly exists. As one surveys the corpus commonly identified as Hebrew narrative—for example, Genesis, Judges, Samuel, Kings, Esther—quite often instances of what are normally considered poetic forms appear as part of the narrative's natural flow. One example appears in 2 Sam 5:20b, after David defeats the Philistines at Baal-perizim, he declares "The LORD has broken through my enemies before me like the breakthrough of waters." Within this declaration appears a simile, an explicit comparison of two ideas utilizing the determiner "like." As discussed in chapter 7 below, such a comparison predominantly surfaces in Hebrew poetry and is widely recognized as a characteristic of the genre. However, 2 Samuel is not usually considered poetry by either scholars or translators, but narrative. Another example appears in 1 Chr 20:5, "And there was war with the Philistines again, and Elhanan the son of Jair killed Lahmi the brother of Goliath the Gittite, the shaft of whose spear was like a weaver's beam." Again, in this narrative recitation of a hero's exploits another simile surfaces, the shaft of a spear is *like* a weaver's beam. Similarly, in Gen 12:16, the author arranges a description of the gifts Pharoah provided Abram for taking his wife in a chiastic formation (a literary structure in which lines or words are arranged in a symmetrical mirror-like pattern, see Fig. 2).[7] Verses such as these exemplify instances in which biblical authors

---

7. Lund, "The Presence of Chiasmus in the Old Testament," 107, discusses this example, and various others. Further examples in narrative appear in Klaus, *Pivot Patterns in the Former Prophets*.

composing narrative texts include aspects of Hebrew poetry in their compositions. Consequently, it is tempting to reach the conclusion that no distinction exists between poetry and narrative in the Hebrew Bible, and that the whole Hebrew Bible constitutes the same fabric, elevated prose, where certain parts contain higher concentrations of poetic forms than others.

> Therefore he treated Abram well for her sake;
> and gave him sheep and oxen
> > and donkeys
> > > and male
> > > and female servants
> > and female donkeys
> and camels.
> (Gen 12:16)

FIGURE 2

The present volume maintains the traditional distinctions between prose and poetry, and fully recognizes a world in which the existence of forms and syntax widely considered poetic occasionally find a home in narrative texts. To be sure, the opposite also holds true: Narrative features such as *wayyiqtol* sequences, which are typically associated with Hebrew prose, also occasionally find a home in poetic texts. That said it is important not to downplay the differences in concentration of poetic forms in biblical texts. Certain compositions such as Psalms, Song of Songs, and Lamentations undoubtedly contain a significantly greater concentration of both poetic structure and imagery that separate them from the standard narrative corpus. In the words of Samuel Goh, we know that we are looking at poetry when there is an accumulation of "corroborative characteristics instead of an absolute one."[8]

---

8. Goh determines that when three elements appear—figurative language, parallelism, and terseness—then we have a poetic text (*Hebrew Poetry*, 8). Even this definition, however, fails to distinguish an identifiable line between poetry and prose. Weiss adopts a slightly less conservative view when he identifies imagery or metaphor as being the essential part of poetic expression (*The Bible from Within*, 132). The point here is not to determine which of the authors is right or wrong but to highlight the fact that no fixed empirical measure exists to identify when a biblical text slips from the realms of prose into poetry. Even though the defining line between prose and poetry remains indistinct and difficult to recognize, the present volume still recognizes the existence of both genres in the Bible.

Thus, the texts containing this higher concentration of poetics are recognized in the present volume as Hebrew poetry. However, in the same way that one bluebird does not make it spring, one poetic feature does not make a text poetry.[9]

Having argued for a recognition of poetry, I now proffer further distinctions within this genre. Texts that are deemed poetry (see the following paragraphs) can be further divided into more nuanced substrata. One can consider the poetry of Psalms and Lamentations, for example, as one extant substratum of poetry, and the poetry of the prophetic oracles—those found in Isaiah particularly but also in Jermiah, Ezekiel, Hosea, and Amos—as another. Even though it is still wise to refer to these texts as poetic, they contain their own separate range of nuance, style, and vocabulary. Separate again is the poetry found in wisdom literature, especially in Proverbs, but also in Ecclesiastes and Job.[10] Even though all three of the texts in this subgroup are still considered poetic texts, they differ in style, structure, and vocabulary. With particular regard to the uniqueness of wisdom literature, readers are advised to consult appendix 2.

1.5 Where Is Poetry?

Having accepted the existence of poetry in the Hebrew Bible, we turn now to the question of where poetry appears in the Old Testament, or more specifically, what texts are included in the present volume's poetic corpus. Examples of poetry in this book include texts from Psalms, Job, Lamentations, Isaiah, Jeremiah, Ezekiel, Proverbs, Ecclesiastes, Song of Songs, and selections from the Minor Prophets. In addition to these, the more ancient poetic texts embedded within narratives are referenced, including Gen 49; Exod 15; Num 22–24; Deut 32–33; Judg 5; 1 Sam 2; and 2 Sam 22. From time to time an even smaller group is referenced, the short bursts of poetry that occasionally

---

9. This is not intended to be an exhaustive description of Hebrew poetry's qualitative values. For further discussions on the topic, bearing in mind that scholars are not unified in their interpretations, see Alter, *Biblical Poetry*; Goh, *Hebrew Poetry*; Lunn, *Word-Order Variation*; and Watson, *Classical Hebrew Poetry*.

10. Although disagreeing with my subdivisions here, the Masorah of the Hebrew text recognizes differences in Hebrew poetry, separating Job, Psalms, and Proverbs from the rest of poetic literature via the addition of *oleh veyored*, a more emphatic disjunctive marker than the *atnakh*.

appear deeply embedded in narrative texts. Here we find excerpts including, but not limited to, Gen 4:23; 25:23; Num 21:27–30; Josh 6:26; 10:12–13; and 2 Sam 1:19–27.[11] English translations fail to consistently depict texts in this last group as being poetic, but their literary configuration regarding their structure, vocabulary, and style certainly connect them more to Israel's poetic traditions than to prose.[12]

1.6 Poetic Units

Exegetes employ a variety of terms to identify and label poetic units and divisions. Often the pragmatic differences between those terms remain extremely nuanced. Unfortunately, the Hebrew poets themselves failed to leave us detailed instructions about the structure and terminology they employed as they designed and crafted their compositions. Amidst the ancient Hebrew writings and inscriptions in our possession, from the monarchy to the Dead Sea Scrolls, a detailed handbook that stipulates the breakdown of individual poetic units and the terms for describing poetic lines remains lost to modern scholarship. Consequently, contemporary labels for the elements of a Hebrew poem have been adopted from Greek and Latin literature and applied to Hebrew poetry. As one would expect, the precise alignment of Greek poetry, for example, with Hebrew poetry is not perfect. In this regard, there is a sense in which modern exegetes force a later construct on an ancient text that is not fully compatible with the paradigm from a different culture. In light of the various labeling schemes adopted by the numerous commentators and exegetes, it is important for the present volume to outline the terms adopted to discuss the elements of a poetic text.

The most basic component of the poem is the word, or to be more

---

11. Reading through this volume, the careful student will undoubtedly detect a slight propensity toward examples drawn from the Psalms. The reason for this is because the Psalter contains the largest reservoir of pure poetic texts in the Bible. This exhibited propensity is not intended to devalue the quality of other poetic texts. Although the present volume may exhibit a tendency to lean on the Psalter, numerous illustrations are still drawn from every corner of the Hebrew Bible.

12. Note that many of these shorter bursts of poetry embedded in narrative are not indented as poetry. In the EVs, translators generally align prose texts with a strict left justification, whereas poetic texts have the second colon in a couplet indented. The indentations often witnessed in the English translations of the Bible are constructs created by the translators of the text.

precise, the Hebrew word. Every Hebrew poem in the Old Testament consists of individual words, and they bear a variety of characteristics that must be noted in poetic analysis. Words can be singular, plural, or dual; masculine or feminine; and in either an absolute or construct state, and they are, for the most part, based on a triliteral root system. Words may appear once, twice, or multiple times in a verse or poem, and the repetition of words—and Hebrew roots—frequently serves important structural and semantic functions within a poetic unit.

The next largest component is the colon, which receives different names from different authors.[13] The colon (or line) in Hebrew poetry is a defined unit demarcated with specific signs and markers in the MT.[14] Consequently, the length of a specific colon remains consistent through all English translations and exegetical works on the Hebrew Bible. Cola usually appear in related pairs, called bicola; however, at various points biblical poets isolate individual cola and use them as independent and unconnected elements in Hebrew verse. When this situation occurs, it is called a monocolon. An example appears in Song 6:10: "Who is this that grows like the dawn?" This cola remains isolated from the following colon even though the two cola form a complete thought together.[15]

Cola are usually grouped together in verses, which are also consistently and concretely demarcated in the MT with a specific marker (see below). For the most part, verses consist of a one bicolon, which contains two cola and may be referred to as a couplet, but in rarer instances they contain three or more cola. An example of a three-cola (or tricolon) verse appears in Ps 85:8[9]:

אֶשְׁמְעָה מַה־יְדַבֵּר הָאֵל ׀ יְהוָה	I will hear what God the Lord will say;
כִּי ׀ יְדַבֵּר שָׁלוֹם אֶל־עַמּוֹ	for he will speak peace to his people,
וְאֶל־חֲסִידָיו	to his godly ones;
וְאַל־יָשׁוּבוּ לְכִסְלָה׃	but let them not turn back to folly.

---

13. Authors sometimes used the terms "stich" and "hemistich," borrowed from Greek and Latin literature, to describe bicola and cola. See Cuddon, *Literary Terms*, 681.

14. The following section discusses these in more detail.

15. The monocolon as a structural feature stands on its own as a strophe. Watson, *Classical Hebrew Poetry*, 170–74, further divides monocola into three categories, the standard a-b-c pattern, the synonymous a-a'-a" structure (as in Jer 4:2b, "In truth, in justice, and in righteousness"), and the a-b-a' chiastic monocolon, as displayed in Ps 57:1[2], "Be gracious to me, O God, be gracious to me."

The strophe is a somewhat elusive textual unit consisting of a collection of related cola that falls approximately between the verse and stanza in size. It is an arbitrary division, and the Hebrew of the MT fails to define concretely strophic boundaries. Consequently, one can find variances in the strophic length depending on an exegete's interpretation of a biblical text. A strophe may consist of a single colon, in rare instances, or be as large as multiple verses. Naturally, a degree of overlap exists between strophe and verse delimitations, and the boundaries of a verse, as demarcated in the MT, may coincide with that of a strophe.

The largest division of a poetic unit is the stanza,[16] which may constitute a collection of strophes. As with the strophe, the MT's cantillation marks do not designate stanza boundaries, and other criteria are employed to determine the start and end of each stanza.[17] Stanzas vary in size depending on the length of poetic units, and English translations do not agree upon their divisions.

Colon	Strophe	Stanza	Poetic Unit
Colon 1	Strophe 1	Stanza 1	Poetic Unit
Colon 2			
Colon 3	Strophe 2		
Colon 4			
Colon 5			
Colon 6	Strophe 3	Stanza 2	
Colon 7			
Colon 8			
Colon 9	Strophe 4		
Colon 10			
Colon 11	Strophe 5	Stanza 3	
Colon 12			
Colon 13	Strophe 6		
Colon 14			

---

16. Certain scholars refer to this as a verset. See, for example, Cuddon, *Literary Terms*, 758.
17. See chapter 10 for further discussion of how to divide texts into stanzas.

Taking Ps 44 as an example, the JPS 1984 divides the composition into five stanzas (vv. 1–9, 10–17, 18–23, and 24–27). The NASB, on the other hand, divides the same composition into five stanzas, but the divisions differ (1–3, 4–8, 9–16, 17–19, 20–26).[18] The figure above presents the various divisions in relation to each other.

Below (see Fig. 3), Ps 1 is presented with annotation reflecting the various levels of potential divisions.[19]

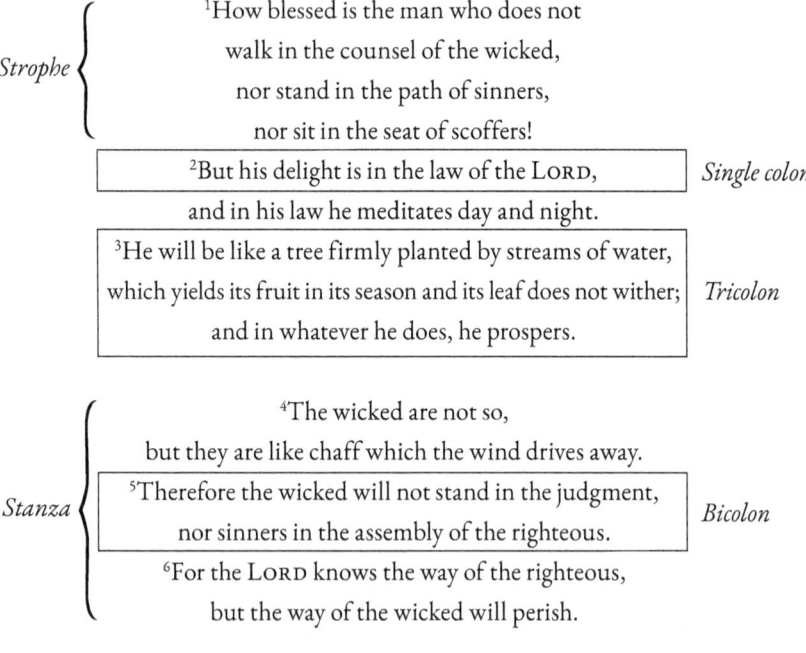

FIGURE 3

Further Reading: Chisholm, *Exegesis to Exposition*, 169–82; Fokkelman, *Reading Biblical Poetry*; Geller, "Theory and Method"; Goh, *Hebrew Poetry*; James, *Invitation to Biblical Poetry*; Kugel, *Idea of Biblical Poetry*, 1–95;

---

18. Notwithstanding the differences in verse number between the two versions, the translators clearly did not agree on the stanza divisions.

19. The strophic division here aligns with Goh's interpretation of the psalm (*Hebrew Poetry*, 116). However, a good case exists for the first strophe containing vv. 1–2.

Longman, *How to Read the Psalms*; Lunn, *Word-Order Variation*; Meek, "Structure of Hebrew Poetry"; Meir, "Pentateuchal Poetry"; Muraoka, *Emphatic Words*; O'Connor, *Hebrew Verse Structure*; Schökel, *A Manual*; Watson, *Classical Hebrew Poetry*.

PART 2

Lexical Building Blocks

2

Masoretic, Syntactic, Lexical, and Morphological Features of Poetry

When compared to prose, Hebrew poetry exhibits distinct characteristics with respect to word formation, vocabulary, and the use of the Masoretic cantillation marks. The following chapter discusses important areas where poetry diverges from prose. Although the discussion in this chapter highlights numerous features that appear in poetry, it is essential to recognize that these features do not serve as definitive or absolute indicators of poetry, because some may occasionally appear within prose texts. Nevertheless, their predominant occurrence in poetic contexts justifies their general classification as hallmarks of poetry. In analyzing poetic texts, it is advisable to assess the cumulative presence of these features rather than relying on individual occurrences in isolation.

2.1 Masoretic Divisions

An important difference between certain poetic texts in the Old Testament and narrative texts concerns the division of verses into individual poetic lines, or cola. The Masoretes—Jewish scribes responsible for the copying and transmitting of the MT—carefully inserted into the texts they copied a hierarchy of cantillation marks—musical notations—that help readers and translators to identify and divide individual verses.[1] The cantillation marks

---

1. For a full description of these markers see Futato, *Basics of Hebrew Accents*. See also Tov's description in *Textual Criticism*, 62–65. It is important to remember that neither the cantillation marks

fundamentally divide into two categories, disjunctive and conjunctive. Disjunctive markers separate words or groups of words into smaller units, in a similar way that commas and semicolons divide sentences in English. Conjunctive markers join words and word groups together, creating tightly knit lexical units—perhaps the closest equivalent in English is the regular dash. Both conjunctive and disjunctive markers are categorized hierarchically according to strength.[2]

Regarding the analysis of poetry, the disjunctive markers, those that separate, serve the most important function. The *silluq* combined with the *sof pasuq* indicate the strongest disjunctive marker—for both prose and poetry—and they divide texts into verse divisions. The *silluq* is a vertical line that appears underneath the accented syllable [ֽ], and it appears together with a symbol resembling a colon in English grammar, the *sof pasuq*. Psalm 23:1 exemplifies its appearance in a poetic text. The final word in the Hebrew text below reveals a vertical line (the *silluq*) to the left of the *qamets* under the final syllable, and at the end of the verse appear the two vertical dots of the *sof pasuq*:

יְהוָה רֹעִי לֹא אֶחְסָר׃   The LORD is my shepherd, I shall not want.

Whether in prose or poetry, this combination of cantillation marks indicates the end of a verse, irrespective of the verse length. Within poetic verses, however, the secondary disjunctive markers differ in certain instances from prose texts. In prose, the strongest secondary disjunctive cantillation mark is the *atnakh*, which looks like a small wishbone [֑] placed underneath the accented syllable in a Hebrew word. Consider the prose text of Ps 88:6[7]:

---

nor the vowel points appeared in the original Hebrew of our biblical texts. The consonantal tradition from the Dead Sea Scrolls plainly demonstrates this fact. It is difficult to determine a precise date for when the accents and vowels were added (or even if they were added at the same time). The earliest date for their addition is the beginning of the fifth century CE. For a discussion of the date of their addition see Sanders and de Hoop, "Masoretic Accentuation."

2. Here it is useful to think of the punctuation system in English where the full stop serves as the most prominent divider, and the semicolon functions beneath it, with the comma functioning below that.

| שַׁתַּ֗נִי בְּב֣וֹר תַּחְתִּיּ֑וֹת | You have put me in the lowest pit, |
| בְּ֝מַחֲשַׁכִּ֗ים בִּמְצֹלֽוֹת׃ | in dark places, in the depths. |

The *atnakh* sits under the *yod* in the word תַּחְתִּיּ֑וֹת, "lowest," and functions as the primary means for dividing the verse into two sections or cola. The first colon, "You have put me in the lowest pit," is Ps 88:6[7]a, and the remaining phrases, "In dark places, in the depths," constitutes Ps 88:6[7]b. The *atnakh*, therefore, serves as the main divisional marker for the verse in this instance. The *atnakh* functions as the second strongest disjunctive marker in Hebrew narrative texts, along with a significant portion of poetic texts, including prophetic poetry—the poetry of Isaiah, Jeremiah, Hosea, Obadiah, and Zephaniah, for example. However, for three books the situation differs: Job, Proverbs, and Psalms. These three books are known as the אמ"ת, *emeth*,[3] books—an acronym stemming from their Hebrew names אִיּוֹב (Job), מִשְׁלֵי (Proverbs), and תְּהִלִּים (Psalms). In these three compositions another cantillation mark, *oleh veyored* (see Fig. 4) functions as the strongest disjunctive marker when it appears. Consequently, when dividing poetry in the three *emeth* books, it is important to identify whether *oleh veyored* is present, and if so, to use that marker as the primary point of division in the verse.[4] Psalm 88:8[9] provides an example of its use:

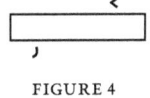

FIGURE 4

הִרְחַ֣קְתָּ מְיֻדָּעַ֣י מִמֶּ֑נִּי	You have removed my acquaintances far from me;
שַׁתַּ֣נִי תוֹעֵב֣וֹת לָ֑מוֹ	you have made me an object of loathing to them;
כָּ֝לֻ֗א וְלֹ֣א אֵצֵֽא׃	I am shut up and cannot go out.

Unlike a narrative text, the primary division in Ps 88:8[9] occurs with the *oleh veyored*, which appears in the lexical unit מִמֶּ֑נִּי, "from me." After this, the *atnakh*, under the *lamed* in the word לָ֑מוֹ, further divides the remaining clause, creating a three-cola verse (i.e., a tricolon). When *oleh veyored* is absent

---

3. *Emeth* is a Hebrew word meaning "truth."
4. These cantillation marks form part of the MT; consequently, they should be rendered consistently in every English translation's attempt to reflect Hebrew poetry.

from a verse, then the *atnakh* remains the strongest disjunctive marker. This can be seen from Ps 85:3[4]:

| אָסַפְתָּ כָל־עֶבְרָתֶ֑ךָ | You withdrew all your fury; |
| הֱשִׁיב֥וֹתָ מֵחֲר֥וֹן אַפֶּֽךָ׃ | you turned away from your burning anger. |

In Ps 85 above, due to its brevity, *oleh veyored* was not employed; consequently, the *atnakh* remains the primary disjunctive marker. Although *oleh veyored* usually appears on a single word or lexical form, in certain instances the two symbols appear separated over two words. An example of this phenomenon appears in Ps 1:3:

וְֽהָיָ֗ה כְּעֵץ֮ שָׁת֪וּל עַֽל־פַּלְגֵ֫י מָ֥יִם	He will be like a tree firmly planted by streams of water,
אֲשֶׁ֤ר פִּרְי֨וֹ ׀ יִתֵּ֬ן בְּעִתּ֗וֹ	which yields its fruit in its season
וְעָלֵ֥הוּ לֹֽא־יִבּ֑וֹל	and its leaf does not wither;
וְכֹ֖ל אֲשֶׁר־יַעֲשֶׂ֣ה יַצְלִֽיחַ׃	and in whatever he does, he prospers.

Here the *oleh veyored* symbols split across the construct form פַּלְגֵי מָיִם. However, although it appears in this split format, it still serves as the foremost disjunctive marker within Ps 1:3.[5]

One cannot overemphasize the importance of accurately recognizing the *atnakh* and *oleh veyored* cantillation marks when analyzing Hebrew poetry. Dividing verses accurately into individual cola remains one of the most important early stages of poetic analysis, and it can only be achieved through proper recognition of these disjunctive markers.[6]

---

5. Overall, the cantillation marks discussed above are part of a larger system of disjunctive markers used in the MT. The *atnakh*, *silluq*, and *oleh veyored* constitute the three strongest disjunctive markers within this system. For the remainder of the present volume, Hebrew verses are divided and presented according to these primary cantillation marks. However, occasionally some of the secondary markers may be used for longer cola. For an overview of the disjunctive groupings see Futato, *Basics of Hebrew Accents*, 18. This short volume further describes how the cantillation marks are used for interpretation. Further treatment of the accents can be found in Tov, *Textual Criticism*, 62–65.

6. Notably, the written appearance of these verse divisions reflects a relatively late phenomenon, ca. the fifth century CE. Sanders and de Hoop, "Masoretic Accentuation," provide a more detailed treatment of their origins. Basically, this means that such divisions were not formally used during the biblical period. That said, one can assert that they reflect a reliably transmitted reading tradition that should still be honored as a dependable reflection of how ancient Israelites divided poetry.

2.2 Syntactic Features

Terse Syntax

Quite often, Hebrew poetry, as opposed to prose, omits particles such as the definite article, the definite direct object marker אֶת, and prepositions. Although certain texts recognized as prose may occasionally exhibit this characteristic, the phenomenon manifests itself more in texts widely acclaimed as poetic. Psalm 34:8[9] provides an example of the terse nature of poetry with the omission of an expected relative pronoun:[7]

טַעֲמוּ וּרְאוּ כִּי־טוֹב יְהוָה	O taste and see that the LORD is good;
אַשְׁרֵי הַגֶּבֶר [אֲשֶׁר] יֶחֱסֶה־בּוֹ	how blessed is the man [who] takes refuge in him!

In this example, the relative pronoun, inserted in brackets, does not appear in the Hebrew text; despite its absence, however, it is implied in the translation.[8] In normal circumstances, the prose equivalent of this phrase includes some form of the relative pronoun. Another example of the relative pronoun's omission appears in Jer 13:20b (emphasis added):

אַיֵּה הָעֵדֶר [אֲשֶׁר] נִתַּן־לָךְ	Where is the flock *that* was given you,
צֹאן תִּפְאַרְתֵּךְ	your beautiful sheep?

The relative pronoun "that," in italics above, is not explicitly represented in the Hebrew text. As with the previous example, English translations of this verse, however, all include a relative pronoun even though it remains absent from the Hebrew text. In addition to the relative pronoun, Hebrew poetry similarly omits the definite article with regularity. Judges 5:4a provides a clear example:

יְהוָה בְּצֵאתְךָ מִשֵּׂעִיר	LORD, when you went out from Seir,
בְּצַעְדְּךָ מִשְּׂדֵה אֱדוֹם	when you marched from the field of Edom,
[הָ]אֶרֶץ רָעָשָׁה	[the] earth quaked ...

---

7. Joüon §158a.
8. Most commonly EVs, such as the ESV and NASB, include the relative pronoun.

In Judg 5:4a, the poet omits the definite article הַ from the word אֶרֶץ, earth, even though it is expected grammatically.⁹ Deuteronomy 12:24b provides an example of the prose equivalent:

| עַל־הָאָרֶץ תִּשְׁפְּכֶנּוּ כַּמָּיִם | You shall pour it [blood] out on *the* ground like water. (NASB, emphasis added) |

Here the definite article appears attached to the word אֶרֶץ, "earth/ground," where it is expected. Exodus 9:14b demonstrates another instance of the prosaic form:

| תֵּדַע כִּי אֵין כָּמֹנִי בְּכָל־הָאָרֶץ | So that you may know that there is none like me in all *the* earth. (emphasis added) |

Once again, the definite article הַ appears before the word אֶרֶץ "earth."¹⁰ As with the definite article, Hebrew poets are prone to omit prepositions in their compositions. An example appears in Isa 42:22b:

| הָיוּ לָבַז וְאֵין מַצִּיל מְשִׁסָּה וְאֵין־אֹמֵר הָשַׁב | They have become prey with none to deliver them, and spoil, with none to say, "Give them back!" |

In Isaiah, the expression "to become" consists of the verb "to be," הָיָה, together with the preposition לְ. Ordinarily, in Hebrew prose, writers adopt the preposition, in this case *lamed*, with the first indirect object בַּז, "plunder," in addition to the second indirect object מְשִׁסָּה, "spoil," thus rendering the hypothetical sequence, הָיוּ לָבַז . . . לִמְשִׁסָּה . . . . However, due to the terse nature of Hebrew poetry, the expected preposition on the second indirect object is lacking. Genesis 1:26b represents the expected use of a verb governing multiple indirect objects that each have the preposition, in this instance בְּ (shaded below), before them:

---

9. Witnessed in numerous English versions—e.g., NASB, ESV, NIV, and NLT.
10. See also 2 Sam 12:2, which provides an example of the prose equivalent.

וְיִרְדּוּ בִדְגַת הַיָּם	And let them rule over the fish of the sea
וּבְעוֹף הַשָּׁמַיִם	and over the birds of the sky
וּבַבְּהֵמָה	and over the cattle.

The verb רָדָה, in this instance, adopts the preposition בְּ for each noun that it governs, and in each case the preposition appears—humanity has dominion over fish, birds, beasts, etc. This marks the normal expected usage and repetition of the preposition, as opposed to the poetic proclivity to omit later repetitions of the preposition. Another example of a poet's omission of prepositions appears in Isa 15:8 (emphasis added):[11]

כִּי־הִקִּיפָה הַזְּעָקָה אֶת־גְּבוּל מוֹאָב	For the cry of distress has gone around the territory of Moab,
עַד־אֶגְלַיִם יִלְלָתָהּ	its wail *goes as far as* Eglaim and its
וּבְאֵר אֵילִים יִלְלָתָהּ	wailing *even to* Beer-elim.

In Isaiah, the preposition appears in the first expression, עַד אֶגְלַיִם, "as far as Eglaim," describing the distance the people's cry travels. Although it explicitly appears at the beginning of the second colon, it remains absent from the beginning of the third colon. The parallelism in Isa 15:8c implies the repetition of the preposition, but the writer avoids its explicit usage.

A cursory comparative survey of 1 Kgs 1–20 and Pss 1–101[12] (see Fig. 5) further reveals Hebrew poetry's propensity to omit particles and prepositions. The table below compares the usage of the particle אֵת, the definite article הַ, and the relative particle אֲשֶׁר between the representative poetic and prose passages. The comparison demonstrates that these particles have a noticeably lower frequency in poetry than they do in prose.[13] It is important for the exegete to remember the scarcity of these particles and

---

11. See also Isa 48:9 with the preposition לְמַעַן.
12. These ranges appear random, but they both contain the same number of words, which makes them more comparable: 1 Kgs 1–20 has 16,804 words and Pss 1–101 contain 16,804 words.
13. In the same way that poetry omits particles and some prepositions, verbs are often omitted when psalmists employ ellipsis in bicola. See below for further discussion.

stand-alone prepositions so they can insert them when needed for correct translation.[14]

	1Kgs 1–20	Pss 1–101
אֵת	512	62
אֲשֶׁר	364	66
הַ	1247	210

FIGURE 5

2.3 Lexical Features

Wayyiqtol Frequency

Appearance of the *wayyiqtol* form (*waw* consecutive with imperfect) in Hebrew poetry is noticeably rare when compared to its usage in Hebrew prose.[15] A quick comparison between an extended segment of prose, 1 Kgs 1–20, and a similar sized portion of poetry, Pss 1–101, reveals the differences.[16] The psalms exhibit 190 occurrences of the verb form, whereas 1 Kgs reveals 930 instances. In this relatively substantial sample size, it is easy to distinguish the Hebrew poets' aversion to the *wayyiqtol*. The presence, or lack thereof, of the *wayyiqtol* form presents one of the more obvious features that define Hebrew poetry. However, it is crucial to remember that the *wayyiqtol* can, on occasion, surface in poetry. Most often, the authors of extended narrative poetry adopt the *wayyiqtol* to convey a sense of progression in their compositions, as seen in Ps 106:30:

---

14. Unfortunately, the terseness of Hebrew poetry intensifies parataxis (the placement of clauses or phrases one after another without words indicating the relationships between them). Consequently, Hebrew poetry is slightly more difficult to read, and the relationship between cola requires contemplation.

15. Related to the appearance of *wayyiqtol* is the deviant word order that frequently appears in poetic texts. On the whole, the expected word order in prose texts is VSO (verb→ subject→ object). Hebrew poets more often than not disrupt this expected sequence with various options. For a closer look at the poetic word patterning and their functions, see Lunn, *Word-Order Variation in Biblical Hebrew Poetry*.

16. Both texts contain approximately the same number of words.

| וַיַּעֲמֹד פִּינְחָס וַיְפַלֵּל | Then Phinehas stood up and interposed, |
| וַתֵּעָצַר הַמַּגֵּפָה | And the plague was stayed. |

Vocabulary

Several words and morphological forms tend to appear more frequently in Hebrew poetry than prose. Although the words and forms discussed in this section are important for establishing a specific text's poetic profile, it is important to remember that they are not all unique to poetry, despite their prevalence in poetic texts. The words discussed in the present section only constitute part of a larger profile of poetic literature.

At the beginning of Ps 78, in the first verse, the psalmist implores his audience to pay special attention to his words:

| הַאֲזִינָה עַמִּי תּוֹרָתִי | Give ear my people to my teaching |
| הַטּוּ אָזְנְכֶם לְאִמְרֵי־פִי | Incline your ear to the words of my mouth. |

The psalmist selects two words in this single verse that primarily appear in poetic texts. The verb translated as "give ear," הַאֲזִין, is the *hiphil* form from the noun אֹזֶן, meaning "ear." As a verb, this word predominantly surfaces in poetry—Gen 4:23 (1x); Exod 15 (1x); Num 23 (1x); Judg 5 (1x); Job (6x); Psalms (15x); Proverbs (1x); Isaiah (8x)—and even though it occasionally appears in nonpoetic texts, its distribution in prose pales in comparison (2 Chr [1x]; Neh [1x]). The standard prosaic root employed to express hearing or listening is שָׁמַע, as a *hiphil* causative or *qal* factitive, as witnessed in a variety of locations such as 2 Kgs 17:40: "However, they did not listen [שָׁמֵעוּ], but they did according to their earlier custom."

The other poetic lexical form of interest found in Ps 18:31[30] is אִמְרָה "word." For the most part, this noun's distribution is restricted to poetic couplets in the Hebrew Bible—Gen 4:23 (1x); Deut 32–33 (2x); 2 Sam 22 (1x); Psalms (26x); Proverbs (1x); Isaiah (5x); Lamentations (1x). In standard Hebrew prose the more common equivalent noun is derived from the root דבר, as witnessed in 2 Sam 7:7a: "Wherever I have gone with all the sons of Israel, did I speak a word [דָּבָר] with one of the tribes of Israel . . . ?" Some of the more common poetic words are listed in the table below:

חָוָה	he declared	מָחַץ	he shattered
פָּעַל	he made/did	חֶמֶר	wine
שָׁתַל	he planted	טֶרֶף	prey
צָעַד	he marched	כַּבִּיר	mighty
נֹגַהּ	brightness	זַעַם	indignation
קָנָה[17]	he created	חָרוּץ/פָּז	gold

It is important to emphasize once again that the distribution of the words above across the Hebrew Bible is not exclusive to poetic texts, and a few of the words occasionally surface in prose texts. Consequently, to establish the poetic character of a passage, one cannot simply identify a single instance of one of the words listed above. As mentioned in the introduction, the identification of a poetic text develops through the recognition of multiple poetic forms, including vocabulary, in a single verse.

Aramaic Words

Certain Aramaic words represent another resource in the biblical poets' toolkit. Often, but not always, psalmists apparently feel compelled to revert to Aramaic counterparts when compiling parallel cola, where the need arises for a matching synonym for the second colon. Consider the following from Ps 25:4 (emphasis added):

דְּרָכֶיךָ יְהוָה הוֹדִיעֵנִי	Make me know your ways, O Lord;
אֹרְחוֹתֶיךָ לַמְּדֵנִי	teach me your *paths*.

Here the psalmist first employs the standard prose word for "way," דֶּרֶךְ, in the first colon but switches to the Aramaic word, אֹרַח, in the second colon to generate a suitable word pair. As a noun, אֹרַח almost exclusively appears in poetic texts.[18] In the Aramaic portions of Daniel, the same word (albeit pointed as אֳרַח) is used to denote a way or path.[19] When employing Aramaic

---

17. This word is extremely common in prose; the context here relates to God as creator, creating heaven and earth, or humanity.
18. Genesis 49; Judg 5; Job, Psalms, Proverbs, Isaiah, and Micah.
19. See Dan 4:34 and 5:23. Cf. BDB 1082b (the Aramaic section).

terminology, psalmists do not consistently reserve the Aramaic word for the second colon, as witnessed by Ps 103:15 (emphasis added):

אֱנוֹשׁ כֶּחָצִיר יָמָיו	As for *man*, his days are like grass;
כְּצִיץ הַשָּׂדֶה כֵּן יָצִיץ	as a flower of the field, so he flourishes.

Here the psalmist adopts the form אֱנוֹשׁ as his primary word to denote man, humankind. Under usual circumstances in Hebrew prose, one would expect to find the word אָדָם to reflect humankind in this context. The form אֱנוֹשׁ, or אֱנָשׁ, is the standard Aramaic word for denoting man or humankind. Daniel 1–6 attests to its frequency in Aramaic.[20] In addition to the examples cited above, the more common Aramaic words employed by Hebrew poets appear in the table below:

	Aramaic	Hebrew Prose Equivalent
Prov 23:9	מִלָּה	דָּבָר
Isa 21:14	אָתָה	בָּא
Num 24:16	חָזָה	רָאָה

2.4 Morphological Features

2.4.1 Rare Suffixes

Hebrew poets frequently preserve rarer Hebrew morphology, word forms appearing more sparingly in prose. One prominent feature relates to the unexpected suffixes appearing on certain verbs, nouns, and even prepositions. Occasionally, the extended form of the 2ms suffix appears; thus, instead of the expected ending ךָ-, we find the presumed poetic alternative כָה-.[21] Psalm 141:8 provides an example:

---

20. See for example, Dan 2:10, 38; 3:10; and 4:13. Cf. Jastrow, *Dictionary*, 53a.
21. See Joüon §61i.

כִּי אֵלֶיךָ יְהוִה אֲדֹנָי עֵינָי	For my eyes are toward you, O Lord, my Lord;
בְּכָה חָסִיתִי אַל־תְּעַר נַפְשִׁי	in you I take refuge; do not leave me defenseless.

In the second colon, the psalmist directly addresses God with a plea shaped with 2ms suffixes. Usually, one expects to find the form בְּךָ to represent the direct address, "in you . . . ," but in this case the poet elects to employ the longer poetic form, בְּכָה. A similar situation appears in Exod 15:11, where the poet declares, מִי־כָמֹכָה בָּאֵלִם, "Who is like you among the gods?" The expected form expressing the direct 2ms address is כָּמֹךָ; however, the songwriter in this instance employs the poetic equivalent כָּמֹכָה with the enclitic *he*.

Another poetic suffix employed by certain authors is מוֹ- (occasionally מוּ-), representing the 3mp object suffix.[22] An example appears in Exod 15:7b (emphasis added):

תְּשַׁלַּח חֲרֹנְךָ	You send forth your burning anger,
יֹאכְלֵמוֹ כַּקַּשׁ	and it consumes *them* as chaff.

Usually in prose, the 3mp object suffix prefers the form ם-, as in Lev 11:42b:

לְכָל־הַשֶּׁרֶץ הַשֹּׁרֵץ	Concerning any swarming thing that swarms
עַל־הָאָרֶץ לֹא תֹאכְלוּם	on the ground, you shall not eat *them*.

However, in the case of Exod 15:7b, the songwriter employs the ending מוֹ-. The meaning and function of the suffix remain the same, but the morphology varies in poetic texts like this. Another example appears in Ps 2:3, where the poetic form appears as a pronominal suffix, as opposed to the object suffix in the previous example:

---

22. This form was originally considered archaic, but since the work of scholars such as Bloch, one should understand it as a poetic form. See Bloch, "The Third-Person Masculine Plural Suffix Pronoun," 147–70.

נְנַתְּקָה אֶת־מוֹסְרוֹתֵימוֹ	Let us tear apart their fetters
וְנַשְׁלִיכָה מִמֶּנּוּ עֲבֹתֵימוֹ	and cast away their cords from us!

The noun עֲבֹת, "cords," uses the pronominal suffix מוֹ- as a reference to the kings of the earth who desperately desire to emancipate themselves from subjugation to the Lord and his anointed. The suffix is not restricted to the noun in Hebrew poetry, but it appears also with prepositions, as in the case of Lam 1:19b:

כִּי־בִקְשׁוּ אֹכֶל לָמוֹ	While they sought food for themselves
וְיָשִׁיבוּ אֶת־נַפְשָׁם	and to restore their lives.

In the expression "for themselves," the expected form of the preposition is לָהֶם, as in Exod 5:7, "let them go and gather straw for themselves [לָהֶם]." However, the author of Lamentations, in this instance, opts for the rarer poetic form. Furthermore, one should note that the same suffix appears on certain prepositions representing the 3ms suffix, as seen in Job 22:2:

הַלְאֵל יִסְכָּן־גָּבֶר	Can a vigorous man be of use to God,
כִּי־יִסְכֹּן עָלֵימוֹ מַשְׂכִּיל	or a wise man be useful to him?

In this instance, the poetic suffix מוֹ- appears on the preposition עַל and translates "him," reflecting the 3ms suffix.[23] Although this rare ending appears on nouns and prepositions, and sometimes with different interpretations, it is still more common in poetic texts.

2.4.2 Poetic Prepositions

Prepositions in Hebrew poetry routinely experience further alterations. Hebrew poets periodically opt for an extended form for certain independent prepositions. For example, instead of the preposition עַל, for "over/upon,"

---

23. See also Job 6:16.

the slightly longer form of עֲלֵי appears. Consider Jacob's blessing in Gen 49:22 (emphasis added):

בֵּן פֹּרָת יוֹסֵף	Joseph is a fruitful bough,
בֵּן פֹּרָת עֲלֵי־עָיִן	a fruitful bough *by* a spring;
בָּנוֹת צָעֲדָה עֲלֵי־שׁוּר	its branches run *over* a wall.

The preposition representing both "over" and "by" above appears in Hebrew as עֲלֵי and not as the expected form עַל, visible later in Gen 50:1: "Then Joseph fell on [עַל] his father's face." Another example of the extended poetic form appears in Ps 108:9[10] (emphasis added):

מוֹאָב סִיר רַחְצִי	Moab is my washbowl;
עַל־אֱדוֹם אַשְׁלִיךְ נַעֲלִי	*over* Edom I shall throw My shoe;
עֲלֵי־פְלֶשֶׁת אֶתְרוֹעָע	*over* Philistia I will shout aloud.

For the preposition in these instances, no difference exists in meaning or function when compared with the prosaic counterparts. The difference purely reflects a morphological variation in the poetic context. Like the preposition עַל, the word אֶל, "to/unto," undergoes a similar transformation in poetry, resulting in the form אֱלֵי. An example appears in Job 29:19 (emphasis added):

שָׁרְשִׁי פָתוּחַ אֱלֵי־מָיִם	My root is spread *out to* the waters,
וְטַל יָלִין בִּקְצִירִי	and dew lies all night on my branch.

Here Job opts for the extended poetic form אֱלֵי to express "out to." A noted feature of this extended form of the preposition, however, is that its limited appearance is restricted to the book of Job, and the author fails to incorporate it consistently. For most of the composition, Job appears comfortable fielding the expected prose form of the preposition, as witnessed in Job 30:22a: "You lift me up to [אֶל] the wind and cause me to ride. . . ."

A third preposition appearing in a longer poetic form is the Hebrew word עַד, "until," which certain poets similarly adjust with the addition of the *yod*. Job 7:4 provides an example:

אִם־שָׁכַבְתִּי וְאָמַרְתִּי	When I lie down I say,
מָתַי אָקוּם	"When shall I arise?"
וּמִדַּד־עָרֶב	But the night continues,
וְשָׂבַעְתִּי נְדֻדִים עֲדֵי־נָשֶׁף	and I am continually tossing until dawn.

Here Job opts for the extended poetic form, עֲדֵי, to express the temporal preposition "until." Unlike the preposition אֱל, the poetic form of עֲדֵי arises in texts outside of Job, as with Ps 104:23:

יֵצֵא אָדָם לְפָעֳלוֹ	A man goes forth to his work
וְלַעֲבֹדָתוֹ עֲדֵי־עָרֶב	and to his labor until evening.

In expressing the end of a man's workday, the psalmist elects to use the longer form of the preposition, עֲדֵי, instead of the expected and more common form עַד. As with the previous prepositions, Hebrew poets are not bound to appropriating the poetic variations, and they frequently adopt the expected prose forms, even to the point of mixing both in a single composition.

To conclude this chapter, it is essential to emphasize that identifying the morphological and lexical adjustments commonly found in Hebrew poetry constitutes merely the initial step in the comprehensive process of poetic analysis. As Wilfred Watson aptly asserts, "It is not merely enough to single out, identify and label a whole range of poetic devices ... but it is only the beginning and unless continued, leads nowhere."[24] This foundational principle of poetic analysis retains its relevance and applicability throughout the subsequent sections of this volume.

Questions for Consideration: How many of the characteristics described in this chapter appear in the text? How often does the poet choose standard forms over poetic forms? Do any of the poetic forms in the text under consideration contribute to rhyme or assonance? Are the poetic morphological alterations used consistently throughout the examined text? What effect do

---

24. Watson, *Classical Hebrew Poetry*, 30–31.

omitted particles or prepostions have (e.g., do they improve the symmetry of two cola?)

Further Reading: Joüon, *A Grammar*; Futato, *Basics of Hebrew Accents*; *GKC*; Sanders and de Hoop, "Masoretic Accentuation"; Lunn, *Word-Order Variation*; Meek, "The Structure of Hebrew Poetry";[25] Revell, "Pausal forms."

---

25. This relatively old work discusses more nuanced elements of Hebrew poetry that distinguish it from prose.

PART 3

Structural Poetics

3

Parallelisms

The present chapter explores the concept of parallelism, or more accurately, parallelisms, because the term encompasses a variety of distinct forms identified within the field of Hebrew poetry. The discussion focuses on the most prominent types of parallelism recognized in scholarly literature, highlighting their distinctive features within poetic texts. Beyond classifying these types of parallelism, the chapter also addresses two essential components frequently associated with the technique: the use of word pairs and the phenomenon known as the ballast variant. These elements play a crucial role in shaping and sequencing components in parallel cola. Before diving into the specifics of parallelism and its accompanying elements, it is necessary to outline a few fundamental features of poetic lines that are instrumental in clarifying our understanding of parallelism.

The basic structural unit of Hebrew poetry is the colon, also called a line, which constitutes a collection of words in a verse. In most cases an individual colon is demarcated by an *atnakh* or *oleh veyored* Masoretic marker. As stated earlier, these marks occur within the Hebrew Bible and are therefore standard across all English translations of the Bible. The term parallelism describes one of many relationships two cola may exhibit. It is recognized that the word parallelism itself was appropriated from the world of mathematics and, therefore, to some degree reflects only an imprecise description for Hebrew poetry. That said, unfortunate as it may be, it remains a widely accepted term employed for discussing structural aspects, specifically cola relationships, of Hebrew poetry.[1]

---

1. In Robert Lowth's 1778 introduction to Isaiah, he refined his ideas on Hebrew verse and established the idea of parallelism. He states, "Parallel lines may be reduced to three sorts—parallels

At a rudimentary level, parallelism denotes the sequential alignment of two cola in a poetic text where the two cola, or parallel elements, exhibit a degree of repetition in form or meaning. In most cases only two cola are involved, and they are usually aligned consecutively; however, certain instances exist where three or more cola are aligned in parallel formation. Thus, it is possible to identify a tricola pattern, using three cola, and quatrains, four-cola alignments. In each of these cases, the cola are still referred to as being in parallel. Furthermore, cases arise where the related parallel cola deviate from a consecutive arrangement, thus creating the phenomenon called "distance parallelism," which signifies the departure from the contiguous alignment of cola within the poetic structure.[2]

When analyzing parallelism in poetic texts, more than simply recognizing the corresponding cola, it is important to ask, "What aspect of the related cola is repeated?" The relationship or poetic connection between the cola may be characterized in semantic, syntactic, and even grammatical terms. For the most part, semantic analysis carries the most significance when establishing the function of parallelism. To be sure, semantic parallelism has historically received the lion's share of attention in scholarly work. That said, although syntactic and grammatical parallelisms are underrepresented in the literature, their identification and analysis remain important to the examination and interpretation of Hebrew poetry.

---

synonymous, parallels antithetic, and parallels synthetic" (*Isaiah*, 6). His work and theories of Hebrew verse at the time were extremely important, and in many respects he elevated Hebrew poetic studies to a place of prominence in the world of biblical scholarship. Since his introduction to Isaiah, however, especially in the last thirty years, his ideas have been refined, developed in numerous directions, and even refuted. Recent scholarship has highlighted areas where his threefold categorization is inadequate, at best. Consequently, a variety of other frameworks for analyzing poetic lines have been proposed. Works such as O'Connor's *Hebrew Verse Structure* laid down the foundations for understanding cola relationships as being appositional. And this idea is reaffirmed by Holmstedt in "Hebrew Poetry." Holmstedt attempts to dislodge the idea of "parallelism" as a description from scholarly thinking to the point that he explicitly states, "I offer in this study a linguistic proposal for the relationship of poetic lines, and so intend to finish the wholesale replacement of parallelism that O'Connor initiated" (p. 619). Despite such valiant efforts, to date, the terms "parallelism" and the types "synonymous," "antithetical," and "synthetic" (also called "formal") remain etched in popular usage, despite their inadequacies. Consequently, I shall still be using these terms throughout the present volume, albeit avoiding Lowth's strict sense and more as a point of reference to readers who may be familiar with Lowth's terms. It is important to remember that cola relationships are far more sophisticated than those originally described by Lowth.

2. Examples are provided below.

3.1 Word Pairs

Word pairs are established pairs of words that habitually appear in consecutive cola.[3] The task of establishing their origin remains elusive, and, to be sure, the likelihood is that many of the pairs appearing in the Old Testament were not created by Israelites but borrowed from surrounding cultures.[4] The first word in the pair—often designated in the present volume with a lowercase "a"—appears in the first colon, and the second word in the pair—designated with "b"—appears in the following colon. Their appearance in consecutive cola generates a notable cohesion between the poetic units. Generally, three criteria are used to establish the existence of a word pair.[5] First, the words must belong to the same class of words, i.e., nouns, verbs, adjectives, etc., so if the a-word is a verb then its corresponding b-word also appears as a verb. Second, they must appear in parallel cola, which are usually consecutive. Third, they must appear with relative frequency in biblical literature.[6] Consider the following verse from Ps 39:12[13]a (emphasis added):

שִׁמְעָה־תְפִלָּתִי יְהוָה *Hear* my prayer, O Lord,
וְשַׁוְעָתִי הַאֲזִינָה and *give ear* to my cry.

In this verse, the word pair consists of "hear" (a-word) and "give ear" (b-word). Both words are verbs, and they appear together in parallel cola. Furthermore, they often appear together in consecutive, parallel cola in Hebrew poetry (see, for example, Job 34:2; Pss 17:1; 49:2; and Joel 1:2). Another example appears in Ps 2:1 (emphasis added):

---

3. This phenomenon also has other designations, such as "fixed pairs," "parallel pairs," and even "standing pairs," but they all relate to the same concept.
4. This is apparent from the common pairs in Ugaritic; see Watson, *Classical Hebrew Poetry*, 128–43; Segert, "Parallelism in Ugaritic Poetry," 302–4; and Yoder, "A-B Pairs." Of course, word pairs are not restricted to Semitic literature; they are commonly found within the English language. Thus, for example, we have known pairs such as "flesh and blood," "mother and father," "bread and butter." Naturally, there is an overlap and word pairs in biblical and Semitic literature are also known and established in the English language, such as "heaven and earth" and "silver and gold."
5. These criteria are listed in Watson, *Classical Hebrew Poetry*, 128, and though imperfect, they provide appropriate guidelines for studying Hebrew Poetry.
6. Concerning this third criterion, if an identified or suspected word pair rarely appears in biblical literature, it is possible to validate its existence from other Semitic texts, such as Ugaritic or even Akkadian.

לָמָּה רָגְשׁוּ גוֹיִם	Why are the *nations* in an uproar
וּלְאֻמִּים יֶהְגּוּ־רִיק	and the *peoples* devising a vain thing?

Here the a-word "nations" in the first colon corresponds with the b-word "peoples" in the second, creating the word pair, rendering the schematic a//b. In both cola the corresponding words are nouns, and as a pair they appear often in the Hebrew Bible, as witnessed by Ps 105:44 and Prov 13:34. A notable phenomenon concerning word pairs concerns the second word in the pair: The b-word usually represents the rarer of the two words. Furthermore, the b-word is most often represented as one of the poetic words, discussed above, that is predominantly confined to poetry.[7] In addition to common nouns, proper nouns may also be included as word pairs. An example appears in Num 23:18:

קוּם בָּלָק וּשֲׁמָע	Arise, O Balak, and hear;
הַאֲזִינָה עָדַי בְּנוֹ צִפֹּר	give ear to me, O son of Zippor!

Here the central character in the first colon, Balak, is paired with the patrilineal formula, "son of Zippor." A slight adjustment is noticeable here, however, because the second colon employs two words to reflect the a-word in the first colon. This phenomenon, called an augmented pair, is reflected elsewhere in poetry. The relationship between word pairs like this can be represented by the notation a//ab. Another example appears in Exod 15:4:

מַרְכְּבֹת פַּרְעֹה וְחֵילוֹ	The chariots of Pharaoh and his army
יָרָה בַיָּם	he has cast into the sea;
וּמִבְחַר שָׁלִשָׁיו	and the choicest of his officers
טֻבְּעוּ בְיַם־סוּף	are drowned in the Sea of Reeds.

The initial recollection of the destructive waters appears simply as "sea" in the first colon, but this is augmented in the second colon by the corresponding phrase "Sea of Reeds," rendering two segments in the b-word. A slight change appears in this example when compared to the example in

---

7. See the previous section's discussion on poetic vocabulary.

Num 23. The word pair here constitutes a proper noun coupled with a common noun.

The final issue deserving attention concerns word-pair semantics. Contrary to the examples discussed above, the words do not have to be synonymous. Consider how certain word pairs operate in English. Expressions like "tooth and nail" constitute a word pair, but the two words involved are not synonymous. Similar pairings exist in Hebrew poetry, and an example appears in Ps 85:11[12]:

| אֱמֶת מֵאֶרֶץ תִּצְמָח | Truth springs from the earth, |
| וְצֶדֶק מִשָּׁמַיִם נִשְׁקָף: | and righteousness looks down from heaven. |

Here the psalm utilizes a common word pair found both in prose and poetry, heaven and earth. Although this pair represents a well-recognized unit, the individual elements cannot be viewed as synonymous, and one could argue they are more akin to opposites.[8] Notwithstanding their opposed meanings, they still appear as a word pair in poetry. One should note that even though the examples cited thus far separate the elements of the pair over two cola, the pairs may also appear together, separated by a *waw* in Hebrew. The same word pair mentioned above in Ps 85 similarly appears in a single colon in Ps 115:15:

| בְּרוּכִים אַתֶּם לַיהוָה | May you be blessed of the LORD, |
| עֹשֵׂה שָׁמַיִם וָאָרֶץ: | maker of heaven and earth. |

The final type of word pair worthy of note at this stage is one that produces numerical parallelism. In this case, the word pair consists of two

---

[8]. Tracking the development of Hebrew word pairs is difficult, to say the least, but they may have developed from composite expressions that appeared either together or joined by the *waw* ("and") conjunction. Consider, for example, the word pair "heaven and earth," which appears together, separated by a *waw* in Gen 14:19; Ps 69:34; and Ps 115:15, but as a split form across cola in Gen 27:28; Job 38:33; and Ps 57:6. It is hard to discern which came first, the word pair or the parallel pair, but identifying the origins is not critical to recognizing them and understanding how they work in poetry. Additionally, various genres appear to adopt their own pairs, as noted by Schökel, *A Manual*, 62. Prophetic literature, Psalms, and Proverbs rely on certain word pairs within their respective genres. For more on this phenomenon, see Melamed, "Break-Up of Stereotype Phrases." And more recently, Tsumura, "Literary Insertion," argues for a more general literary device of AXB, where A and B are set grammatical or semantic units—such as an established word pair—and X is a word, phrase, clause, or discourse that slots in between. Within this framework it is easy to recognize the breaking up of a composite pair.

numbers, but the numbers are not the same. Instead, the b-word incrementally advances the a-word by one, generating a schematic of a//a+1. Deuteronomy 32:30a presents an example of this type of parallelism:

| אֵיכָה יִרְדֹּף אֶחָד אֶלֶף | How could one chase a thousand, |
| וּשְׁנַיִם יָנִיסוּ רְבָבָה | and two put ten thousand to flight. |

In this instance, the number "one" appearing in the first colon corresponds with the number "two" in the second. Together, as a word pair, they play a crucial role in binding the two cola into a parallel pair. Other number pairs emerge elsewhere in similar sequences, as seen from Prov 6:16:

| שֶׁשׁ־הֵנָּה שָׂנֵא יְהוָה | There are six things that the LORD hates, |
| וְשֶׁבַע תּוֹעֲבוֹת נַפְשׁוֹ | yes, seven that are an abomination to him. |

Here the numbers six and seven appear in the consecutive cola, contributing toward their parallel relationship. With respect to the sequencing of this type of word pair, the smaller of the numbers frequently appears in the first colon.[9] Numerical parallelism like this commonly appears in wisdom literature, especially Proverbs, although it is not entirely restricted to this genre.[10] Overall, Hebrew poets employ word pairs to help create poetry, as seen above, and their appearance engenders a robust bond between consecutive and parallel cola. Identifying the word pairs employed by psalmists contributes toward understanding and distinguishing the poet's character and tendencies.

3.2 Synonymous Parallelism

The term synonymous parallelism commonly designates degrees of repetition that occur between two or more cola.[11] At least three categories of synony-

---

9. For more examples see Job 5:19 (6 // 7); Ps 62:12 (1 // 2); Hos 6:2 (2 // 3); Amos 1:3 (3 // 4).

10. Further information on this type of parallelism appears in O'Connell, "Telescoping N + 1 Patterns"; Roth, "Numerical Sequence," 300–11; and Weiss, "Pattern of Numerical Sequence."

11. Although Lowth's original definition of this term and his understanding of it has undergone significant revision, criticism, and discussion over the years, the term "synonymous parallelism" unfortunately remains in use today.

mous parallelism can be distinguished: semantic, grammatical, and syntactic. This section first focuses on semantic parallelism, which is by far the most researched and most noticeable feature of Hebrew poetry. Although biblical poetry does not usually rhyme as such, unlike English poetry, the idea of synonymous parallelism could be described as semantic rhyming between two or more cola. Usually, two elements in the first colon are echoed or repeated in the second (see Fig. 6)

a	b
a′	b′

FIGURE 6

When identifying and discussing semantic parallelism, the first thing to note is the degree of semantic overlap between two or more cola. Additionally, one must note the emphatic seconding character that poets often reserve for the second colon. Thus, the relationship between two cola, A and B, is that of "A is so, and what's more, B."[12] This emphatic element of the second colon implies that the two (or more) parallel cola are not truly synonymous because the exact thought and expression is not precisely equal in both parts. Consider, for example, Ps 145:10 (emphasis added):

		a		b
יוֹד֣וּךָ יְ֭הוָה כָּל־מַעֲשֶׂ֑יךָ	All	your works	shall	give thanks to you, O Lord,
וַ֝חֲסִידֶ֗יךָ יְבָרֲכֽוּכָה	and	your godly ones	shall	bless you.
		a′		b′

Ostensibly, v. 10b echoes the sentiment that everything God has created will offer thanks to him, their creator, with adoration. A closer look, however, reveals an intensification between "all your works" in colon A and "your godly ones" in colon B. The designation of מַעֲשֶׂ֑יךָ, "your works," includes animals, birds, fish, and land mammals, in addition to people of every nation.

---

12. See Kugel's discussion of the parallel line in *Idea of Biblical Poetry*, 103.

Such a broad designation narrows in the second colon by the corresponding term חֲסִידֶיךָ, "your godly ones," representing a more specific subset of its corresponding pair. One could further argue that the verbs for "give thanks," יָדָה, and "bless," בָּרַךְ, reflect a degree of intensification, with "bless" constituting a "more general form of powerful speaking than its pair."[13] Another example arises in Ps 51:5[7]:

הֵן־בְּעָווֹן חוֹלָלְתִּי	Behold, in iniquity I was brought forth,
וּבְחֵטְא יֶחֱמַתְנִי אִמִּי	and in sin my mother conceived me.

The psalmist in this verse expresses his perception of the unfathomable depths of his sinful nature and desire to disobey. The statement begins in colon A by suggesting that long ago, from the days of his birth, sin engulfed him. Then in colon B the image intensifies from a temporal perspective by suggesting that even before his birth, at conception, sin overwhelmed him.[14]

One notable manifestation of the intensification between cola was mooted in our discussion of word pairs, and the fact that the rarer and more poetic word forms usually appear in the second colon of parallel couplets. Appearing in this position lends to a slightly more emphatic character to the second colon, furthering the notion of "what's more, B."

In addition to the varying degree of intensity synonymous cola exhibit with respect to word pairs, other variances and differences are notable when comparing two parallel cola. The following examples explore the divergences between parallel lines. One end of the extreme appears in Ps 105:6:

זֶרַע אַבְרָהָם עַבְדּוֹ	O seed of Abraham, his servant,
בְּנֵי יַעֲקֹב בְּחִירָיו	O sons of Jacob, his chosen ones.

In this example, the level of repetition is remarkably complete when considering the number of elements in each colon both contain three words. Furthermore, the correspondence between each word is notable. Focusing on the English translation, "seed" corresponds well with "sons," both

---

13. Here see Kugel, *Idea of Biblical Poetry*, 7.
14. The idea of intensification frequently appears in Hebrew poetry; cf. Job 13:1 and Isa 44:22.

representing the fruit of the womb. Then Abraham parallels Jacob, both forefathers of the Hebrews. Finally, "servant" corresponds with "chosen ones," which reflect single words in Hebrew: עֶבֶד and the plural of בָּחִיר. So, in this couplet both the number of words and their semantic overlap correlate well between the cola.[15] It is possible to schematize this close relationship as a—b—c // a'—b'—c', reflecting a strict level of correspondence. This precise level of congruence is rare and thus should be noted when analyzing poetry. To create this level of parallelism the poet would have spent a little extra creative energy in his arrangement. It is therefore likely that he wanted his readers to pay special attention to that part of his composition.

Another similar example of these matched elements surfaces in the depiction of God dramatically parting the seas for the Israelites in Ps 106:22:

| נִפְלָאוֹת בְּאֶרֶץ חָם | Wonders in the land of Ham |
| נוֹרָאוֹת עַל־יַם־סוּף | and awesome things by the Sea of Reeds. |

The "wonders," נִפְלָאוֹת, in colon A correspond with the "awesome things," נוֹרָאוֹת, in colon B. Similarly, the "land of Ham," אֶרֶץ חָם, a poetic designation for Egypt, parallels "Sea of Reeds," יַם סוּף, in the second colon, which additionally demonstrates the relationship of "what's more" discussed earlier. A slight degree of variance in this instance appears with the nature of the preposition modifying the nouns of place. Colon A employs the inseparable preposition בְּ, "in," which attaches itself to the construct אֶרֶץ חָם, "land of Ham," creating a single lexical item. Contrasting this, the corresponding preposition "by" in colon B is represented with the separable preposition עַל. Despite this minor variance, the level of correspondence between the number of words used and semantic relationship between the two is remarkably precise. Another variation of exact repetition appears in Judg 5:27a:

| בֵּין רַגְלֶיהָ כָּרַע נָפַל שָׁכָב | Between her feet he bowed, he fell, he lay; |
| בֵּין רַגְלֶיהָ כָּרַע נָפָל | between her feet he bowed, he fell. |

---

15. Note also the grammatical and syntactic correspondence: a-words are construct nouns, b-words are personal names, and c-words are construct nouns with singular suffixes.

Here the songwriter adopts more than just a semantic repetition; he exactly replicates words from colon A to colon B. The only minor, and yet discernable, variance appears at the end of colon A. Judges 5:27b thus exemplifies a relatively rare example of parallelism, exhibiting an extreme level of repetition. It is possible to argue here that the poet exhibits a diminished creative capacity in creating this verse. After all, he seems to repeat artlessly most of the words from one colon into another. However, due to the repetition's precision and the scarcity of this type of duplication in Hebrew poetry, the poet creates a notable emphatic structure that readers are wise to register if they hope to appreciate the beauty of the poetry found in Scripture. Furthermore, because of the repetition, structures like this draw the reader's attention to the point of variance, "he lay." Since it has not been repeated, the clause develops into a crucial part of the image that the author seeks to convey.

Perhaps the most common sequencing of synonymous parallelism involves ellipsis—the intentional omission of verbs, subjects, or other grammatical components from colon B that can be inferred from colon A. In these cases, it is usually the first word in colon A that finds no visual representation in colon B, even though its presence is implied. Consider Ps 96:3:

סַפְּרוּ בַגּוֹיִם כְּבוֹדוֹ Tell of his glory among the nations,
בְּכָל־הָעַמִּים נִפְלְאוֹתָיו his wonderful deeds among all the peoples.

The imperative verb סַפְּרוּ, "tell of," opens v. 1 and addresses the גּוֹיִם, "nations," in the first colon. Moving to the second colon, however, even though the word "tell of" is absent, its force remains evident in the second colon. Thus, colon B is understood as "[tell of] his wonderful deeds among all the peoples," despite the omission of the verb "tell of." This means of expressing synonymous parallelism unquestionably dominates the various forms of synonymous parallelism in the Old Testament. Another example appears in Ps 103:1:

בָּרְכִי נַפְשִׁי אֶת־יְהוָה Bless the LORD, O my soul,
וְכָל־קְרָבַי אֶת־שֵׁם קָדְשׁוֹ and all that is within me, *bless* his holy name.

Here the psalmist exhorts every part of his body, everything that contributes to his humanity, to overcome his lingering despondency and praise the Lord. To accomplish this, the verse begins with the word "bless," which precedes the word נַפְשִׁי, "my soul," denoting his mind and will. Following these opening words is the vocative address to the Lord. The second colon omits the imperative verb בָּרֲכִי, "bless," but it is nonetheless implied. Thus, colon B exhorts the corresponding elements to "my soul"—"all that is within me"—to bless the Lord, or as stated in the second colon, "his holy name." Through this slightly more complex sequencing, it is possible to discern the pattern a—b—c // b′—c′,[16] which is typical of synonymous parallelism. In addition to verbs, other parts of speech may be omitted. Isaiah 14:4b demonstrates another possibility (emphasis added):

| אֵיךְ שָׁבַת נֹגֵשׂ | How the oppressor has ceased, |
| שָׁבְתָה מַדְהֵבָה | *and how* fury has ceased! |

In v. 4b, Isaiah's levels his proclamation against the king of Babylon and his armies. Instead of the interrogative pronoun, אֵיךְ, "how," appearing in both segments, the poet only utilizes it in the first colon. Despite its omission, however, its force undoubtedly applies to the second colon too, as evidenced by the English translation. Schematized, the present cola once again presents the pattern a—b—c // b′—c′, where the initial element, "a," the interrogative, remains absent from the second colon. Another example of note concerns Num 23:19a:

| לֹא אִישׁ אֵל וִיכַזֵּב | God is not a man, that he should lie, |
| וּבֶן־אָדָם וְיִתְנֶחָם | nor a son of man, that he should repent. |

Here Numbers records the words of the gentile prophet, Balaam, who explains a crucial aspect of God's character to Balak, the king who hired him to curse the Israelites. Two instances of ellipsis warrant an explanation in this text. First is the omission of the negative particle לֹא "no/not," which applies to both cola, despite its omission from colon A; consequently, the second colon

---

16. Within this schema, "the Lord" equates to "his holy name."

is in fact negated. Second, the word אֵל, God, the subject of both clauses, appears in only the first colon. Notwithstanding the physical omission of both words in v. 19b, their force or presence still influences the reading of colon B. Thus, the second colon can be rendered "[God is not] a son of man, that he should repent." Despite the omission of the particle and noun, the familiar correspondence of elements creating parallelism still exists. In this case, "man" corresponds with "son of man,"[17] and "lie" corresponds with "repent."

Finally, consider Ps 37:36, which discusses the fate of the wicked man:

| וַיַּעֲבֹר וְהִנֵּה אֵינֶנּוּ | Then he passed away, and behold, he was no more; |
| וָאֲבַקְשֵׁהוּ וְלֹא נִמְצָא | I sought for him, but he could not be found. |

This verse deserves mention because it represents the opposite end of the semantic correspondence spectrum. Here the level of semantic overlap between the cola is exceedingly subtle in comparison to the examples discussed earlier. Although both cola express the wicked man's evanescence, little can be said concerning the degree to which the psalmist employs matching word pairs. The expressions "then he passed away" and "I sought for him" bear no semantic correspondence at all. Despite the lack of semantic congruity between the individual words in the two cola, a fundamental idea is repeated: the wicked man disappears. The purpose of adducing this somewhat obtuse example is to demonstrate the varying scale of cohesiveness that can exist between two synonymously connected cola.

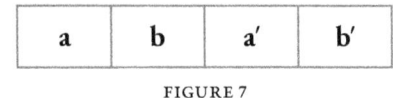

FIGURE 7

3.3 Internal Half-Line Parallelism

Synonymous parallelism need not exist solely between two cola; it often occurs within a single colon. The same principle applies where elements in the first part of the colon are echoed or repeated in the second part

---

17. For other examples of this pairing see Job 35:8; Ps 80:18; and Prov 8:4.

(see Fig. 7). Watson terms this phenomenon internal half-line parallelism.[18] Despite the lack of research on this poetic structure,[19] it appears frequently throughout Hebrew poetry. Judges 5:3a below demonstrates its features:

שִׁמְעוּ מְלָכִים הַאֲזִינוּ רֹזְנִים   Hear, O kings; give ear, O rulers!

This verse presents a clear example of internal half-line parallelism, exhibiting a pattern of a—b // a'—b', without ellipsis. The Hebrew text uses four words, and all of them participate in the verse structure. Further points of correspondence consolidate the verse pattern, such as plural imperative forms denoting the "a" elements, and plural common nouns reflecting both "b" elements. Note that the basic characteristics of synonymous parallelism still apply. Both pairs of corresponding words exhibit a degree of semantic overlap; furthermore, they both constitute established word pairs in the Old Testament.[20] The primary differentiating feature of this structure is that the synonymous parallelism all appears within a single colon, and is not split between cola, as discussed above. Consider the variations in Prov 10:9a:

הוֹלֵךְ בַּתֹּם יֵלֶךְ בֶּטַח   He who walks in integrity walks securely.

Proverbs 10:9 represents another strict example of the phenomenon. However, in this rendition of the sequence, two additional points deserve mention. First is the repetition of the root הלך in both sections of the colon, one as a participle and the other as an imperfect. Ordinarily, two separate roots appear with an overlapping semantic plane. Second is the repetition of the *bet* at the beginning of the "b" elements. Together, these factors contribute to an instance of alliteration, the repetition of initial consonants in a limited space.[21]

Due to the relative lack of research on internal half-line parallelism, it is currently difficult to establish unequivocal evidence in support of its rhetorical and structural function. Watson mentions three potential uses that are

---

18. See Watson, "Internal Parallelism."
19. As mentioned by Watson, "Internal Parallelism," 365. A discussion of the structure also appears in Avishur, *Stylistic Studies of Word-Pairs*.
20. For hear // give ear, see Gen 4:23; Num 23:18; Ps 39:12; Isa 1:2; and 32:9; for kings // rulers see Ps 2:2; Prov 8:15; 31:4; Hab 1:10.
21. A more complete discussion appears later in the second section.

worth noting.²² First, it may be used to open or introduce a section in a text, a stanza in a psalm, or a logical unit within an extended prophecy. Second, it may be used as a refrain in a poetic unit. Third, it may be used to effect proverbial sayings, even as witnessed in the second example above, which was bolstered by the alliteration.

3.4 Tricola Examples

a	b
a′	b′
a″	b″

FIGURE 8

Synonymous parallelism on occasion extends beyond two cola, with the repeated thought continuing over three consecutive cola (see Fig. 8). Exodus 15:8, in the Song of the Sea, demonstrates one example of the phenomenon:

וּבְרוּחַ אַפֶּיךָ נֶעֶרְמוּ מַיִם	At the blast of your nostrils the waters were piled up,
נִצְּבוּ כְמוֹ־נֵד נֹזְלִים	the flowing waters stood up like a heap;
קָפְאוּ תְהֹמֹת בְּלֶב־יָם	the deeps were congealed in the heart of the sea.

The song depicts God's role in subduing the Sea of Reeds, dividing it to make way for Israel to pass through in the final stage of their emancipation. Verse 8 dwells on the sea's response to God's rebuke, stylized by the breath of his nostrils. To recount the incident poetically, the author repeats a single idea in three different ways. In essence, the sea split, allowing the Israelites to pass on dry land, and the author dwells on this single idea, revealing different dimensions of the same incident. The same principles of parallelism discussed above apply to the present verse though with three cola being used instead

---

22. See Watson, "Internal Parallelism," 383.

of two. The writer uses three words, one in each colon, to describe waters of the sea, מַיִם, ("waters"), נֹזְלִים, ("flowing waters"), and תְּהֹמֹת, ("deeps"). Furthermore, like the preceding examples, ellipsis finds a place in the verse. The adverbial phrase אַפֶּיךָ בְּרוּחַ ("at the blast of your nostrils") only appears at the beginning of the first colon, but its force lingers over the second and third colon too. Thus, for example, the second colon conveys the sense *at the blast of your nostrils*, the flowing waters stood up like a heap." Another example of a tricolon's semantic parallelism appears in Ps 135:16–17a:

פֶּה־לָהֶם וְלֹא יְדַבֵּרוּ	¹⁶They have mouths, but they do not speak;
עֵינַיִם לָהֶם וְלֹא יִרְאוּ׃	they have eyes, but they do not see;
אָזְנַיִם לָהֶם וְלֹא יַאֲזִינוּ	¹⁷they have ears, but they do not hear.

In this denouncement of the nations' gods, the psalmist enlists three parallel cola to emphasize the limited capabilities of foreign idols, which were undoubtedly competing with the worship of Israel's God. The repetition in these verses requires little explanation. Each line begins by articulating the facial features of an idolatrous image. This is followed by a negated verbal clause, stressing the inability of the features to function in their expected ways.

In addition to three cola, four consecutive cola are occasionally constructed in accordance with the rules of synonymous parallelism (see Fig. 9). An example appears in Isa 24:19–20a:

רֹעָה הִתְרֹעֲעָה הָאָרֶץ	¹⁹The earth is broken asunder,
פּוֹר הִתְפּוֹרְרָה אֶרֶץ	the earth is split through,
מוֹט הִתְמוֹטְטָה אָרֶץ׃	the earth is shaken violently.
נוֹעַ תָּנוּעַ אֶרֶץ כַּשִּׁכּוֹר	²⁰The earth reels to and fro like a drunkard.

a	b
a′	b′
a″	b″
a‴	b‴

FIGURE 9

The passage presents no difficulty to the reader with respect to the repetition; especially conspicuous is the precisely repeated element אֶרֶץ, "earth." Additionally, the psalmist employs a verb in each colon reflecting an aspect of the earth's violent reaction. The example here is especially noteworthy because of the repetition of the root in the opening two words of each colon.

3.5 Distant Parallelism

So far the examples of synonymous parallelism presented have involved consecutive cola. Instances arise, however, where the expected repetition occurs in noncontiguous cola, producing a phenomenon called distant parallelism. Although distinctly rarer than the other types of synonymous parallelism discussed above, its presence deserves mention. Most commonly with this structural feature, the parallel couplet appears at the beginning and the end of poetic compositions, especially in the psalms. A very strict example of this appears in Ps 8:

יְהוָה אֲדֹנֵינוּ מָה־אַדִּיר שִׁמְךָ O Lord, our Lord,
בְּכָל־הָאָרֶץ how majestic is your name in all the earth!
(v. 1[2]a)

. .
. .
. .

יְהוָה אֲדֹנֵינוּ מָה־אַדִּיר שִׁמְךָ O Lord, our Lord,
בְּכָל־הָאָרֶץ how majestic is your name in all the earth!
(v. 9[10])

In this example, the parallelism occurs in the form of exact repetition in the opening and closing words of the psalm. Another example of the same phenomenon appears in Ps 103, although here the corresponding words are fewer.[23]

---

23. In essence, these examples generate instances of inclusion and envelope figure, structural techniques discussed later in chapter 5.

בָּרֲכִי נַפְשִׁי אֶת־יְהוָה	Bless the Lord, O my soul. (v. 1a)
. .	
. .	
. .	
בָּרֲכִי נַפְשִׁי אֶת־יְהוָה:	Bless the Lord, O my soul. (v. 22b)

In the same way two consecutive cola are labeled synonymous parallelism when presented sequentially, it is logical to adopt similar terminology when the parallel cola are separated by more than one verse; that is, when a literary distance exists between the corresponding cola.

Psalm 105:8–9, 42 demonstrates another example, one involving less repetition and where the repeated elements do not appear at the literary extents of the composition.

זָכַר . . . בְּרִיתוֹ . . .	He remembered . . . his covenant . . .
אֶת־אַבְרָהָם	with Abraham. (vv. 8–9)
. .	
. .	
. .	
כִּי־זָכַר אֶת־דְּבַר קָדְשׁוֹ	For he remembered his holy promise with
אֶת־אַבְרָהָם	Abraham. (v. 42a)

In the example above, the parallel elements appear within the body of the composition, as opposed to the extremities, as in the previous examples. Furthermore, the correspondence between the parallel elements remains imprecise, and not directly repetitive. Although the repetition of "with Abraham" and "he remembered" is present, the lexical representation of God's oath to Abraham finds two different expressions, "his covenant" and "his holy promise."

Psalm 132:9, 16 present a third example of the phenomenon (emphases added):

כֹּהֲנֶיךָ יִלְבְּשׁוּ־צֶדֶק	Let your **priests** be <u>clothed</u> with righteousness,
וַחֲסִידֶיךָ יְרַנֵּנוּ:	and <u>let your godly ones sing for joy</u>. (v. 9)

וְכֹהֲנֶיהָ אַלְבִּישׁ יֶשַׁע Her **priests** also I will <u>clothe</u> with salvation,
וַחֲסִידֶיהָ רַנֵּן יְרַנֵּנוּ׃   and her <u>godly ones will sing aloud for joy</u>.
(v. 16)

Again here, near exact correspondence exists between the words and expressions "priests," "clothe," and "godly ones sing for joy." This direct repetition draws the reader's attention to the parallel couplets even though they are separated by six verses. Additionally, however, a degree of variance deserves mention, with the metaphorical clothing finding an alternative expression. In v. 9, it is צֶדֶק, "righteousness," but in v. 16 it is יֶשַׁע, "salvation." The clergy being clothed with virtue proclaiming their happiness is the repeated idea between the cola.[24]

At least two functions of distant parallelism have been recognized. First, poets may adopt it to create a larger structural framework for their composition, employing the feature to create a stanza division. Ideally, however, it is still wise to pursue supporting evidence for determining stanza divisions to avoid falsely identifying textual divisions that were not intended by the author. Psalmists further employ distant parallelism to generate inner textual allusions.[25] The example discussed above, Ps 105, demonstrates the usage. Within this long composition, the psalmist introduces a crucial thematic element early in the psalm, God's covenant with Abraham, to give his descendants the land of Israel. Subsequently, the psalm delineates numerous literary-historical events, exemplifying how God remains faithful to his covenant. Then, toward the end of the psalm, v. 42, the psalmist alludes back to the words of God's promise, vv. 8–9, via distant parallelism. The repetition toward the end of the psalm reminds the reader of the central thematic idea introduced at the beginning. It is possible to think of this usage as a localized version of inner-biblical allusion.[26]

---

24. Other examples cited in Wendland, *Analyzing the Psalms*, 108–34, are Pss 132:2, 11; 22:1–11 (semantic); Pss 22:22, 25; 78:10–11, 17, 32, 40, 56.

25. The topic of inner-biblical allusion is discussed below in ch. 9.

26. Wendland, *Analyzing the Psalms*, 108–31, engages with this topic well. He classifies the

3.6 Grammatical Parallelism (Synonymous)

The feature of synonymous parallelism occurs on more than just the semantic level, as the examples above have illustrated. Other deeper classifications of parallelism exist, reflecting various degrees of grammatical, linguistic, and even phonological synonymity. As the discussion continues exploring some alternative types of synonymous parallelism, it is important to note that grammatical parallelism, in each of its forms, does not exclude semantic parallelism. Consequently, two or more levels of parallelism may exist within a single couplet, and in certain instances Hebrew poets supplement semantic correspondence with various forms of grammatical parallelism.

When speaking of grammatical parallelism, we are referring to the sequencing of parts of speech—nouns, substantives, verbs, prepositions, etc.—as they appear in consecutive parallel cola.[27] Just as poets semantically sequence words in rhythmic parallel style, they align the parts of speech to similarly generate a reading rhythm. Consider the following example from Ps 103:10:

| לֹא כַחֲטָאֵינוּ עָשָׂה לָנוּ | He has not dealt with us according to our sins, |
| וְלֹא כַעֲוֹנֹתֵינוּ גָּמַל עָלֵינוּ | nor rewarded us according to our iniquities. |

A cursory evaluation of this verse reveals that the psalmist took time to align, almost perfectly, the grammatical parts of the verse. The sequence for both cola contains the following sequence: neg.part.→prep.→n. phr.+1cp suf.→v.→prep.+1cp suf. The variation between the cola remains a moot point: the addition of the *waw* prefixing the negative particle in colon B along with the slightly longer prepositional form עַל at the end of the colon. Notwithstanding such slight alterations, an undeniable pattern emerges when reading these cola. Another example appears in Prov 14:33:

---

adoption of this poetic feature in terms of its structural usage. Wendland determines four primary uses: first, enclosure, yielding a pattern of a—X—a' (at the start and end of a psalm); second, aperture, yielding a—X, a'—X (opening individual units); third, closure, X—a, X—a' (at the close of stanzas); fourth, juncture, X—a, a'—X. Despite these definitions, clear and unarguable instances of this poetic feature remain elusive.

27. The challenges of determining concrete and provable instances of grammatical distant parallelism currently lie outside of contemporary scholarship's reach, although the possibility is intriguing.

בְּלֵב נָבוֹן תָּנוּחַ חָכְמָה	Wisdom rests in the heart of one who has understanding,
וּבְקֶרֶב כְּסִילִים תִּוָּדֵעַ	but in the hearts of fools it is made known.

In this instance, the proverb's author adopts the sequence prep.→n./const.→n.→v./impf. The main differences between the two cola are the addition of the noun חָכְמָה, "wisdom," in the first colon, and the *waw* conjunction at the beginning of colon B.[28] Despite these variances, unmistakable and purposeful parallel sequencing exists between the cola. Proverbs 14:33 highlights a particularly important aspect of grammatical parallelism: It can exist independently of semantic parallelism. Verse 33 presents the reader with an instance of grammatical synonymous parallelism; however, from a semantic perspective the verse reveals antithetical parallelism.[29] In short, the grammatical relationship between the cola reveals a synonymous relationship; however, this differs from the semantic correspondance, which reveals an antithetical relationship. The variance in this verse highlights the need for students to devote attention to both the surface and deeper structural levels of poetic lines because they do not necessarily correspond with each other.

Isaiah 2:4a presents us with another example:

וְשָׁפַט בֵּין הַגּוֹיִם	And he will judge between the nations,
וְהוֹכִיחַ לְעַמִּים רַבִּים	and will render decisions for many peoples.

Grammatically, the sequence above reflects the order: conj.→v.→ prep. → n.pl. The type of preposition appearing in each colon disrupts the similarity between them: Colon A adopts an independent/separable preposition, בֵּ, whereas colon B favors the inseparable preposition לְ. Consequently, colon B adds a ballast variant—in the form of the adjective, רַבִּים, "many"[30]—to compensate for the line length.[31]

---

28. One may further mention the plural-singular noun differences and the *qal* vs. *niphal* verb stems, but these are inconsequential at this stage.

29. See below.

30. See below for a further discussion on the concept and need for the ballast variant.

31. It is important to note that synonymous parallelism, as discussed above, is not a mutually exclusive phenomenon—either appearing in the semantic domain or the grammatical (or even

3.7 Ballast Variants

As they composed poetry, Hebrew poets assiduously implemented lexical adjustments to line lengths to create a sense of balance between cola. Readers seldom stumble across situations where bicola are severely unbalanced, exhibiting a vast difference between the number of words appearing in each colon. For example, readers are unlikely to find a bicolon with two words in colon A and ten words in colon B. Ordinarily, when a difference occurs between the number of words in parallel cola, it is tolerably minor, one or two words, perhaps. Most often, when poets are faced with the threat of unbalanced line lengths, when the line length differs by a single word, they include an additional lexical item to help balance the lines.[32] The additional word is called a ballast variant, and it creates a sense of order and visual uniformity to Hebrew couplets. An illustration of this phenomenon surfaces in the layout of Ps 15:1 (emphasis added):

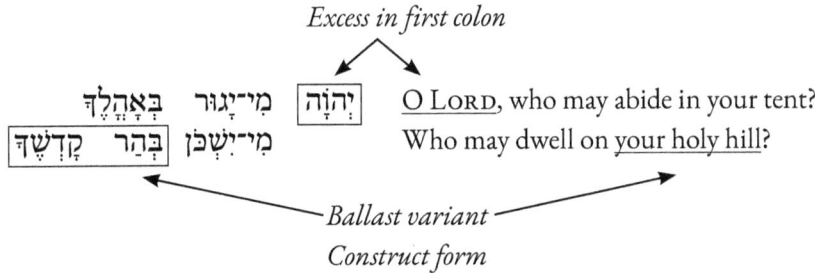

Verse 1 exhibits an instance of semantic synonymous parallelism, and it is not difficult to locate the three repeating segments in each colon: the interrogative (מִי), an expression of dwelling (יָגוּר and יִשְׁכֹּן), and phraseology depicting God's dwelling (אׇהֳלֶךָ and קׇדְשֶׁךָ). The first colon, however, opens

---

phonological). Diverse strata of parallelism frequently coexist, permeating grammatical, linguistic, and even phonological dimensions. It is not uncommon to find instances of grammatical parallelism enhancing and augmenting instances of semantic parallelism. Consequently, a comprehensive examination of each instance of parallelism necessitates teasing out the nuanced interplay between various potential levels of correspondence.

32. Watson adopts the term "*isocolic*" principle to describe the need for balancing. He further observes that when a disparity exists between the number of words in a line, colon B is customarily longer than colon A, according to the law of increasing members (Watson, *Classical Hebrew Poetry*, 343).

the verse with the vocative address, "O Lord," which is not repeated in the second colon and creates a four-word colon. With the addressee only implied in colon B, if left alone, it would only contain three words, in contrast to the four-word colon opening the verse. To remedy the situation, the psalmist adds a ballast variant—in this instance, a modification to the expression relating to the holy place, a construct chain utilizing two words, קָדְשְׁךָ בְּהַר, "your holy hill." Accordingly, the couplet maintains the semantic parallelism and preserves the lexical balance between the individual lines.[33] Consider also Judg 5:28b (NASB, emphasis added):

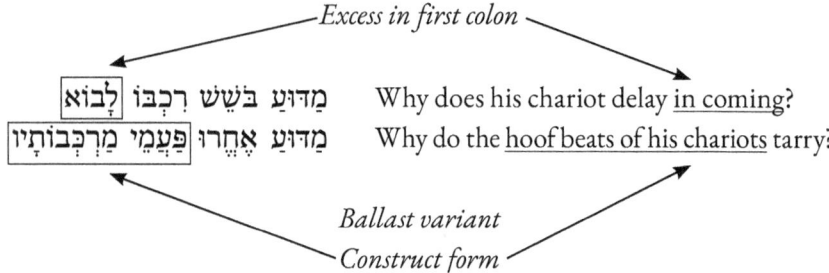

Because the final word in colon A, the infinitive construct form with inseparable preposition, לָבוֹא, "in coming," has no counterpart in colon B, even though it is implied, the construct expression "hoofbeats of his chariots" appears as the ballast variant. The construct form generates an additional, balancing lexical element. Of note here are the syllabic characteristics of colon B. Even though it contains the same number of words as colon A, it remains noticeably longer because of the added 3ms suffix to the plural noun, which increases the syllable count. This couplet highlights a phenomenon that Watson describes as the law of increasing members. In essence, it describes the propensity of Hebrew poets to extend the second of two couplets to make it longer than the first.[34]

---

33. Technically one could argue that the noun "hill" represents the ballast variant, but this does not shed meaningful light on the discussion.

34. Concerning these phenomena—the ballast variants and the law of increasing members—there are no absolutes. Therefore, instances appear that defy these heuristic rules and observations. So, we find instances such as Pss 3:4; 4:3; and Isa 5:2 and what Watson (*Classical Hebrew Poetry*, 345) refers to as a reverse ballast variant in Hos 4:13.

3.8 Phonological Parallelism

Phonological parallelism constitutes another identifiable category of parallelism. It occurs when poets select and pair two similar-sounding words in consecutive cola, similar to the sequencing of standard semantic word pairs. Repeating similar phonological elements in this way represents the closest representation of English rhyme in Hebrew poetry. To be sure, identifying concrete and irrefutable examples of phonological parallelism remains elusive. Because of the organic phonological similarity between some Hebrew verb stems, in addition to standard noun patterns, it is difficult to ascertain with any degree of certainty whether a poet intended to formulate a phonologically parallel pair or whether the pair arose through happenstance. Despite this potential setback, however, with due diligence and comprehensive scrutiny one can still identify this poetic technique. An example of phonological parallelism appears in Ps 78:33:

וַיְכַל־בַּהֶבֶל יְמֵיהֶם   So he ended their days in futility
וּשְׁנוֹתָם בַּבֶּהָלָה   and their years in sudden terror.

In the English translation, the elements of interest in this couplet are "in futility" and "in sudden terror." The Hebrew words for these expressions are undeniably comparable with regard to both morphology and phonology. Not only are the forms בַּהֶבֶל and בַּבֶּהָלָה similar, where each word contains the same letters, they further reflect a comparative pronunciation, *bahebel*, and *babbehalah*. Notably too, in this example, the psalmist implements the phonological and morphological similarity to reinforce the couplet's semantic parallelism. Both cola highlight the reality of a sudden and hopeless end to existence. Consider also Mic 5:10[9]b:

וְהִכְרַתִּי סוּסֶיךָ מִקִּרְבֶּךָ   I will cut off your horses from among you
וְהַאֲבַדְתִּי מַרְכְּבֹתֶיךָ   And destroy your chariots. (NASB)

The divine proclamation of destruction in this verse reveals an instance of morphological parallelism between final words of the bicolon. The prepositional phrase in colon A, מִקִּרְבֶּךָ, *miqqirbeka*, "from among you" corresponds with the suffixed noun מַרְכְּבֹתֶיךָ, *markeboteka*, "from your chariots." The appearance of these similar phonological elements at the end of the cola compares with how the word pairs appeared in the previous example.[35] Furthermore, without too much imagination one can extend the phonological parallelism to include the first words of the bicolon: Both constitute *hiphil* 1cs verbs, prefixed with a *waw*. The resulting similarity between the cola, viewing it purely with a phonological lens, has an overall sequence of a—b // a'—b'. A third example of phonological parallelism appears in Job 8:11:

הֲיִגְאֶה־גֹּמֶא בְּלֹא בִצָּה   Can the papyrus grow without a marsh?
יִשְׂגֶּה־אָחוּ בְלִי־מָיִם: Can the rushes grow without water?

This verse similarly exhibits a phonological pattern of: a—b // a'—b'. The first corresponding elements constitute words within the same verbal stem class, *qal*, and conjugation, imperfect 3ms. Together they produce the corresponding sound pairs, *yig'eh*, and *yisgeh*. Furthermore, the latter parts of each colon contain a phonological pair: The preposition plus negative particle couplet, בְּלֹא, *belo'*, which corresponds with the adverbial particle בְּלִי, *beli*.

When identifying phonological parallelism,[36] students and exegetes alike must exercise extreme caution! If, for example, only a single version of the feature appears in a particular composition or textual unit, then it is advisable to exercise circumspection before concluding an intentional formation of phonological parallelism is intended. On the other hand, if a reader notices an author's propensity to play with words, their sounds, and meanings, then a robust case can be offered for an intentional instance of this phenomenon.

Because unequivocal examples of phonologically paired couplets are not widespread in Hebrew poetry, phonological parallelism can be interpreted as a tool employed by psalmists to accentuate a specific verse or expression. Consequently, readers should ask two important questions when they discover instances of this phenomenon. First, "Can a distinctive degree of

---

35. Undoubtedly, an overlap exists here with respect to wordplay, and that topic is discussed later. Phonological parallelism as described here, and in other places, encroaches into the area of assonance.

36. For other examples see Ps 69:13; Prov 5:15; 6:15; and Zeph 1:13; and Berlin, *Biblical Parallelism*, 103–24.

importance be assigned to this couplet, regarding the text's or pericope's overall meaning?" Second, "Are any other emphatic structures assigned to the verse that highlight a crucial part of the poet's message?" Even though a poet may inadvertently include phonological parallelism in his composition, the opportunity for uncovering additional aspects of emphasis should not be overlooked.

3.9 Emblematic Parallelism

A poetic technique called emblematic parallelism deserves a brief mention at this point.[37] It traverses the boundary between the structural features and poetics in biblical Hebrew.[38] In essence, it constitutes a simile that an author spaces between two consecutive cola. The poet positions a figurative image, the emblem, in the first colon and transfers the image into the practical scenario the author seeks to communicate in the second colon. An example of the technique appears in Ps 42:1[2] below:

| כְּאַיָּל תַּעֲרֹג עַל־אֲפִיקֵי־מָיִם | As the deer pants for the water brooks, |
| כֵּן נַפְשִׁי תַעֲרֹג אֵלֶיךָ אֱלֹהִים׃ | so my soul pants for you, O God. |

In this verse, the emblem consists of the image of the deer panting, thirsting for water in a dry and arid desert. The image conveys a sense of deep dependency and reliance; if the deer fails to locate water and drink in such a harsh climate, it will surely die. In the second colon, the image transfers to the psalmist's actual situation. The level of utter desperation conjured in colon A applies to the psalmist's desperate need for God, his presence and protection, in colon B. Emblematic parallelism, despite the appearance here in Ps 42, more commonly appears in the apothegms of Proverbs. Consider, for example, Prov 11:22:

---

37. Throughout the years, this feature has been commonly discussed in the literature as a type of parallelism, modifying the work of Lowth. For further discussions, see Berlin, "Parallelism"; Greenstein, "How Does Parallelism Mean?," 41–70; Loewenstamm, "The Expanded Colon"; and Watson, *Classical Hebrew Poetry*, 150–56.

38. Technically, it could be discussed in either this section or the following section on poetics.

נֶ֣זֶם זָ֭הָב בְּאַ֣ף חֲזִ֑יר   As a ring of gold in a swine's snout
אִשָּׁ֥ה יָ֝פָ֗ה וְסָ֣רַת טָֽעַם   so is a beautiful woman who lacks discretion.

In the verse above, the wisdom writer conjures up the comical but vivid image of a precious and shining object in a place where it does not belong and is not appreciated. The same then transfers to the real-life situation, the beautiful woman, whose physical outward appearance conflicts with her behavior. Again, a simile remains central to the formation of the parallelism, it is split between the two cola, with the emblem appearing first.[39]

Questions for Consideration: How many repeated elements appear between the parallel pair? How semantically close in meaning are the repeated elements? How intense is the repetition between the cola? What main idea is repeated between the parallel cola? Where does half-line parallelism appear in the text—opening a stanza, closing a stanza? How precise is the repetition? Does it appear at a crucial point of the composition? Which word pairs appear in the text? Are the word pairs common in the rest of biblical literature? (Adopting a less common word pair may signify a degree of creativity in the poet's work.) Is the word pair used in the expected word order, or is it reversed? (Modifying the word order may generate dissonance, drawing the reader's attention.)

Further Reading: Avishur, "Stylistic Studies of Word-Pairs"; Berlin, *Biblical Parallelism*; Dell and Forti, "Two are Better than One"; Greenstein, "How Does Parallelism Mean?"; Grossberg, "Noun/Verb Parallelism"; Holmstedt, "Hebrew Poetry"; Kugel, *Idea of Biblical Poetry*; O'Connor, *Hebrew Verse Structure*; Tsumura, *Vertical Grammar*; Watson, *Classical Hebrew Poetry*; Yoder, "A-B Pairs."

---

39. For further examples, see Prov 10:26; 25:11, 13.

4

Pivoting Patterns

It is possible to categorize several verse structures under the composite heading of pivot patterns. These are patterns within cola, strophes, or stanzas that exhibit a literary hinge, a word or a phrase that creates an axis at the center of a poetic unit, generating what could be described as a turning point within a text. In relation to our travel metaphor, the pivot pattern reflects a U-turn, circling back on your journey to take another look at an interesting site. As you drive past a stately home, for example, it may be necessary to make a U-turn and retrace your steps to take a better look at the building and the grounds. Alternatively, you may wish to turn around a corner to survey the beauty of the structure's side that you cannot quite see from the main road. In either case, it is necessary to pivot, or turn back, to provide an additional dimension to the object of interest. The most common, and important, of these pivoting structures is chiasmus, and due to its importance, an additional section appears in this discussion that elaborates on how biblical poets employ chiasmus in their compositions.

4.1 Chiasmus

a	b
b'	a'

FIGURE 10

Chiasmus is another verse structure that resembles semantic parallelism in certain aspects, and one could argue that an overlap exists between the two verse patterns. Chiasmus, like synonymous parallelism, exhibits a degree of repetition between two cola, and synonymous word pairs are common to both structures. The reversed order of repeated elements (schematized in Fig. 10), however, distinguishes chiasmus from synonymous parallelism. Thus, a typical sequencing of synonymous parallelism appears as a—b // a'—b'. Chiastic patterns occur when the second colon inverts the sequence of repeated elements, yielding the pattern a—b // b'—a'. In this way, it deviates from the expected synonymous parallel pattern that occupies most poetic couplets. To demonstrate this structure, let us first consider Isa 22:22b:

וּפָתַח וְאֵין סֹגֵר	When he opens no one will shut,
וְסָגַר וְאֵין פֹּתֵחַ׃	When he shuts no one will open. (NASB)

This special kind of chiasmus demonstrates the workings of the word reversals.[1] Each of the three words in colon A is repeated in colon B, but in reversed order. It is possible to schematize the verse as a—b—c // c'—b'—a'. Isaiah 22:22b represents a special example because of the precise word repetition; chiasmus is not always formulated in this way. This verse additionally highlights an important feature of Hebrew poetic structures: more than a single structure may appear in a single verse. Even though, as discussed, the verse above presents an instance of semantic chiasmus, its presence does not discount instances of other structural features. In addition to chiasmus, v. 22 exhibits a distinct instance of grammatical synonymous parallelism. The sequence, conj.→*qal* pf.→conj.→neg. part.→*qal* ptc., repeats in both cola, yielding an instance of syntactic synonymous parallelism. Although the alternative layering of structural techniques fails to reflect the usual situation, it raises a potential scenario to which readers should pay attention.

Another example of chiasmus appears in Ps 78:43:

אֲשֶׁר־שָׂם בְּמִצְרַיִם אֹתוֹתָיו	When he performed his signs in Egypt
וּמוֹפְתָיו בִּשְׂדֵה־צֹעַן׃	and his marvels in the field of Zoan.

---

1. Watson, *Classical Hebrew Poetry*, 205, refers to this type of chiasmus as mirror chiasmus.

Here the psalmist poetically details the Lord's miraculous undertakings performed in Israel's emancipation from Egypt. In this instance, the repetition of words in the bicolon contrasts with the strictness witnessed in the previous example. The verse begins with a temporal clause and verb combination, "When he performed." The chiastic structure, however, fails to repeat these elements. The structure's "a" components constitute "Egypt [מִצְרַיִם]" and "the field of Zoan [שְׂדֵה צֹעַן]," which both reference the geographical stage upon which the acts of deliverance transpired. Representing the structure's "b" components are the words "signs [אוֹתוֹת]" in the first colon and "marvels [מוֹפְתִים]" in the second colon. Together, the two cola present the chiastic pattern a—b // b'—a'.

Psalm 78:43 illuminates a frequently occurring negative characteristic of English translations of poetic texts. For the sake of readability, English translations regularly realign a Hebrew poet's original chiastic order, rendering the cola as synonymous parallelism. Consequently, an improved rendering of the original Hebrew word order reads, "When he performed in Egypt his signs, and his marvels in the field of Zoan." For those primarily engaged with the English translations, it is important to remember that alterations like this directly affect the interpretation and understanding of a poetic work.[2]

Another example of this obscured word ordering appears in Ps 105:45:

בַּעֲבוּר יִשְׁמְרוּ חֻקָּיו	So that they might keep His statutes
וְתוֹרֹתָיו יִנְצֹרוּ	And observe His laws,
הַלְלוּ־יָהּ׃	Praise the LORD! (NASB)

Like the example in Ps 78, the initial words in Ps 105:45, "so that [בַּעֲבוּר]," are omitted from colon B. Although the NASB presents an a—b // a'—b' pattern, with "keep" and "observe" as corresponding "a" elements, and "statutes" and "laws" corresponding "b" elements, the Hebrew reflects a distinctive chiastic arrangement. Reorganizing the English to harmonize with the Hebrew text (emphasis added) renders, "So that they might **keep** *statutes*, and his *laws* **observe**," reflecting the expected a—b / b'—a' chiastic word order.

---

2. For readers without knowledge of biblical Hebrew, it is advisable to utilize an interlinear Bible to uncover potentially obscured but significant word ordering in the original language.

Consider another example, this time from Lam 3:22 (emphases added):

חַסְדֵי יְהוָה כִּי לֹא־תָמְנוּ   The **lovingkindnesses** of the LORD
                                                                        indeed <u>never cease</u>,
כִּי לֹא־כָלוּ רַחֲמָיו׃   for they <u>never fail</u> his **compassions**.

In Lam 3:22, even though a chiastic sequencing is detectable, the correspondence between the lexical items—highlighted with the bold text equating to "a" and the underline relating to "b"—remains more obscure than the earlier examples of the structure. Here it is not possible to detect a clean one-for-one correspondence between the lexical items. The couplet exhibits an easily identifiable correspondence between the "a" components, "lovingkindnesses [חֲסָדִים]" and "compassions [רַחֲמִים]," because the Hebrew language represents both concepts with single words. The second component, however, constitutes three parts: the particle כִּי, a negative particle, לֹא, and a verb expressing ceasing. Consequently, even though chiasmus exists, the schema to illustrate it necessitates modification to, a—bcd // bcd'—a'.[3]

Chiasmus can also exist within a single colon, in the same style as internal half-line parallelism. Isaiah 3:8a illustrates the possibility:

כִּי כָשְׁלָה יְרוּשָׁלַם וִיהוּדָה נָפָל   For she has stumbled, Jerusalem, and
                                                                         Judah has fallen.

In the verse above, *qal* perfect verbs represent the "a" portion of both segments, כָּשַׁל "stumbled" and נָפַל "fallen," comprising a recognized word pair in biblical Hebrew that possess a noticeable semantic overlap.[4] The "b" components both refer to the inhabitants of the Southern Kingdom: יְרוּשָׁלַיִם, "Jerusalem," and יְהוּדָה, "Judah." Together, with the omission of the particle כִּי, "for," the colon presents the chiastic pattern a—b // b'—a' (schematically represented in Fig. 11). Unlike the previous examples, however, the pattern exists within the confines of a single colon.

---

3. A sequence of this type is called a split-member chiasmus. For further examples see Prov 7:12 and Isa 11:1; see also Watson, *Classical Hebrew Poetry*, 203.

4. See, for example, Ps 27:2; Isa 31:3; and Jer 46:12.

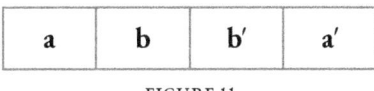

FIGURE 11

4.2 Tricola Chiasmus

Structurally, chiastic patterns may extend vertically beyond two cola and into three or more. In a single colon, one or more lexical elements may subsequently span a tricolon, for example, yielding a colon pattern of repeated elements, ABA'.[5] Consider, Ps 118:15b–16:

יְמִין יְהוָה עֹשָׂה חָיִל׃	[15]The right hand of the LORD does valiantly.
יְמִין יְהוָה רוֹמֵמָה	[16]The right hand of the LORD is exalted.
יְמִין יְהוָה עֹשָׂה חָיִל׃	The right hand of the LORD does valiantly.

In this sequence, the "A" portion of the chiastic sequence consists of the words "does valiantly [עֹשָׂה חָיִל]," which repeats in the first and third colon of the cited portion—ignoring for the time being the words "The right hand of the LORD," which repeats in each colon. In the middle, encapsulated, is the phrase "is exalted [רוֹמֵמָה]," reflecting the pattern's "B" portion.

Another example appears in Isa 56:9 (emphasis added):

כֹּל חַיְתוֹ שָׂדָי	All you beasts of the field,	A
אֵתָיוּ לֶאֱכֹל	come to eat.	B
כָּל־חַיְתוֹ בַּיָּעַר׃	All you beasts in the forest.	A'

Here the words "all beasts [חַיָּה כֹּל]," in addition to the corresponding pronominal suffix, constitutes the outer layers, the "A/A'" portion of the ABA' formation. The first colon adopts "of the field," the location of the beasts, and the second uses the semantic equivalent "in the forest."[6] The words "Come to eat," form the middle, "B," element.

---

5. This pattern is frequently referred to as chiastic in the literature but may also be viewed as an envelope figure.

6. This word pair appears elsewhere in Pss 80:14 and 96:12. Here, although rare, it is also possible to add the category of phonological chiasmus. Two examples cited by Schökel, *A Manual*, 24, are Isa 40:4 and 61:3.

Psalm 12:3–4[4–5] extends further, presenting a four-cola example of chiasmus (emphasis added):

יַכְרֵת יְהוָה כָּל־שִׂפְתֵי חֲלָקוֹת	³May the Lord cut off all flattering **lips,**	A
לָשׁוֹן מְדַבֶּרֶת גְּדֹלוֹת׃	the **tongue** that speaks great things;	B
אֲשֶׁר אָמְרוּ לִלְשֹׁנֵנוּ נַגְבִּיר	⁴who have said, "With our **tongue** we will prevail;	B′
שְׂפָתֵינוּ אִתָּנוּ מִי אָדוֹן לָנוּ׃	our **lips** are our own; who is lord over us?"	A′

The excerpt above contains a psalmist's words of prayer against threatening enemies that focus on ending the hostile and minatory words spoken against the supplicant. The chiastic sequencing in the above verses appears in four consecutive cola, yielding an A—B // B′—A′ pattern. Here the quatrain fails to exhibit a single central element, as with the previous three-cola version, but instead reflects two pivoting components, repetition of the word "tongue [לָשׁוֹן]" in the second and third colon. The cola containing the words "lips [שְׂפָתַיִם]" envelop the two central cola containing "tongue [לָשׁוֹן]." Isolating these two words in their current order produces the chiastic pattern: lips—tongue // tongue—lips.

4.3 Functions of Chiasmus

Fortunately, numerous scholars have dedicated significant time and attention to discussing the forms and functions of chiasmus in both prose and poetry. Concerning poetry specifically, theories have been proposed explaining how poets employ chiasmus to create verse and composition structure and to express meaning within poetic units. The paragraphs below, beginning with the structural use of chiasmus, discuss the more prominent uses of chiasmus.

4.3.1 Opening Poetic Units

Chiasmus, particularly when appearing in individual verses, can serve to open either individual psalms or, perhaps more commonly, poetic units within longer compositions. In the first verse of Hab 2, as the prophet waits for a reply from the Lord, he says (emphases added):

עַל־מִשְׁמַרְתִּי אֶעֱמֹדָה	On my <u>guard post</u> I will **stand**
וְאֶתְיַצְּבָה עַל־מָצוֹר	and **station myself** on <u>the rampart</u>.[7]

In the opening words of this oracle, the chiastic pattern occurs over two cola with two repeated elements, a—b // b'—a'. Nouns reflecting a location for standing watch constitute the outer limits, representing "a" and "a'" of the chiasmus, "guard post [מִשְׁמֶרֶת]" and "rampart [מָצוֹר]." The inner portion of the structure contains verbs of standing, "stand [עָמַד]" and "station myself [הִתְיַצֵּב]."

Also, Ps 92, a song of praise, contains the chiastic sequence: "morning [בֹּקֶר]"—"lovingkindness [חֶסֶד]" // "faithfulness [אֱמוּנָה]"—"night [לַיְלָה]." In this example, the outer elements, instead of reflecting semantic equivalents, are characterized by nouns reflecting a time of day.

לְהַגִּיד	To declare
בַּבֹּקֶר חַסְדֶּךָ	in the **morning** <u>your lovingkindness</u>
וֶאֱמוּנָתְךָ בַּלֵּילוֹת׃	and <u>your faithfulness</u> in the **night**.
	(v. 2[3], emphases added)

A third example of chiasmus surfaces in the beginning of Ps 19, a magnificent hymn of praise celebrating creation and God's law:

הַשָּׁמַיִם מְסַפְּרִים כְּבוֹד־אֵל	<u>The heavens</u> **tell** of <u>the glory of God</u>;
וּמַעֲשֵׂה יָדָיו מַגִּיד הָרָקִיעַ׃	and <u>the work of his hands</u> **declare** the *expanse*.
	(v. 1[2], emphases added)

In this example, three elements create the chiastic arrangement over two cola, displaying the pattern a—b—c // c'—b'—a'. The outer segment, representing "a" and "a'," adopts semantically equivalent nouns serving as

---

7. Many of my own translations appear in this section because of the English versions' propensity to alter the word order for the sake of perceived clarity.

the subjects of their respective clauses.[8] Rather than a person, or a nation, Ps 19 portrays the heavens and the expanse, or firmament, as declaring God's majesty. Moving inward, the next concentric element, the "b" and "b'" portions, contain verbs of declaration, "tell [מְסַפְּרִים]" and "declare [מַגִּיד]." The conjugation of these verbs—both are active participles—reinforces the semantic overlap between them. The chiastic structure's central element, represented by "c" and "c'," constitutes the object of each clause. They both contain descriptions or a reflection of what God has created. The expression כְּבוֹד אֵל, "the glory of God," in this context conveys the idea of the glorious wonders God has created. The second colon rephrases the same notion through the expression מַעֲשֵׂה יָדָיו, "the work of his hands."

4.3.2 Closing Poetic Units

In addition to opening stanzas, chiastic patterns frequently serve to conclude poetic units, appearing either at the end of psalms or shorter pericopae within longer segments. This represents one of the more common functions of chiasmus. An unmistakable example appears at the end of Ps 1:6:

| For the LORD knows the way of the righteous, | כִּי־יוֹדֵעַ יְהוָה דֶּרֶךְ צַדִּיקִים |
| but the way of the wicked will perish. | וְדֶרֶךְ רְשָׁעִים תֹּאבֵד׃ |

In this instance, both semantic and grammatical correspondence contribute to the chiastic effect. After the particle כִּי, "for," the psalmist uses the verb "knows," which corresponds with the final verb, תֹּאבֵד, "will perish." Although both words cannot be viewed as semantic equivalents, they belong to the same lexical class, verbs. Together they represent the "a/a'" portion of the chiastic sequence, a—b // b'—a'. The central elements, "b/b'," contain two construct chains, "way of the righteous [דֶּרֶךְ צַדִּיקִים]" and "way of the wicked [דֶּרֶךְ רְשָׁעִים]." For the most part, the sequence represented in v. 6 is grammatical, v.—const.//const.—v. No readily identifiable semantic congruity exists between the verbs "knows [יוֹדֵעַ]" and "will perish [תֹּאבֵד]." Furthermore, the individual nouns "wicked [רְשָׁעִים]" and "righteous [צַדִּיקִים]" are considered

---

8. This situation staunchly resists translation into English because the expected order in English clauses is S→V→O. To maintain the chiastic arrangement, however, the Hebrew orders the second colon O→V→S, which presents difficulties for English readers to understand.

opposites. That said, the head noun in both construct forms reflects correspondence in the form of exact repetition, the word "way [דֶּרֶךְ]."

Another example of chiasm ending a psalm appears in Ps 27:14:

קַוֵּה אֶל־יְהוָה	Wait for the Lord;	A
חֲזַק וְיַאֲמֵץ לִבֶּךָ	be strong and let your heart take courage;	B
וְקַוֵּה אֶל־יְהוָה׃	yes, wait for the Lord.	A'

This verse differs slightly from the previous example regarding the type of chiasmus employed. Rather than concluding with the a—b // b'—a' pattern, the psalmist employs the longer structural ABA' form to generate his composition's conclusion. In this example, the clause "wait for the Lord [קַוֵּה אֶל־יְהוָה]" creates the envelope around the second colon.

4.3.3 Creating Midpoint

In addition to the beginning and concluding texts, poets sometimes position instances of chiasmus to signify the middle of a pericope. In Prov 1:20–33, the sage presents the reader with an extended metaphor portraying Lady Wisdom as she cries out in the streets to attract the attention of any who would listen as they pass. In addition to the call, however, she warns the reader of the fate awaiting those who reject her call. At the midpoint of her oration, readers are faced with chiastic wording that communicates Lady Wisdom's response when those who reject her words fall to a catastrophic end:

גַּם־אֲנִי בְּאֵידְכֶם אֶשְׂחָק	I at your calamity will laugh;
אֶלְעַג בְּבֹא פַחְדְּכֶם׃	I will mock when your dread comes. (Prov 1:26)

Even though the English translations generally obscure the wording, the Hebrew reflects an unmistakable chiastic ordering, a—b // b'—a'. The correspondence in this instance primarily operates on a grammatical level, n.—v. // v.—n. However, a degree of semantic correspondence serves to reinforce the grammatical structure. Hebrew poetic texts elsewhere attest the word pairs "calamity [אֵיד]" // "dread [פַּחַד]" and "mock [לָעַג]" // "laugh [שָׂחַק]."[9]

---

9. See Job 31:23; Pss 2:4; and 59:8, respectively.

Because chiasmus presents a pivoting structure, creating a central literary hinge, it constitutes an appropriate midpoint in longer literary units.

Another example appears in Ps 51:2[4]:

| הַרְבֵּה כַּבְּסֵנִי מֵעֲוֺנִי | Thoroughly wash me from my iniquity |
| וּמֵחַטָּאתִי טַהֲרֵנִי | and from my sin cleanse me. |

This verse appears in the middle of the first stanza of the Hebrew text, vv. 1–8[3–10]. Syntactically, the repeated elements in this example are remarkable. Apart from the elided adverb "thoroughly [הַרְבֵּה]," the bicolon exhibits an extensive level of congruity between its corresponding elements. The table below highlights the correlation between the cola:

piel impv.→1cs obj.suf.f   *mem* prep.→n.sg.→1cs suf.
mem prep.→n.sg.→1cs suf.   *piel* impv.→1cs obj.suf.

The established word pairs further solidify the chiastic structure, creating a semantic correspondence between the cola. An argument could also be made for the established word pairs "wash [כָּבַס]" // "cleanse [טָהַר]" and "iniquity [עָוֺן]" // "sin [חַטָּאת]."[10]

In addition to chiasmus's structural function, it can participate in conveying meaning in poetic texts; thus, chiasmus can have an expressive use.[11] In this way, chiasmus's predominantly structural feature enhances other poetic devices employed by psalmists. The discussion below examines important categories of expressive chiasmus.

4.3.4 Expressing Contrast

Poets sometimes employ chiasmus to express or highlight contrasts in their compositions. Use of chiasmus in this context is particularly common in wisdom poetry. Consider Prov 13:25a:

| צַדִּיק אֹכֵל לְשֹׂבַע נַפְשׁוֹ | The righteous has enough to satisfy his appetite |
| וּבֶטֶן רְשָׁעִים תֶּחְסָר | but the stomach of the wicked is in need. |

---

10. See Job 10:14; Ps 51:9; and Lam 5:7, for example.
11. See Watson, *Classical Hebrew Poetry*, 205, for this definition.

In this aphorism, the writer draws a direct contrast between the righteous and the wicked regarding their supply of food. As a general rule of life, the righteous have enough to sate their appetites, but those who practice wickedness are deprived of food and adequate nourishment. Within this verse the chiastic pattern a—b // b′—a′ surfaces in the sequence of righteous—appetite // stomach—wicked. In this instance, the correspondence between the a-words is that of a noun reflecting moral character.[12]

This use of chiasmus is not restricted to wisdom poetry, however, and another example of this usage appears in Gen 9:6a, tucked away in a sea of narrative, as part of God's commands to Noah concerning laws governing humankind:

שֹׁפֵךְ דַּם הָאָדָם	Whoever sheds man's blood,
בָּאָדָם דָּמוֹ יִשָּׁפֵךְ	by man his blood shall be shed.

The injunction here concerns the murderer, one who slays another man in anger for selfish or malicious reasons. Generating the chiasmus are the words "shed [שָׁפַךְ]"→"blood [דָּם]"→"man [אָדָם]," which are reversed in the second colon. The contrast relates to the man who commits murder, killing another man, and the retribution that he recieves. One can conceptualize this in terms of an act of injustice contrasted with justice. The punishment of that man, the killer himself, is death at the hands of another man—presumably after a judicial process has transpired. Another aspect of contrast in this statement concerns an action and its consequence. The actions of a killer return to him in the form of his own death sentence.

4.3.5 Emphasis

Another use of chiasmus, and perhaps one of the more common functions, arises when poets aim to emphasize a crucial part of their poem or stanza. Often this function coincides with chiasmus appearing as the last verse of the stanza or composition, an emphatic position. In this way, the structural deployment of the poetic feature coincides with its expressive function. An example of this phenomenon appears in Ps 105:45 (emphases added):

---

12. For further examples in wisdom poetry, see Prov 10:13, 12:20, and 13:24.

בַּעֲבוּר יִשְׁמְרוּ חֻקָּיו	So that they might **keep** <u>his statutes</u>
וְתוֹרֹתָיו יִנְצֹרוּ	and <u>his laws</u> **observe,**
הַלְלוּ־יָהּ׃	praise the Lord!

Here the psalmist occupies himself with recounting the kind and benevolent acts of God toward his people throughout their history from the promise of land to Abraham to the fulfillment of that promise to his offspring. Carefully, the psalmist reserves his most emphatic point for the final verse.[13] All of the merciful acts God performed on behalf of his people were not without obligation. God accomplished them so that his people, the Israelites, would keep and observe his covenant laws. To emphasize this lesson in the final verse, the psalmist adopts a chiastic structure. The psalmist's use of chiasmus—see the corresponding elements highlighted above in bold and underlined—is not restricted to this verse. Throughout his composition, the psalmist at various strategic points creates emphasis with this poetic device. In his description of the patriarchs' nomadic days, when they were vulnerable as they wandered the land of Canaan, despite the dangers from the peoples, God remained faithful to his promise to Abraham by protecting them. At the end of the pericope detailing the patriarchal adventures, the psalmist cites the words of God that emphasize his rebuke of the nations and his protective care of his people. This emphatic quote appears in chiastic formation:

אַל־תִּגְּעוּ בִמְשִׁיחָי	Do not touch my anointed ones,
וְלִנְבִיאַי אַל־תָּרֵעוּ׃	and to my prophets do no harm. (Ps 105:15)

---

13. A survey of biblical literature reveals that the final words of a pericope often create the most impactful part of a textual unit, leaving a lasting impression on the reader, and constituting the portion authors intend to be remembered. On a larger scale, it is notable that prophecies frequently conclude with positive words to avoid leaving the audience with an overly negative and thus hopeless feeling (see, for example, Mic 7:18–20; Zeph 3:14–20; Hag 2:20–23). Etiological texts also reserve word associations until the end of the story (e.g., Gen 32:32, why Israelites do not eat the sinew of the hip; Gen 11:9, the naming of Babylon from "confusion"; Exod 17:7, Massah and Meribah). This idea frequently appears in psalms, where the psalmists often reserve the main point of their message for the conclusion of their compositions. For example, Ps 1:6 emphasizes the fates of the righteous and wicked in the last verse. Additionally, the main point of Ps 78—the selection of Judah and David—is revealed at the end, as is the prophetic warning of Ps 95. New Testament parables reflect the same idea, where the point or main teaching of the parable remains hidden until the end. See Luke 10:30–37 (esp. v. 37) and 20:9–17.

The chiasmus in this verse is concise and strict, where almost all the elements partake in the structure. Furthermore, the syntactic reversal corresponds well with the semantic reversal, reinforcing it. Grammatical chiasmus appears in the sequence: negated v.—n.pl.+1cs // n.pl.+1cs—negated v. This fundamental structure, however, is reinforced by both nouns being prefixed with prepositions. Despite the semantic correspondences ("touch [נָגַע]" // "harm [רָעַע]" and "anointed ones [מָשִׁיחַ]" // ("prophets [נָבִיא]") failing to appear elsewhere in biblical literature, within the confines of v. 15 they constitute appropriate and logical pairings. In v. 15, the emphatic nature of the chiasmus intensifies through the contrasting synonymous parallelism found in the previous verses. The choice of synonymous parallelism generates a rhythm that is broken by the chiastic insertion, which in turn solidifies the words of the rebuke.

Psalm 1:6 presents another example (emphases added):

| כִּי־יוֹדֵעַ יְהוָה דֶּרֶךְ צַדִּיקִים | For the LORD **knows** <u>the way of the righteous</u>, |
| וְדֶרֶךְ רְשָׁעִים תֹּאבֵד | but <u>the way of the wicked</u> **will perish**. |

The chiasmus appearing in v. 6 is primarily grammatical, consisting of v.—const.phr. // constr.phr.—v. Even though the underlined noun phrases correspond in part, both depicting human behavior, no semantic correspondence exists between the verbs, in bold. In v. 6, one of the main reasons for claiming an emphatic application of chiasmus relates to its placement in an emphatic position in the psalm, the final verse of the composition. Here it is worth emphasizing again that the chiasmus by itself is not the trigger for interpreting an emphatic use of the structure, but the context in which the chiasmus appears.[14]

4.3.6 Reversal of State

Another recognized application of chiasmus is to contribute toward the expression of a reversal of state. In using chiasmus this way, the poets articulate a reversal through the meaning of the words chosen, in addition to their sequencing. An example appears in Mal 4:6[3:24] (emphases added):

---

14. Ceresko, *Psalmists and Sages*, 43–48, further discusses the idea of chiasmus as an emphatic tool.

וְהֵשִׁיב לֵב־אָבוֹת עַל־בָּנִים	He will restore the heart of the **fathers** to their <u>children</u>
וְלֵב בָּנִים עַל־אֲבוֹתָם	And the hearts of the <u>children</u> to their **fathers**.

The crossing of words in this instance involves the sequencing: a—b // b'—a'. Here Malachi emphasizes the restoration and reunion of children to their fathers, and fathers to their children, changing the state from a present reality of disunion to one of union. By reversing the order of the keywords in the verse, the psalmist additionally highlights the reversal of state that will occur in fulfilment of the prophecy. Verse 24, in essence, reiterates the same sentiment from two opposing perspectives, one from the children's vantage point and the other from the fathers'. Despite the two perspectives, the verse promotes the same act of reunion. It is therefore possible to assert, with some reservation, that a level of further emphasis arises from this chiastic sequencing. Recognizing multiple functions of chiasmus within a single verse, therefore, should be considered a possibility when interpreting poetic structures.[15]

Zephaniah 3:19, another prophetic text, provides a further example (emphases added):

הִנְנִי עֹשֶׂה אֶת־כָּל־מְעַנַּיִךְ	Behold, I will deal with all your
בָּעֵת הַהִיא	oppressors at that time
וְהוֹשַׁעְתִּי אֶת־הַצֹּלֵעָה	**I will save** the <u>lame</u>
וְהַנִּדָּחָה אֲקַבֵּץ	and the <u>outcast</u> **I will gather**.

In this verse, Zephaniah communicates God's words to the people of Judah, detailing a future era when he will remove the threats and oppression of his people. The emphasis, in this instance, emerges in the restored states of the lame and outcast. Under the benevolent care of the Lord, both maltreated segments of society will be restored and freed from oppression. The chiasmus in this example surfaces at both grammatical and semantical layers.

---

15. The reversal of state also finds expression in larger chiastic structures. See Gaines's discussion on Lam 1:21–26 in *The Poetic Priestly Source*, 56.

Grammatically, the pattern in the second and third lines equate to v.—n. // n.—v., although the verb forms alternate from *weqatal* to *yiqtol*. Semantically, both word pairs, יָשַׁע* [to save] // קָבַץ [to gather] and צָלַע [lame] // נָדַח [outcast], are attested elsewhere in biblical literature.[16]

4.3.7 Enhancing Merismus

Scholars have recognized that on occasion poets adopt chiasmus to enhance a poetic technique called merismus, which expresses two opposite parts of an entity to signify its entirety.[17] An example of this application of chiasmus appears in Ps 121:6 (emphases added):

יוֹמָם הַשֶּׁמֶשׁ לֹא־יַכֶּכָּה	By **day** the <u>sun</u> will not smite you,
וְיָרֵחַ בַּלָּיְלָה	nor the <u>moon</u> by **night**.

The words in this verse serve to highlight the protective power of God from the natural elements. The author of Ps 121 adopts polar opposites, day and night, to articulate the entirety of each day, to communicate the notion of consistency. Coinciding with the merismus, v. 6 reveals the chiastic pattern: day [יוֹם]—sun [שֶׁמֶשׁ] // moon [יָרֵחַ]—night [לַיְלָה], where each element is represented by a noun. The chiastic structure reinforces the semantic opposition in the reversed noun order: day the opposite of night, and sun the opposite of moon. In contrast to the examples discussed above, the corresponding elements of this chiastic pattern do not function as semantic equivalences.

Psalm 78:14 similarly constructs a chiastic structure involving day and night (emphases added):

וַיַּנְחֵם בֶּעָנָן יוֹמָם	Then he led them with **the cloud** by <u>day</u>
וְכָל־הַלַּיְלָה בְּאוֹר אֵשׁ׃	and all the <u>night</u> with **a light of fire**.

Once again, the emphasis in this example is on the constant fidelity of the divine presence in leading the Israelites. The chiasmus schematizes as:

---

16. See Ps 106:47 and Mic 4:6 respectively.
17. See below for a further explanation and examples of this feature.

leading manifestation—time of day // time of day—leading manifestation. The psalmist implements the chiastic sequence together with the merismus, day and night, representing temporal continuity. Unlike the example in Ps 121, however, the author of Ps 78 adopts the notion of continuity to depict the Lord's careful guidance of Israel throughout their desert sojourn. The two examples of chiasmus paired with merismus cited here serve as a reminder that more than a single poetic form may occupy a single verse. Consequently, readers and interpreters must be tuned to multiple layers of structural and poetic features resting within a single composition.

Another occasional function of chiasmus relates to its appearance in nonconsecutive cola, referred to as distant chiasmus, where it serves to create inner-textual allusions.[18] Consider the following lines from Ps 78:

| בְּנֵי־אֶפְרַיִם נוֹשְׁקֵי רוֹמֵי־קָשֶׁת | The sons of Ephraim were archers equipped with bows, |
| הָפְכוּ בְּיוֹם קְרָב׃ | yet they turned back in the day of battle. (v. 9) |

| וַיִּסֹּגוּ וַיִּבְגְּדוּ כַּאֲבוֹתָם | But turned back and acted treacherously like their fathers; |
| נֶהְפְּכוּ כְּקֶשֶׁת רְמִיָּה | they turned aside like a treacherous bow. (v. 57) |

The psalm, another historiographic composition, retells instances of Israel's past, persistent disobedience in light of God's faithfulness to them.

---

18. Ceresko, "The Function of Chiasmus," 2, mentions that chiasmus sometimes creates an envelope around small collections of verses, unifying short collections of verses within a stanza. This function may hold true for vv. 4 and 6 regarding the word pair: בָּנִים — דּוֹר אַחֲרוֹן // דּוֹר אַחֲרוֹן — בָּנִים. Although linking the idea of past generations together looks plausible, two factors militate against the proposition. First, the subsection is not recognized by scholarship, and second, a number of other words are repeated in vv. 4 and 6 (סָפַר and בָּנִים are written twice in v. 6). Kalimi further demonstrates that this phenomenon was employed by the Chronicler in his rewriting of Samuel and Kings. He dedicates a chapter to the phenomenon in *Reshaping*. Kalimi recognizes several instances of both the Chronicler's reuse and chiastic reordering of Samuel and Kings. Seidel documented numerous instances between Isaiah and Psalms where chiastic sequencing functions as a tool for invoking biblical allusion (see "Maqbillot Ben Sefer Yeshaya"). Weiss further discusses the same phenomenon within individual literary units in *The Bible from Within*, 116–17, where he cites numerous examples from Ezekiel and Isaiah (e.g., Isa 8:16, 20; 51:17, 22; Ezek 8:12; 9:9; 16:6–7, 22).

Verse 9 recalls an instance when the sons of Ephraim "were archers equipped with [רָמָה] bows [קֶשֶׁת]" and yet "turned back [הָפַךְ] in the day of battle." Complementing this sequence of words, in v. 57 the psalmist recounts Israel rebelling against God, acting just like their fathers; they "turned aside [נֶהְפְּכוּ] like a treacherous bow [רְמִיָּה כְּקֶשֶׁת]." Between these two verses, repetition of the three Hebrew words—or homophones to be more accurate, since רְמִיָּה, meaning "deceit," does not share the same root as רָמָה, meaning "cast/shoot"—appears in chiastic order, presenting the pattern a—b—c // c′—b′—a′. The inverted repetition here functions as an intentional poetic device conjoining two incidents in the psalm: the Ephraimite's rebellion-induced retreat and Israel's treacherous betrayal after entering the land. By effecting this connection, the psalmist associates the behavior of the generation who were divinely emancipated from Egypt with that of their descendants who entered and conquered the promised land. Thus, the psalmist illuminates Israel's pervasive disobedience: the generation that conquered the land were no better than the rebellious Ephraimites.

4.4 Terraced Pattern

a	b	
	b′	c

FIGURE 12

Another pivoting pattern for discussion is the terraced pattern, perhaps one of the more neglected structural devices discussed in Hebrew poetry. Schematically, it presents the pattern: a—b // b′—c, where the "b" element reflects a repeated word or phrase that appears at the end of the first colon and the beginning of the second (see Fig. 12). An example appears in Judg 5:23b (emphasis added):

| כִּי לֹא־בָאוּ לְעֶזְרַת יְהוָה | Because they did not come <u>to the help of the LORD</u>, |
| לְעֶזְרַת יְהוָה בַּגִּבּוֹרִים: | <u>to the help of the LORD</u> against the warriors. |

In this instance, the writer pronounces a curse upon the inhabitants of Meroz because they failed to aid the Lord's warriors. The repeated element here consists of the underlined phrase, "to the help of the Lord," which appears at the end of colon A and the beginning of colon B. Although it reflects a degree of repetition, like synonymous parallelism, the nonrepeated words accelerate the sense of forward movement as the reader progresses through the song.

Another example appears in Ps 115:12a:

| יְהוָה זְכָרָנוּ יְבָרֵךְ | The Lord has remembered us; he will bless us; |
| יְבָרֵךְ אֶת־בֵּית יִשְׂרָאֵל׃ | he will bless the house of Israel. |

In this song, the psalmist asserts his confidence in the Lord and his favor toward his people. Unlike the previous example, the repeated element consists of a single Hebrew word, the verb יְבָרֵךְ, "he will bless," which appears at the end of colon A and the beginning of colon B. Despite the English version's addition of the final "us," the Hebrew text repeats the verb verbatim, the same root, stem, and conjugation.

Psalm 135:12 presents another instance of the poetic structure:

| וְנָתַן אַרְצָם נַחֲלָה | And he gave their land as a heritage, |
| נַחֲלָה לְיִשְׂרָאֵל עַמּוֹ | a heritage to Israel his people. |

As a climactic point in this narrative psalm, the psalmist depicts the pinnacle of God's blessing to Israel, bestowing upon them the land of the Canaanites as an inheritance. The repeated word נַחֲלָה, "heritage," ends colon A and opens colon B, creating the pivot point and staircase effect. In Ps 135, unlike Ps 115, the repeated element is a noun and not a verb.

On occasion, the terraced effect breaches the confines of a bicolon, and the biblical authors unfold the terrace across three or more cola. Consider the following from Ps 98:4–5:

הָרִיעוּ לַיהוָה כָּל־הָאָרֶץ	⁴Shout joyfully to the Lord, all the earth;
פִּצְחוּ וְרַנְּנוּ וְזַמֵּרוּ׃	break forth and sing for joy and sing praises.
זַמְּרוּ לַיהוָה בְּכִנּוֹר	⁵Sing praises to the Lord with the lyre,
בְּכִנּוֹר וְקוֹל זִמְרָה׃	with the lyre and the sound of melody.

In this beautifully constructed quatrain, the psalmist carefully constructs the first pivot in colon B with the word זַמֵּר, "sing praises." He proceeds to incorporate another pivoting word at the end colon C, בְּכִנּוֹר, "with the lyre." The culminating literary effect is a double-stepped terrace.[19]

4.5 Staircase Parallelism

a	b	
a'	c	

FIGURE 13

Staircase parallelism is another type of pivot pattern employed by biblical authors. The staircase effect stems from the sequence a—b // a'—c, where "a" serves as the hinge (see Fig. 13). Within the sequence, the "a" portion of the formation may constitute a noun, noun phrase, verb, or clause, and it repeats at the beginning of colon A and colon B. Unlike the terraced pattern, staircase parallelism repeats the first element in each bicolon. The staircase effect typically, but not always, stems from an extension in colon B, an added element that extends it beyond the length of colon A. Psalm 77:16a presents one example where the length of both cola is the same:

רָאוּךָ מַּיִם אֱלֹהִים   The waters saw you, O God;
רָאוּךָ מַּיִם יָחִילוּ   the waters saw you, they were writhed.

Here the psalmist chronicles the sea's violent response to the appearance of God in his majesty. The words רָאוּךָ מַּיִם, "the waters saw you" repeat at the beginning of colon A and colon B. Notice here, however, that the second element in each colon differs. Colon A explicitly declares God as the object of the sea's anguished response. The second colon omits the object but

---

19. For other examples of terraced patterns see, Jud 5:23; Pss 98:4–5; 116:1; Prov 30:1; Song 2:15; and Isa 38:11.

balances the line with the verb יָחִ֫ילוּ, "they were in anguish."[20] The first verse of another hymn of praise, Ps 96:1–2a, presents a further example:

שִׁ֥ירוּ לַֽיהוָ֗ה שִׁ֣יר חָדָ֑שׁ	[1]Sing to the LORD a new song;
שִׁ֥ירוּ לַֽיהוָ֗ה כָּל־הָאָֽרֶץ׃	sing to the LORD, all the earth.
שִׁ֥ירוּ לַֽיהוָ֗ה בָּרֲכ֥וּ שְׁמ֑וֹ	[2]Sing to the LORD, bless his name.

Here in vv. 1–2a, an exhortation to sing a new song to the Lord, the psalmist repeats the imperative שִׁ֥ירוּ לַֽיהוָ֗ה, "sing to the LORD," in all three cola, generating the literary pivot linking the three cola. After the repeated elements, each colon incorporates different phrases to complete their respective lines. Colon A specifies what the addressees must sing, "a new song," but colon B details the identity of those being addressed, "all the earth," and colon C specifies an object of the blessing, God's name. As with the terraced pattern, poets occasionally expand the staircase to encompass three or more cola. A single example from Num 24:3b–4a can demonstrate this extension:[21]

נְאֻ֤ם בִּלְעָם֙ בְּנ֣וֹ בְעֹ֔ר	[3b]The oracle of Balaam, the son of Beor,
וּנְאֻ֥ם הַגֶּ֖בֶר שְׁתֻ֥ם הָעָֽיִן׃	[4]and the oracle of the man whose eye is opened;
נְאֻ֕ם שֹׁמֵ֖עַ אִמְרֵי־אֵ֑ל	the oracle of him who hears the words of God.

Numbers 24:3b–4a elucidates the process in which the prophet, Balaam, receives his oracle from the Lord. To announce the vision, the writer positions the word נְאֻם, "oracle," three times at the start of each successive colon, which ultimately generates the literary hinge for the staircase formation. The overall pattern created here slightly extends the original schema, creating the sequence: a—b // a'—c // a"—d.[22]

---

20. By including the verse's final colon, "Also the deep trembled," one could argue for an instance of chiasmus, with the reversal of terms for "anguish" and "sea" (waters—anguish // trembled—the deep).

21. Technically, the previous example in Ps 96 also fits the tri-cola pattern if we include v. 2, which also begins "Sing to the LORD."

22. For further examples of staircase parallelism, see Jud 5:12; Pss 29:1–2; 96:7–9; Prov 31:2; and Song 6:9.

4.6 Janus Parallelism

Another pivoting structure that appears less frequently in the Hebrew Bible is Janus parallelism. Unlike the structures discussed thus far, Janus parallelism constitutes an acutely sophisticated pattern that necessitates a knowledge of Hebrew. The verse structure hinges around two meanings of a single word in three consecutive Hebrew cola, where the keyword appears in the central colon. Thus, colon A creates a parallel relationship using a word with one meaning in colon B. However, colon B, using the same word with a different meaning, continues to forge a parallel relationship with colon C. Song of Songs 2:12 presents a relatively clear example of this technique:

הַנִּצָּנִים נִרְאוּ בָאָרֶץ	The flowers appear on the earth,
עֵת הַזָּמִיר הִגִּיעַ	the time of singing/<u>pruning</u> has come,
וְקוֹל הַתּוֹר נִשְׁמַע בְּאַרְצֵנוּ	<u>and the voice of the turtledove is heard in our land.</u> (Song 2:12, emphasis added)

The keyword serving as a hinge in this example is the Hebrew זָמִיר, which translates to either "pruning" or "singing."[23] Because colon A mentions "flowers ... on the earth," the preferred translation of זָמִיר is pruning—the task of pruning relates directly to the flourishing of flowers and plant life. Consequently, in the first bicolon, the connective word pair comprises flowers-pruning. Moving to the second bicolon, and an alternative meaning of זָמִיר, "song," emerges. Because the time of "singing" has arrived—the second meaning of זָמִיר—the sound of the turtledoves echoes throughout the land. Thus, for colon B and colon C the connective word pair results in singing turtledoves, because both of these words convey the notion of sound.

Jeremiah 2:14–15 presents another example of this rare phenomenon:[24]

---

23. As a potential aid to identifying this poetic technique, the ESV includes a footnote for this word, sharing its alternative meaning. When English translations provide such help, readers without the knowledge of Hebrew may potentially identify instances of Janus parallelism.

24. See Watson, *Classical Hebrew Poetry*, 159.

הַעֶבֶד יִשְׂרָאֵל אִם־יְלִיד בַּיִת הוּא	¹⁴Is Israel a slave? Or is he a homeborn servant?
מַדּוּעַ הָיָה לָבַז׃	Why has he become a contempt/prey?
עָלָיו יִשְׁאֲגוּ כְפִרִים	¹⁵The young lions have roared at him,
נָתְנוּ קוֹלָם	they have roared loudly.
וַיָּשִׁיתוּ אַרְצוֹ לְשַׁמָּה	And they have made his land a waste;
עָרָיו נִצְּתָה מִבְּלִי יֹשֵׁב׃	his cities have been destroyed, without inhabitant. (emphasis added)

In this example, the keyword בַז generates the literary hinge. Translating בַז as "contempt" aligns the content of colon C with colon A and colon B. thus, the reader understands that Israel has become contemptible and receives the status of a lowly servant. In the second half of the strophe, the psalmist portrays Israel as a victim, the object of a destroying agent. Here it is better to interpret בַז, as "prey," because it corresponds with the context of devastation and ruin, congruent with the context of the final four lines.²⁵ Because Janus parallelism remains a complicated and challenging feature to isolate with surety, ongoing scholarly efforts are essential to uncover more examples in biblical literature.²⁶

Questions for Consideration: How often is chiasmus used in the text? Is it used in a reversal of state? Where does it appear in the text—opening a stanza, closing a stanza, midpoint of a stanza? Does it appear in an emphatic position? Does it frame a specific stanza? What is the nature of the hinge (repeated word, root, semantic overlap)? Do the bicola used in a terraced pattern or staircase pattern appear at a climactic point in the composition?

---

25. Here the NASB preserves the meaning "prey." Unfortunately, however, it fails to preserve the alternative meaning in its footnotes.

26. That said, the work of Noegel deserves mention because he has intentionally sought to discover how Janus parallelism is used specifically in the book of Job. His conclusions suggest that Janus parallelism functions as a practical demonstration of wit as the essence of wisdom. Concerning Janus parallelism in Job, he states, "The numerous displays of word-wise wit in the book of Job are to be seen not as mere literary embellishments and flares of poetic style but rather as demonstrations of wit and one-upmanship . . . such word manipulation should be understood as the very essence of wisdom" ("Janus Parallelism," 320). For further discussions of Janus parallelism, see Carasik, "Janus Parallelism"; Ceresko, "Janus Parallelism"; Rendsburg, "Janus Parallelism"; Tsumura, *Vertical Grammar*; Tsumura, "Janus Parallelism."

Further Reading: Ceresko, "The Function of Chiasmus"; Ceresko, "Janus Parallelism"; Klaus, "Pivot Patterns in the Former Prophets"; Lund, "The Presence of Chiasmus"; Lund, *Chiasmus in the New Testament*; Noegel, "Janus Parallelism"; Paul, "Polysemous Pivotal Punctuation"; Rendsburg, "Janus Parallelism." Watson, *Traditional Techniques.*

5

Enveloping Structures

Enveloping structures can be understood as literary frames that surround specific segments of texts that biblical authors seek to demarcate. For the most part, they constitute repeated elements that stand at the beginning and end of the segmented text. In certain instances, as discussed below, the repeated elements appear three or more times in a textual unit, thus dividing the text into specific units. In these instances, it is easier to identify stanza divisions because the authors convey with absolute clarity where each stanza begins and ends via the repeated element. The repeated elements in these structures may constitute a word, a root, semantically equivalent ideas, or even a whole verse.

5.1 Envelope Figure

The term envelop figure in the present context describes a poetic technique in which repeated elements—usually words or phrases, or even a verse—appear at the beginning and ending of a poetic unit.[1] An important factor in the identification and determination of an envelope figure is that the framing lexical tag only appears twice in the text under examination. Because other poetic devices present various similarities to the envelope figure, failure to identify two lexical tags leads to confusion in identifying

---

1. Obviously, this feature is not restricted to poetry, like many of the other features discussed. Kalimi devotes a chapter in his book to describing how the Chronicler employs the feature (*Reshaping*, 295–324).

the correct form.[2] Regarding the Psalter, because each psalm represents an independent unit, the lexical tags surface in the opening and closing verses of the psalms. Perhaps the most often cited example appears in Ps 8:

| יְהוָה אֲדֹנֵינוּ מָה־אַדִּיר שִׁמְךָ בְּכָל־הָאָרֶץ | O Lord, our Lord, how majestic is your name in all the earth! (v. 1[2]a) |

. .
. .
. .

| יְהוָה אֲדֹנֵינוּ מָה־אַדִּיר שִׁמְךָ בְּכָל־הָאָרֶץ: | O Lord, our Lord, how majestic is your name in all the earth! (v. 9[10]) |

The author of Ps 8 adopts a complete verse, duplicates it, and places one at the beginning of the composition, and the other at the end. To create the envelope figure, the psalmist refrains from repeating the verse elsewhere in the psalm.

Another example appears is Ps 103:

| בָּרֲכִי נַפְשִׁי אֶת־יְהוָה... | Bless the Lord, O my soul... |
| בָּרֲכִי נַפְשִׁי אֶת־יְהוָה... | Bless the Lord O my soul... (vv. 1–2) |

. .
. .
. .

| בָּרֲכִי נַפְשִׁי אֶת־יְהוָה: | Bless the Lord, O my soul! (v. 22b) |

In this example, the lexical frame constitutes a single colon as opposed to a whole verse. Still, the repeated element בָּרֲכִי נַפְשִׁי אֶת־יְהוָה, "Bless the Lord, O my soul," only appears at the beginning of the composition, vv. 1–2, and at the end, v. 22, creating a frame for the song. The framing element for the envelop may be even shorter, one word in length.

Consider the example in Ps 29 (emphasis added):

---

2. Watson, *Classical Hebrew Poetry*, 283, is one of the few scholars who emphasizes this distinctive feature of the envelope figure.

| הָבוּ לַיהוָה כָּבוֹד וָעֹז | Ascribe to the Lord glory and strength. (v. 1b) |

. .
. .
. .

| יְהוָה עֹז לְעַמּוֹ יִתֵּן | May the Lord give strength to his people. (v. 11a) |

Instead of a colon, or even a phrase, the psalmist in this composition opts for a single word to create the envelop figure. Both the psalm's opening and closing verses include the Hebrew word עֹז, "strength." The fact that the word "strength" does not repeat elsewhere in the composition confirms the case for envelope figure in this instance.

5.2 Refrain

In certain instances, a repeated phrase or clause occurs more than twice; i.e., more than at the beginning and end of the poetic unit. Repetitions like this with a poetic text are called a refrain. The refrain, unlike the envelope figure, appears multiple times in a text, and may possess a structuring role in a textual unit,[3] generating stanzas. Usually, poets avoid positioning refrains at the beginning of their compositions, preferring to place them in the main body of the text or at the end. Refrains can essentially be divided into two categories, strict and variant. An example of a strict refrain appears in Ps 67 (emphasis added):

אֱלֹהִים יְחָנֵּנוּ וִיבָרְכֵנוּ	1[2]God be gracious to us and bless us,
יָאֵר פָּנָיו אִתָּנוּ סֶלָה׃	and cause his face to shine upon us—Selah.
לָדַעַת בָּאָרֶץ דַּרְכֶּךָ	2[3]That your way may be known on the earth,
בְּכָל־גּוֹיִם יְשׁוּעָתֶךָ׃	your salvation among all nations.
יוֹדוּךָ עַמִּים אֱלֹהִים	**3[4]Let the peoples praise you, O God;**
יוֹדוּךָ עַמִּים כֻּלָּם׃	**let all the peoples praise you.**

---

3. See Watson, *Classical Hebrew Poetry*, 295.

יִשְׂמְחוּ וִירַנְּנוּ לְאֻמִּים	4[5]Let the nations be glad and sing for joy;
כִּי־תִשְׁפֹּט עַמִּים מִישׁוֹר	for You will judge the peoples with uprightness
וּלְאֻמִּים בָּאָרֶץ תַּנְחֵם סֶלָה:	and guide the nations on the earth. Selah.
יוֹדוּךָ עַמִּים אֱלֹהִים	5[6]**Let the peoples praise you, O God;**
יוֹדוּךָ עַמִּים כֻּלָּם:	**let all the peoples praise you.**
אֶרֶץ נָתְנָה יְבוּלָהּ	6[7]The earth has yielded its produce;
יְבָרְכֵנוּ אֱלֹהִים אֱלֹהֵינוּ:	God, our God, blesses us.
יְבָרְכֵנוּ אֱלֹהִים	7[8]God blesses us,
וְיִירְאוּ אֹתוֹ כָּל־אַפְסֵי־אָרֶץ:	that all the ends of the earth may fear him.

Psalm 67 implements the couplet, "Let the peoples praise you, O God; / Let all the peoples praise you," as a refrain. In this relatively succinct hymn of praise, the refrain repeats in vv. 3[4] and 5[6], but does not appear either at the psalm's opening or close. Because no variation exists in the repeated words, it is called a *strict* refrain. Another example of a strict refrain appears throughout Amos 4, with the words "Yet you have not returned to Me [וְלֹא־שַׁבְתֶּם עָדַי]" (see vv. 6, 8, 9, 10, and 11). Psalm 107 presents another example of a strict refrain, with words replicated verbatim and interspersed throughout the psalm. Four times in this relatively long composition, the author cites, יוֹדוּ לַיהוָה חַסְדּוֹ וְנִפְלְאוֹתָיו לִבְנֵי אָדָם, "Let them give thanks to the LORD for his lovingkindness, / And for his wonders to the sons of men!" (vv. 8, 15, 21, and 31).

Most of the time, however, the level of repetition in the Old Testament, although still distinguishable, fails to display the level of precision in the examples cited above. These *variant* refrains display degrees of alterations in the repetition as it appears throughout the poetic unit. An example appears in Ps 99:

יוֹדוּ שִׁמְךָ גָּדוֹל וְנוֹרָא	Let them praise your great and awesome name;
קָדוֹשׁ הוּא:	holy is he. (v. 3)
.	.
.	.
רוֹמְמוּ יְהוָה אֱלֹהֵינוּ	Exalt the LORD our God

> וְהִשְׁתַּחֲווּ לַהֲדֹם רַגְלָיו
> קָדוֹשׁ הוּא
>
> and worship at his footstool;
> holy is he. (v. 5)
>
> . .
> . .
> . .
>
> רוֹמְמוּ יְהוָה אֱלֹהֵינוּ
> וְהִשְׁתַּחֲווּ לְהַר קָדְשׁוֹ
> כִּי־קָדוֹשׁ יְהוָה אֱלֹהֵינוּ
>
> Exalt the Lord our God
> and worship at his holy hill,
> for holy is the Lord our God. (v. 9)

Throughout this composition, the psalmist intently emphasizes the holiness of God, which he achieves with a variant refrain. It first appears in v. 3, with the declaration קָדוֹשׁ הוּא, "Holy is he." Likewise, in v. 5, with the call to worship at God's footstool, the psalmist adds the refrain to the end of the verse, קָדוֹשׁ הוּא, "Holy is he." In the final verse, however, although the psalm recalls the declaration of God's holiness, the words vary, קָדוֹשׁ יְהוָה אֱלֹהֵינוּ, "Holy is the Lord our God."

Another example of a variant refrain appears in Ps 80:[4]

> [3[4]]אֱלֹהִים הֲשִׁיבֵנוּ וְהָאֵר פָּנֶיךָ וְנִוָּשֵׁעָה
> [7[8]]אֱלֹהִים צְבָאוֹת הֲשִׁיבֵנוּ וְהָאֵר פָּנֶיךָ וְנִוָּשֵׁעָה׃
> [19[20]]יְהוָה אֱלֹהִים צְבָאוֹת הֲשִׁיבֵנוּ הָאֵר פָּנֶיךָ וְנִוָּשֵׁעָה׃

O God, restore us and cause your face to shine upon us, and we will be saved. (v. 3[4])

O God of hosts, restore us and cause your face to shine upon us, and we will be saved. (v. 7[8])

O Lord God of hosts, restore us; cause your face to shine upon us, and we will be saved. (v. 19[20])

---

4. The boundaries occasionally blur when determining whether a refrain is strict or variant. Consider the broader context of the Song of Songs. Here the refrain divides the text into sections of a much longer composition. In vv. 2:7; 3:5; and 8:4, the poet uses the words, "I adjure you, O daughters of Jerusalem, / By the gazelles or by the hinds of the field, / That you do not arouse or awake my love / Until she pleases." Although this exact phrase appears three times throughout the book, serving to divide it into larger sections, it is noteworthy that the phrase "I adjure you, O daughters of Jerusalem" appears in 5:8 without the remainder of the refrain. This partial refrain likely surprises the listening audience accustomed to hearing the complete expression. Further examples for consideration are found in Exod 15:6, 11, 16; 1 Sam 19:25, 27; Ps 126:1, 4; and Isa 29: 5, 16.

Throughout this lament, the psalmist implores God incessantly to restore his people, recalling the Aaronic blessing and leveraging God to act according to his steadfast mercy. Even though the psalm repeats several of the words of the refrain, variations still appear in the way the psalmist addresses God. The first instance, v. 3[4], refers simply to God in the vocative, "O God." Then in v. 7[8] he is called "God of hosts." And finally in v. 19[20] the psalmist reveals the divine name in addition to the epithet "God of hosts." Notwithstanding any potential later wholescale editing that may have been performed on this composition,[5] the refrain noticeably alters as it surfaces throughout the psalm.[6]

5.3 Chorus

The chorus in biblical Hebrew constitutes an infrequent and limited subset of the refrain. It is a phrase or verse that repeats after every verse or line. Unfortunately, biblical Hebrew has only preserved a single example of this technique. Psalm 136 illustrates the only substantial example in biblical literature in an antiphonal hymn. For presumably liturgical purposes, after each successive line, the author invites congregational participation with the words כִּי לְעוֹלָם חַסְדּוֹ, "For his lovingkindness is everlasting." One can conclude that this verse represents an intentional insertion for recitation by a congregation or other participants. Psalm 136 was in all likelihood recited in an antiphonal context in which a lead speaker recited alternate lines and a congregation or audience responded with the repeated chorus.[7]

---

5. Here v. 7[8] may originally have read "Lord of hosts," matching the final occurrence in v. 19. Such a change would have been implemented by the editor responsible for the Elohistic alterations to this portion of the Psalter. In any event, the refrain used in this psalm varies from the beginning to the end.

6. In longer psalms and poetic compositions, one can detect thematic refrains. Consider, for example Ps 78, which periodically inserts statements of Israel's rebellion against God amid the longer depictions of his magnificent acts of mercy. See, for example, vv. 17, 32, 40, and 56. Watson, *Classical Hebrew Poetry*, 285, dissects it further, suggesting inclusion can be created with assonance and gramatical forms such as personal pronouns.

7. Like the refrain, non-repeated verses must also be interpreted in light of the repeated element. For instance, when the psalm states, "For his lovingkindness is everlasting," this phrase should be interpreted in the context of v. 6, "to him who spread out the earth above the waters," where the interpreter must discern how this act reflects the Lord's steadfast love. Similarly, verses such as v. 18, "And slew mighty kings," must be understood in view of the chorus, acknowledging that kings who were destroyed did not perceive the act as one of lovingkindness.

5.4 Inclusion

Another enveloping structure, and perhaps the most common in biblical literature, is *inclusio*,[8] or inclusion. When employing the technique, the psalmist adopts a word, short phrase, or perhaps even a repeated root to create a literary frame that surrounds a poetic segment—a verse, or collection of verses. In this way, inclusion resembles the envelope figure discussed above, but it does not encompass the entire psalm, only a shorter collection of verses.[9] The primary purpose of inclusion, therefore, is to demarcate a segment of text, or possibly even just a single verse.[10] We can schematize the occurrence of an inclusion with "A . . . A'." Isaiah 29:9b demonstrates a short example of the technique:

| שָׁכְרוּ וְלֹא־יַיִן | Drunk they became, but not with wine, |
| נָעוּ וְלֹא שֵׁכָר: | they stagger, but not with strong drink. |

As part of a vivid description of God stifling and frustrating the plans of the nations who come against his people, Isaiah adopts a brief inclusion to capture the divine stupor the Lord will send upon them. Noticeable here, at the beginning and end of the couplet, the poet purposefully employs the root שכר, "Drunk they became [שָׁכְרוּ] . . . strong drink [שֵׁכָר]."[11] The poet has restricted his imagery of drunkenness to this single couplet, and has encapsulated the imagery with two words with the same root, שכר, which conveys drunkenness and intoxication. Thus, the imagery contained in the couplet finds a direct reflection in the words that encapsulate the bicolon.[12]

---

8. This is being included here as part of a discussion of Hebrew poetry, but it is important to note that this feature is also common in prose texts.

9. In the literature, a varying understanding of inclusion and envelope figure is discernable. Consequently, some scholars refer to the envelop figure as inclusion. For the purposes of the present volume, and for students beginning their engagement with poetry, the distinction between the two features is both necessary and beneficial.

10. Overlap clearly exists here with the ABA' chiastic tricolon discussed above. In both instances one detects a framing element generated from repeated words.

11. This kind of repetition, where the first word of a sentence is repeated as the last word, is also called epanalepsis and constitutes, in certain cases, a separate poetic device. It is discussed further in ch. 9.

12. This is an example of a strophic inclusion. Other examples appear in Pss 83:2; 119:65–66a; and Jer 5:21.

Within a longer text, another example of inclusion appears in Ps 105:

וַיָּבֹא יִשְׂרָאֵל מִצְרָיִם Israel came into Egypt;
וְיַעֲקֹב גָּר בְּאֶרֶץ־חָם: and Jacob sojourned in the land of Ham. (v. 23)

. .
. .
. .

שָׂמַח מִצְרַיִם בְּצֵאתָם Egypt was glad when they departed,
כִּי־נָפַל פַּחְדָּם עֲלֵיהֶם: for the dread of them had fallen upon them.
(v. 38, emphasis added)

FIGURE 14

As part of an interpretive, and notably cheerful, recitation of history, the psalmist employs the word מִצְרַיִם, "Egypt," to construct a comparatively sizable inclusion within the composition. The example here, between vv. 23–38, highlights a crucial feature for identifying inclusion. Within any biblical texts, a significant probability arises that words or roots will be duplicated. This natural duplication occurs in Hebrew and any other language. A random page from *The Wall Street Journal*, for example, will exhibit articles in which various words are duplicated. Without careful consideration of texture and content, one could flippantly identify any two instances of a word, or root, and claim an instance of inclusion. It is, therefore, crucial to identify additional details supporting the probability of an inclusion.

Ideally, the content enclosed within the proposed inclusion will distinctly correlate with the framing elements (Fig. 14 schematizes this arrangement). An important question to ask, therefore, is, "Does the framing element of the inclusion correspond with the content within?" It is important, when possible, to identify a connection between the lexemes generating the frame and the content of the framed portion. A closer look at the overarching literary framework of Ps 105 demonstrates this idea. It is important to first note that the word מִצְרַיִם, "Egypt," only appears twice in the psalm, vv. 23 and 38. This generates an ideal scenario because it is somewhat problematic to establish an inclusion if one or more elements of the literary frame appears within the proposed inclusion. The content of the enclosed passage and its relationship to the inclusion marker sheds important light on the author's likely intention. Psalm 105:23–38 recounts events that take place within the geographical region of Egypt. Consequently, the name Egypt demarcates events that took place within the land of Egypt. It first appears when Jacob and his family go down to Egypt and then reappears to depict Israel leaving Egypt after God emancipated them from captivity. A closer inspection of the enclosed passage reveals numerous instances in which the psalmist could have used the word Egypt, but instead opted for an epithet or alternative pronoun.[13] The important lesson, therefore, gleaned from both inclusion examples cited thus far, is that those analyzing poetry are strongly advised to establish a semantic or contextual link between the framing word or phrase of an inclusion and the contents that it frames.[14]

Consider another instance in the oracular hymn, Ps 95 (emphasis added):

אֲשֶׁר בְּיָדוֹ מֶחְקְרֵי־אָרֶץ	[4]In whose hand are the depths of the earth,
וְתוֹעֲפוֹת הָרִים לוֹ׃	the peaks of the mountains are his also.
אֲשֶׁר־לוֹ הַיָּם וְהוּא עָשָׂהוּ	[5]The sea is his, for it was he who made it,
וְיַבֶּשֶׁת יָדָיו יָצָרוּ	and his hands formed the dry land.

---

13. See for example, vv. 30, 32 and 35.
14. This constraint in the determination of inclusion could be viewed as unduly conservative. However, it represents the present author's desire to limit the excessively liberal use of the term, one that virtually claims an inclusion for any two instances of a word appearing in a biblical text.

Verses 4–5 contribute to the psalmist's recognition and adoration of God for his work in creating the earth. It is possible, operating solely within the confines of these two verses, to argue for an instance of inclusion. The section begins with and ends with the word יָד, "hand," which creates the distinguishing literary frame for the encapsulated material. Within the frame, the psalmist lists elements in the created order—the earth's depths, the mountain peaks, the sea, and the dry land—that God has formed with his hands. Although the word "hand" appears later in the psalm, v. 7, it fails to appear within the two instances cited above. Therefore, a robust argument can be made for the localized instance of inclusion in vv. 4–5. Again, the critical point of emphasis here is that other contextual factors must be considered when determining the existence of an inclusion. It is not enough to simply identify two words in a text and argue that an author intended to construct a logically framed textual unit.

An example of inclusion in prophetic writings appears in Jer 5:21 (emphasis added):

שִׁמְעוּ־נָא זֹאת עַם סָכָל וְאֵין לֵב	Now hear this, O foolish and senseless people,
עֵינַיִם לָהֶם וְלֹא יִרְאוּ	who have eyes but do not see;
אָזְנַיִם לָהֶם וְלֹא יִשְׁמָעוּ	who have ears but do not hear.

In these brief condemnatory words that God levels against his people, an inclusion forms from the repeated root, שמע. The opening word שִׁמְעוּ, "hear," is a plural imperative, imploring the "house of Jacob" to heed the following words. English translations slightly obscure the initial position of the root, and they frequently add the word "Now" to represent the particle of interjection; however, the Hebrew text positions the root at the start of the colon. The same root ends the strophe, but this time in the imperfect form. In addition to the lexical root serving as the primary inclusion marker, it is possible to see the words inside as a self-contained semantic unit focusing on the dismal predicament of possessing nonfunctioning facial features.

The final example appears in Joel 2 (emphasis added):

יִרְגְּזוּ כֹּל יֹשְׁבֵי הָאָרֶץ	Let all the inhabitants of the land tremble,
כִּי־בָא יוֹם־יְהוָה	For the day of the LORD is coming;
כִּי קָרוֹב	Surely it is near. (v. 1b, NASB)

. . .
. . .
. . .

כִּי־גָדוֹל יוֹם־יְהוָה וְנוֹרָא מְאֹד	The day of the LORD is indeed great and very awesome,
וּמִי יְכִילֶנּוּ:	And who can endure it? (v. 11b, NASB)

In this longer pericope, the expression יוֹם יְהוָה, "day of the LORD," generates the literary frame for the inclusion, appearing in vv. 1b and 11b. Once again, for the purposes of establishing an inclusion, it is important to note that the same phrase fails to appear within the textual segment. Thus, the inclusion demarcates the prophetic portrayal of impending disaster that the prophet predicted would fall upon the inhabitants of Judah.[15]

A primary function of inclusion is to demarcate specific sections of a poetic text. The isolated segments vary in length and, as witnessed above, may constitute a single couplet, several verses, or even stanzas. When considering the nature of the original and ancient manuscripts, it is not difficult to comprehend the value of inclusion. Unlike English translations, the early manuscripts were not written with verse and chapter divisions, and the individual stanzas received no indication in the Hebrew texts. Inclusion, therefore, served the practical function of informing the reader of how the psalmist sought to divide texts and unify specific themes.

That said, exercising due diligence is firmly advised when adducing inclusion as evidence for a stanza or strophe division. In writing biblical (or any) texts, as mentioned earlier, nothing prevents scribes from using the same word or root in two or more instances simply as part of the writing process. Consequently, a simple identification of a repeated lexeme in a text fails to prove that it subdivides the text into stanzas or strophes. If two repeated words or phrases are identified, then further investigation is needed to determine whether the author intended to construct an inclusion.

---

15. For a further example, see Ps 96, and for prophetic literature, see Olley, "'No Peace.'"

In this way, the identification of repeated words functions as one corroborative characteristic for stanza determination.

Questions for Consideration: What is the nature of the repeated element (a word, a root, a colon, a verse)? Does the content within the frame center around a specific topic? Is the chorus repeated precisely every time it appears, or are there variations? What is the literary relationship between the chorus or refrain and the textual units that it segments?

Further Reading: Alter, *Biblical Poetry*, 105, 115, 118, 124, 128; Goh, *Hebrew Poetry*, 55, 122, 130, 162; Tsumura, *Vertical Grammar*, 38–39, 71–72; Watson, *Classical Hebrew Poetry*, 274, 282–87, 295–96; Wendland, *Analyzing the Psalms*, 53–54, 108.

6

Additional Cola Relationships

Chapter 6 discusses a varied collection of cola relationships that fail to conform to any of the previous structures. The discussion of cola relationships below is not exhaustive. The primary purpose of introducing these potential relationships is to prompt students and aspiring exegetes to pose the critical question: What is the relationship between a colon and its neighbor? In addition to the cola relationships, two additional phenomena are discussed—acrostics and enjambment—that do not fit tidily into any of the previous discussions.

6.1 Antithetical Parallelism

The phenomenon known as antithetical parallelism forms a single strand from the larger fabric of consecutive cola relationships.[1] Often in Hebrew poetry, couplets convey a single thought, despite being written as individual cola, generating a contrasting effect. When two cola appear in this formation, the literature refers to it as antithetical parallelism. For the most part, biblical Hebrew adopts the conjunctive *waw* at the beginning of the second colon to denote the contrasting elements. Consider the following example from Ps 34:19[20]:

| רַבּוֹת רָעוֹת צַדִּיק | Many are the afflictions of the righteous, |
| וּמִכֻּלָּם יַצִּילֶנּוּ יְהוָה: | but the LORD delivers him out of them all. |

---

1. This is discussed further in the next section on Other Relationships.

Verse 19[20] presents the reader with two contrasting situations: the afflictions of the righteous and the Lord's deliverance. Both independent, even conflicting, ideas amalgamate into a unified thought: attempting a righteous life is worthwhile because the Lord delivers the righteous from afflictions. It is important to keep this tension in mind when analyzing antithetical parallelism: despite the contrasting elements, a single and logical unit of thought is still expressed in the couplet. Frequently in biblical wisdom literature, the contrasting antithetical relationships constitute a prominent poetic structure. Proverbs 11:2 provides another example:

בָּא־זָדוֹן וַיָּבֹא קָלוֹן   When pride comes, then comes dishonor,
וְאֶת־צְנוּעִים חָכְמָה   but with the humble is wisdom.

Verse 2 juxtaposes opposite pairs inside this bicolon: pride and humility, dishonor and wisdom. In this verse, the sage contrasts the product of living pridefully against that of living with humility; the couplet sets both ideas in opposition to each other with the contrastive *waw* conjunction. Together, the contrasting cola encourage readers to evaluate which of the two scenarios is more beneficial: be prideful and then suffer dishonor or be humble and know wisdom.

Antithetical parallelism relies on the reader comparing two cola and identifying the relation between them as being contradictory, as seen above. However, when comparing the two cola, sometimes the differences are difficult to determine. Particularly in wisdom poetry, biblical authors adopt a mitigated form of antithesis to convey their meaning. Consider, for example, Prov 17:12:

פָּגוֹשׁ דֹּב שַׁכּוּל בְּאִישׁ   Let a man meet a bear robbed of her cubs,
וְאַל־כְּסִיל בְּאִוַּלְתּוֹ   rather than a fool in his folly.

In the couplet above, readers are still required to derive the lesson by comparing the statements presented in two cola. The author, however, does not present polar opposites for comparison. Instead, he depicts two negative situations—encountering an angry bear and a fool—where one is worse than the other. The message of the verse here is still derived through comparison, but the two cola involved are not contrasted. Interpreters of this verse, therefore, must translate the *waw* conjunction at the start of colon B not as an adversative particle, but as a comparative particle.

Another more explicit example appears in Ps 118:9:

טוֹב לַחֲסוֹת בַּיהוָה   It is better to take refuge in the Lord
מִבְּטֹחַ בִּנְדִיבִים: than to trust in princes.

Again, in Ps 118:9, it is incumbent upon the reader to compare the contents of each colon. However, the writer explicates the comparative relationship between the couplets. The Hebrew construction . . . מ . . . טוֹב, "it is better . . . than . . ." specifically signifies to the reader which situation is better. Both are still to be compared, but one, the former, is explicitly preferred. Like the previous example, the best of the two comparative scenarios appears in the first colon.

6.2 Other Relationships

The explanation of antithetical parallelism leads to the more nuanced discussion of verse relationships. Synonymous parallelism, as discussed earlier, displays a relatively high degree of repetition or restatement between consecutive cola. However, even though the fundamental idea or message of two or more parallel cola exhibit similarities, the cola are never exactly the same. It is fair to say that perfectly matched parallel cola—with identical meaning, and lexical and grammatical correspondence—do not appear in Hebrew poetry. Therefore, to acquire a more nuanced understanding of consecutive cola, one must ask the question, "What is the precise relationship between colon A and colon B?" The ensuing discussion and examples, not intended to be exhaustive, aim to illustrate various options available for understanding and defining the potential relationships between cola.[2]

---

2. Most of the examples discussed in this section fall under Lowth's catchall designation of "parallels synthetic" (see Lowth, *Isaiah: A New Translation*, 6). As we shall see, the relationships in this category are far more nuanced than Lowth suggests, and at this point, Holmstedt's appositional model becomes more relevant. See Holmstedt, "Hebrew Poetry."

6.2.1 General to Specific

One relatively common relationship between cola can be termed "general to specific," where colon A introduces a general idea or topic, and colon B progresses the idea by detailing it further. Consider Ps 8:3[4]:

כִּי־אֶרְאֶה שָׁמֶיךָ מַעֲשֵׂי אֶצְבְּעֹתֶיךָ	When I consider your heavens, the work of your fingers,
יָרֵחַ וְכוֹכָבִים אֲשֶׁר כּוֹנָנְתָּה	the moon and the stars, which you have ordained.

The psalmist begins here in colon A with the general observation of God's work in creation, watching and considering the heavens and the work of God's fingers. Then, in colon B, he specifies examples of the work of God's fingers, i.e., the moon and stars. The general observation in the first colon is specified in the second. Another example of this relationship appears in Ps 78:18, part of an extensive stanza delineating the sins and rebellious deeds perpetrated by Israel during their desert sojourn:

וַיְנַסּוּ־אֵל בִּלְבָבָם	And in their heart they put God to the test
לִשְׁאָל־אֹכֶל לְנַפְשָׁם	by asking food according to their desire.

The psalmist opens in colon A with a general statement recounting the internal heart attitude and sinful thought processes of the Israelites, putting God to the test. Following this, colon B expands upon the mental process, specifically detailing the outcome of their thoughts—they asked, or demanded, food that they desired.

6.2.2 Cause and Effect

Another potential relationship between cola is that of cause and effect. In these instances, an action or a statement in colon A triggers an action or generates a specific set of circumstances that appear in colon B. Consider Job 5:12, below:

מֵפֵר מַחְשְׁבוֹת עֲרוּמִים	He frustrates the plotting of the shrewd,
וְלֹא־תַעֲשֶׂינָה יְדֵיהֶם תּוּשִׁיָּה	so that their hands cannot attain success.

Colon A alerts the reader to God's tendency to hinder the plots and schemes of shrewd and cunning individuals. The effect of this attribute of God is that these same individuals, who plot and scheme, are unsuccessful in their plans. In instances such as Job 5:12, when translators of the English versions interpret the Hebrew text, they explicate the relationship between the two cola. The translation above reads "so that," which interprets the Hebrew *waw*. This constitutes an important technical consideration: when engaging purely with the Hebrew text, additional analytical effort is required to interpret the relationships between cola separated by a *waw*.

6.2.3 Temporal

The relationship between two cola can also be defined as "temporal," which requires an analysis of the timespan that occurs between events mentioned in consecutive cola. Here the indispensable question to ask is, "When do the events of one colon transpire in relation to the events in the following colon?" Consider Ps 106:29–30:

וַיַּכְעִיסוּ בְּמַעַלְלֵיהֶם	²⁹They provoked him to anger with their deeds,
וַתִּפְרָץ־בָּם מַגֵּפָה׃	and the plague broke out among them.
וַיַּעֲמֹד פִּינְחָס וַיְפַלֵּל	³⁰Then Phinehas stood up and interceded,
וַתֵּעָצַר הַמַּגֵּפָה׃	and so the plague was stayed.

In these verses, an undeniable sequence of consecutive events surfaces in the psalmist's recitation. Israel provokes God, then the plague breaks out, then Phineas intercedes, and then the plague is quelled. Events recorded in each colon occur one after the other. Sequencing like this commonly surfaces in the historiographic psalms, those reciting events in Israel's past. Within such psalms, a potential indicator of the sequential layout of the cola appears in the use of *wayyiqtol* verbs, which customarily indicates sequential events in biblical narrative.³ One could view this along similar lines to the cause-effect relationship above, but the specific use of the *wayyiqtol* verb forms highlights the temporally consecutive nature of the cola. Isaiah 40:6 provides another example of temporal sequencing:

---

3. For more on this basic use of the *wayyiqtol*, see Patton, Putnam, and Van Pelt, *Basics of Hebrew Discourse*, 68; and Collins, "Wayyiqtol as 'Pluperfect.'"

קוֹל אֹמֵר קְרָא	A voice says, "Call out."
וְאָמַר מָה אֶקְרָא	Then he answered, "What shall I call out?"
כָּל־הַבָּשָׂר חָצִיר וְכָל־חַסְדּוֹ	All flesh is grass, and all its loveliness is like
כְּצִיץ הַשָּׂדֶה:	the flower of the field.

Here in Isa 40, still in the realm of poetry, the prophet pens a sequence of three consecutive events. First is the acknowledgement of the voice that calls out, then the response seeking information on what to call, and finally the words that are to be spoken. Each event occurs one after the other. Unlike the previous example, however, Isaiah's words are not part of a historiographic recitation, and there are no *wayyiqtols* to guide the reader in interpretation.

Another potential temporal relationship reflects simultaneous action, two events occurring at the same time where the first event appears in colon A and the second event in colon B:

וָאֲחַשְּׁבָה לָדַעַת זֹאת	As I pondered to understand this,
עָמָל הִיא בְעֵינָי	it was troublesome in my sight. (Ps 73:16)

In Ps 73, the psalmist considers the behavior of envious and arrogant individuals, and in v. 16 declares the results of his contemplation. At the same time he pondered their behavior, he became troubled, the two events transpired at the same time. A cursory reading of the Hebrew text fails to intimate simultaneous actions occurring between the cola. Detection of this phenomenon must be achieved through a close reading of the text and an analysis of the potential relationships between cola. If we understand the initial imperfect verb as a durative action, taking up more than an instant of time, then placement of the second verb, the perfect, equates to an instantaneous action. It is logical in this instance, therefore, to place the act of the perfect verb—the psalmist being troubled—as occurring while he pondered, at the same time.

6.2.4 Providing Reason

A causal relationship between cola comprises another potential category for cola relationships. Causal relations exist when colon B is subordinate to colon A, providing a reason or cause for a specific action or statement.

In these instances, it is useful to understand the second colon as a completion or continuation of a thought process. Often, within this category, semantic repetition between the cola diminishes, but syntactic parallelism may still exist. Consider Ps 25:16:

| פְּנֵה־אֵלַי וְחָנֵּנִי | Turn to me and be gracious to me, |
| כִּי־יָחִיד וְעָנִי אָנִי | for I am lonely and afflicted. |

This verse exemplifies a causal relationship between two cola. The second colon provides a reason or cause for the first colon. In colon A, the psalmist requests that God turn his attention to him, focusing on his situation; then colon B provides the reason—he is lonely and afflicted. The sentiment in the second colon does not repeat in the first, as typically witnessed in synonymous parallelism, but adds detail to colon A, completing the thought. In this instance, the explicit discourse marker, the particle כִּי, cues the reader to understand a causative relationship between the statements.[4] Occasionally, poets reverse the clause order, placing the reason before the cause. An example of this is Ps 106:33:

| כִּי־הִמְרוּ אֶת־רוּחוֹ | Because they were rebellious against His Spirit, |
| וַיְבַטֵּא בִּשְׂפָתָיו׃ | He spoke rashly with his lips. (NASB) |

In Ps 106's recitation of the exodus account, while Israel was wandering in the desert, the Israelites, according to the psalmist's rendition, provoke Moses to sin. Perhaps as a point of emphasis, the reason for Moses's rash actions in the subordinate clause appears first—the Israelites rebelled against God's Spirit.[5] After colon A states the reason for Moses's actions, the psalmist reveals Moses's response, he spoke rashly. These cola could just have easily been reversed, "he spoke rashly with his lips because they were rebellions against his Spirit."

At this point, the list of potential relationships could continue with more and more nuanced relationships between cola. Indeed, others have attempted

---

4. See also Pss 34:9 and 39:12.

5. Or possibly Moses's spirit, depending on how one reads this. The capitals provided in the NASB here are obviously not in the original Hebrew.

to categorize such relationships further.[6] For the present volume, however, the examples presented are enough to instill the necessity to examine carefully and attentively the relationships between individual cola and define them accordingly. Furthermore, it is important to remember at this point in the analysis that overlaps exist between categories of cola relationships, and they should not be considered mutually exclusive.

6.3 Acrostics

The acrostic is a structural technique for arranging poetry where the first letter of each colon, or collection of colons, spells out a word or presents successive letters of the alphabet. The number of cola grouped together for each letter varies from composition to composition. Perhaps the most recognized acrostic occurs when the first letter of each verse follows the sequence of the Hebrew alphabet. A prominent example appears in Ps 34. Consider the opening 5 verses:

אֲבָרֲכָה אֶת־יְהוָה בְּכָל־עֵת	1[2]I will bless the Lord at all times;
תָּמִיד תְּהִלָּתוֹ בְּפִי׃	his praise shall continually be in my mouth.
בַּיהוָה תִּתְהַלֵּל נַפְשִׁי	2[3]My soul boasts in the Lord;
יִשְׁמְעוּ עֲנָוִים וְיִשְׂמָחוּ׃	the humble will hear it and rejoice.
גַּדְּלוּ לַיהוָה אִתִּי	3[4]O magnify the Lord with me,
וּנְרוֹמְמָה שְׁמוֹ יַחְדָּו׃	and let us exalt his name together.
דָּרַשְׁתִּי אֶת־יְהוָה וְעָנָנִי	4[5]I sought the Lord, and he answered me,
וּמִכָּל־מְגוּרוֹתַי הִצִּילָנִי׃	and delivered me from all my fears.
הִבִּיטוּ אֵלָיו וְנָהָרוּ	5[6]They looked to him and were radiant,
וּפְנֵיהֶם אַל־יֶחְפָּרוּ׃	and their faces will never be ashamed.

As demonstrated by the black Hebrew letters, each successive verse, every other colon, begins with a successive letter of the alphabet. The first verse

---

6. Patton, Putnam, and Van Pelt, *Basics of Hebrew Discourse*, 252–54, present a list of possibilities like those discussed above. They divide the relationships into two types: continuity and discontinuity. Continuous relationships consist of similarity, contrast, example, temporal, cause and effect, motive, and explanation; and the discontinuous relationship signals a change in the subject of the verb.

begins with *aleph*, the second *bet*, the third *gimel*, and so forth. Notable here is that identification of the acrostic pattern fails to transfer to the English translation. Despite the purportedly literal translations of the Bible—such as the NASB, KJV, and ESV—that strive for strict adherence to the Hebrew text, the acrostic pattern remains imperceptible to them.

Psalm 111 presents another kind of acrostic pattern, consider the following:

אוֹדֶה יְהוָה בְּכָל־לֵבָב	¹ᵇI will give thanks to the Lord with all my heart,
בְּסוֹד יְשָׁרִים וְעֵדָה׃	in the company of the upright and in the assembly.
גְּדֹלִים מַעֲשֵׂי יְהוָה	²Great are the works of the Lord;
דְּרוּשִׁים לְכָל־חֶפְצֵיהֶם׃	they are studied by all who delight in them.
הוֹד־וְהָדָר פָּעֳלוֹ	³Splendid and majestic is his work,
וְצִדְקָתוֹ עֹמֶדֶת לָעַד׃	and his righteousness endures forever.
זֵכֶר עָשָׂה לְנִפְלְאֹתָיו	⁴He has made his wonders to be remembered;
חַנּוּן וְרַחוּם יְהוָה׃	the Lord is gracious and compassionate.
טֶרֶף נָתַן לִירֵאָיו	⁵He has given food to those who fear him;
יִזְכֹּר לְעוֹלָם בְּרִיתוֹ	he will remember his covenant forever.

In this example, consecutive letters of the alphabet remain the defining feature; however, the psalmist opted to arrange them according to successive individual cola as opposed to the successive bicola in Ps 34. The sequential arrangement in acrostics may further extend to encapsulate whole stanzas arranged by successive letters of the Hebrew alphabet. The most cited example appears in Ps 119.

אַשְׁרֵי תְמִימֵי־דָרֶךְ . . .	¹Blessed are those whose way is blameless . . .
אַשְׁרֵי נֹצְרֵי עֵדֹתָיו . . .	²Blessed are those who observe his testimonies . . .
אַף לֹא־פָעֲלוּ עַוְלָה . . .	³They also do no unrighteousness . . .
אַתָּה צִוִּיתָה פִקֻּדֶיךָ . . .	⁴You have ordained your precepts . . .
אַחֲלַי יִכֹּנוּ דְרָכָי . . .	⁵Oh that my ways may be established . . .
אָז לֹא־אֵבוֹשׁ . . .	⁶Then I shall not be ashamed . . .

אֽוֹדְךָ בְּיֹשֶׁר לֵבָב . . .	⁷I shall give thanks to you with uprightness of heart . . .
אֶת־חֻקֶּיךָ אֶשְׁמֹר . . .	⁸I shall keep your statutes . . .
בַּמֶּה יְזַכֶּה־נַּעַר אֶת־אָרְחוֹ . . .	⁹How can a young man keep his way pure? . . .
בְּכָל־לִבִּי דְרַשְׁתִּיךָ . . .	¹⁰With all my heart I have sought you . . .
בְּלִבִּי צָפַנְתִּי אִמְרָתֶךָ . . .	¹¹Your word I have treasured in my heart . . .
בָּרוּךְ אַתָּה יְהוָה . . .	¹²Blessed are you, O Lord . . .
בִּשְׂפָתַי סִפַּרְתִּי . . .	¹³With my lips I have told of . . .
בְּדֶרֶךְ עֵדְוֺתֶיךָ שַׂשְׂתִּי . . .	¹⁴I have rejoiced in the way of your testimonies . . .
בְּפִקֻּדֶיךָ אָשִׂיחָה . . .	¹⁵I will meditate on your precepts . . .
בְּחֻקֹּתֶיךָ אֶשְׁתַּעֲשָׁע . . .	¹⁶I shall delight in your statutes . . .
גְּמֹל עַל־עַבְדְּךָ . . .	¹⁷Deal bountifully with your servant . . .
גַּל־עֵינַי וְאַבִּיטָה . . .	¹⁸Open my eyes, that I may behold . . .
גֵּר אָנֹכִי בָאָרֶץ . . .	¹⁹I am a stranger in the earth . . .
גָּרְסָה נַפְשִׁי לְתַאֲבָה . . .	²⁰My soul is crushed with longing . . .
גָּעַרְתָּ זֵדִים אֲרוּרִים . . .	²¹You rebuke the arrogant, the cursed . . .
גַּל מֵעָלַי חֶרְפָּה וָבוּז . . .	²²Take away reproach and contempt from me . . .
גַּם יָשְׁבוּ שָׂרִים בִּי נִדְבָּרוּ . . .	²³Even though princes sit and talk against me . . .
גַּם־עֵדֹתֶיךָ שַׁעֲשֻׁעָי . . .	²⁴Your testimonies also are my delight . . .

Psalm 119:1–24 contains three stanzas, each containing eight verses. The first letter in each stanza is the same, and each progression in the stanza is marked by a progression in the Hebrew alphabet from *aleph*, which begins the first section, to *bet*, which marks the beginning of the second stanza (vv. 9–11), and *gimel* in the third stanza. The same principle is at work; the textual unit begins with successive letters of the alphabet, but each letter of the alphabet extends to a whole stanza.[7]

Not all acrostics are complete, and a few Hebrew texts exhibit partial acrostic patterns, where poets follow the sequence of the Hebrew alphabet

---

7. Other examples of acrostics appear in Pss 25; 37; 112; 145; Prov 31:10–30; Lam 1–4.

but discontinue the sequencing prior to reaching the last letter. Consider Nah 1:3b–7a:

בְּסוּפָה וּבִשְׂעָרָה דַּרְכּוֹ . . .	³ᵇIn whirlwind and storm is his way . . .
גּוֹעֵר בַּיָּם וַיַּבְּשֵׁהוּ . . .	⁴He rebukes the sea and makes it dry . . .
אֻמְלַל בָּשָׁן וְכַרְמֶל . . .	Bashan and Carmel wither . . .
הָרִים רָעֲשׁוּ מִמֶּנּוּ . . .	⁵Mountains quake because of him . . .
וַתִּשָּׂא הָאָרֶץ מִפָּנָיו . . .	Indeed the earth is upheaved by his presence . . .
לִפְנֵי זַעְמוֹ מִי יַעֲמוֹד . . .	⁶Who can stand before his indignation . . .
חֲמָתוֹ נִתְּכָה כָאֵשׁ . . .	His wrath is poured out like fire . . .
טוֹב יְהוָה	⁷The Lord is good,
לְמָעוֹז בְּיוֹם צָרָה . . .	A stronghold in the day of trouble . . .

In vv. 3b–7a, above, one observes the partial acrostic pattern in bold letters. Although the initial letters of each colon reveal parts of an alphabetic sequencing, it is difficult to ignore the disruptions to the arrangement. After Nah 1:8, patterns like this fail to appear.[8]

A notable feature of biblical acrostics is their apparent imperfection, and understanding why they appear presents certain challenges. Instances such as Ps 119, utilizing the complete Hebrew alphabet in the sequencing recognized today, represent the minority of cases. Routinely, poets appear to disrupt the pattern, rendering an apparent incompleteness. Psalm 34, for example, interrupts the expected alphabetic sequence in vv. 8–9. The psalmist appears to agitate the anticipated order of *he, waw, zayin, khet, tet*, rendering *he, zayin, khet, tet*, with the omission of the *waw*. Moreover, he incorporates

---

8. Pseudo-acrostics or quasi-acrostics also deserve mention. These eleven-line and twenty-two-line poems in the Hebrew Bible were modeled after acrostics, without a successive letter of the alphabet in the first line of each unit. Examples of these acrostics are in Pss 16; 29; 32; and 33. See also Freedman, "Acrostic Poems," esp. 415 (who refers to the phenomenon as non-alphabetic acrostics); Giffone, "'Perfect' Poem," esp. 72; James, "Aesthetics of Biblical Acrostics"; Justiss, "Identifying Alphabetic Compositions"; Pinker, "Nahum 1" (for the validity of Nah 1:2–8 containing a partial acrostic); Watson, *Classical Hebrew Poetry*, 199, who cites twenty-two-line examples in Ps 38 and Lam 5; and eleven-line examples in Job 9:25–35; Jer 5:4–5; and Hos 12:3–6. However, due to the possibility of the appearance of partial acrostics through happenstance, a degree of conflict arises concerning scholarly identification of them. See, for example, Floyd, "The Chimerical Acrostic of Nahum 1:2–10," who denies the existence of the acrostic in Nah 1.

an additional verse at the end of the psalm that unexpectedly begins with the letter *pe*. Overall, even though the composition reveals an undoubtedly intentional structure according to the letters of the alphabet, adjustments have clearly been made to disrupt the sequence.

Another example of this disruption appears in the partial acrostic of Ps 9.[9] According to today's ordering of the Hebrew alphabet, the expected sequence for the initial letters is *aleph, bet, gimel, dalet, he*. However, this composition reflects the ordering of *aleph, bet, gimel, he, waw*, with the omission of the *dalet*. Additionally, the letter-ordering in the acrostics of Lam 2–4 and the partial acrostic Ps 10 reverse the letters *pe* and *ayin*. Furthermore, Ps 25, like Ps 34, omits the expected *waw* line and replaces it with an additional *pe* line at the end. Such disruptions elicit further inquiry into the possible mindset of the Hebrew poets. How could a creative and skilled poet arrange 95 percent of an acrostic poem and fail at one or two points in the alphabetic sequencing? A potential answer to this question lies in a healthy respect for a psalmist's creativity. Perhaps the ancient poets did not omit letters, or reverse their order, because they lacked imagination, or were sloppy in their composition, but because they sought to demonstrate their ingenuity and generate increased reader engagement. This is possible if the disruptions were designed to draw attention to specific parts of the composition, attracting the reader's attention to a potential point of emphasis. In this way, the broken acrostic patterns may serve as highway markers indicating an exit ramp for a point of interest.[10]

Turning to the overall function of acrostics, in all their various guises, three further possibilities arise. First, it has been suggested that acrostics were originally written to facilitate memorization,[11] presumably either for

---

9. If the acrostic pattern appeared in Ps 9 alone, one could describe it as partial. However, if Ps 9 constitutes the first half of Pss 9–10, a single composition, then the acrostic pattern would be complete.

10. There is a sense in which these disruptions, as described above, reflect windows into literary artistry. Alsene-Parker, "The ABCs of Hebrew Acrostic Poems," 3, argues, "It is this openness to adaptation that makes the acrostic form a perfect vessel for artistic creativity.... Rather than being a repetitive or clunky constraint, the alphabetic acrostic form gave the poets a flexible mould within which they could showcase their artistry."

11. This position is reflected in Midrash Lamentations Rabbah 1:1. The acrostic aids memorization so people could recite it easily when commemorating the destruction of the temple. See Assis, "Alphabetic Acrostic in the Book of Lamentations," 712. However, Giffone, "'Perfect Poem,'" 71, denies that possibility.

the poet who recites the song or for the audience who listens.[12] Second, they may have been written to reflect completeness, which is to say demonstrate the psalmist's comprehensive treatment of his topic. An obvious difficulty with this assumption, however, emerges with the phenomenon of partial and quasi-acrostics whose alphabetic sequencing remains incomplete. A quasi-acrostic cannot be interpreted as being comprehensive in treatment because it omits certain letters of the alphabet.[13] Third, the acrostic may simply reflect a poet displaying his skill to his audience, arranging the cola and verses of a thematic unity framed with alphabetic sequencing. A potential problem with this theory relates to the general organization of acrostic poems. Regularly, when poets employ an acrostic organization, other structural poetic features are sacrificed, and tasks such as determining stanza divisions become more challenging for exegetes.

When determining the meaning or the function of an acrostic, therefore, it is advisable to first understand what kind of acrostic appears in the text being examined. Is it complete, with the correct sequencing of the letters? Is the alphabetic sequencing reflected at the start of cola, verses, or stanzas? Is it incomplete with only half of the alphabet used? Is it disrupted, and if so, where? Once the exegete determines the type and character of the acrostic, they should then uncover and discuss any potential links between the acrostic's form and the prominent themes within the composition.

6.4 Enjambment

Enjambment constitutes a disruption in the expected order of syntax. In a sentence, syntax requires that a relatively strong pause occurs to demarcate its termination, usually in the form a full stop or a semicolon in English. Hebrew poetry, on the other hand requires a *hard stop* at the end of its basic

---

12. Although this has been proposed, not all agree. Watson, *Classical Hebrew Poetry*, 191, suggests that the form of the acrostic was designed more for the eye than for the ear.
13. In the case of Nahum, one could counter that the disruption in the sequencings serves to reflect a thematic disruption in the prophet's message. The broken acrostic in Nah 1, therefore, represents chaos, the opposite of completeness, as suggested by Giffone, "'Perfect' Poem," 56. For Giffone, "The acrostic form is essentially an imposition of order onto disorder, a way of making connections where none is apparent or strengthening existing connections" (p. 70).

unit, the line or colon. In most cases, these two scenarios align—with the sentence or clause terminating at the end of the poetic line. However, sometimes the end of a sentence may extend past the boundaries of a single colon.[14] This overflow of one sentence or clause spilling into two cola produces enjambment.[15] An example of the phenomenon appears at Ps 14:2:

יְהוָה מִשָּׁמַיִם הִשְׁקִיף	The Lord looks down from heaven upon
עַל־בְּנֵי־אָדָם	the sons of men
לִרְאוֹת הֲיֵשׁ מַשְׂכִּיל	to see if there are any who understand,
דֹּרֵשׁ אֶת־אֱלֹהִים:	who seek after God.

Verse 2 above comprises part of the psalm's opening, depicting God gazing down from his heavenly vantage point to see if anybody on earth behaves with understanding, seeking him and acting appropriately. The Masoretic markings *oleh veyored*—used here because the Psalter is one of the *emeth* books[16]—followed by an *atnakh* divide the verse into three cola. According to the rules of syntax, the first colon fails to contain the complete sentence, even though the subject and verb are present, it does not reflect the complete thought. The remainder of the sentence is divided into two more cola. The outcome is that the poetic cola divisions disrupt the sentence, splitting it over three cola, deviating from the normal expected structure found in Hebrew poetry. Psalm 116:1 provides another example:

אָהַבְתִּי כִּי־יִשְׁמַע יְהוָה	I love the Lord, because he hears
אֶת־קוֹלִי תַּחֲנוּנָי:	my voice and my supplications.

In v. 1, above, the psalmist professes his love for God because of his ability to hear and presumably respond to the psalmist's cry. The sentence flows over two cola, which are divided by an *atnakh*. This example presents a dramatic slice into the grammatical structure because the second

---

14. This normal situation is referred to as end-stopping. For more on this see Watson, *Classical Hebrew Poetry*, 332–33.
15. One of the more extensive studies on the topic was performed by Dobs-Allsopp, "The Enjambing Line in Lamentations."
16. See ch. 2 concerning this group of texts.

colon constitutes a truncated phrase that wholly depends on the first colon for meaning.[17]

Hebrew poets primarily employ enjambment to disturb the expected presentation of Hebrew poetic syntax. However, further research is required to formulate more precise observations concerning the specific contexts in which it appears. At the bare minimum, exegetes are advised to note occurrences of enjambment when examining poetic texts, and then to suggest how it aligns with the composition's primary themes, movement, and flow. The underlying theory concerning enjambment's appearance is that if a poet determined to disturb an established rhythm, he must have done so with the specific intention of drawing a reader's attention to that part of the composition.

Questions for Consideration: What is the relationship between the cola? Are any verse relationships consistently used by the poet? Are any new (not defined above) relationships apparent? If an acrostic is present, is it complete? What variations exist from the expected sequential alphabetic pattern? Are there missing or transposed letters? Do the disturbances in the expected pattern appear at crucial positions in the composition?

Further Reading: Alsene-Parker, "The ABCs of Hebrew Acrostic Poems"; Assis, "The Alphabetic Acrostic in the Book of Lamentations"; Dobs-Allsopp, "The Enjambing Line in Lamentations"; Floyd, "The Chimerical Acrostic of Nahum 1:2–10"; Freedman, "Acrostic Poems"; Goh, *Hebrew Poetry*, 37, 46–48; Pinker, "Nahum 1."

---

17. Watson, *Classical Hebrew Poetry*, 335, suggests that this feature "serves to break the monotony of end-stopped lines, to assist the forward movement of a poem by creating tension between metre and grammar, and thirdly to bring the verse closer to normal speech rhythms." It is difficult, however, to apply this rationale directly to the feature's contribution toward a composition's meaning.

PART 4

Poetic Technique

7

Basic Imagery

We turn now to discuss a higher and more conceptual layer of poetic formation in the Hebrew Bible. Returning to our house construction metaphor, the relationship between structural poetics and imagery can be understood as analogous to the external structure of a house and its internal furnishings. To create a livable home, both elements are essential. In addition to a sound structural framework and a sturdy, waterproof roof, houses require chairs, beds, carpets, tables, and other furnishings to complete them. Just as these two aspects of building—external structure and furniture—exist in a single house, so too do structural poetics and poetic imagery. The imagery employed by biblical poets adds new layers to the poetic experience. Typically, the images function independently of the structural features in which they are situated. However, in certain instances, the structural features can enhance poetic imagery.[1]

7.1 Imagery

Perhaps the most definitive feature of biblical Hebrew poetry is the frequent employment of poetic imagery, words that transform abstract concepts and deep-seated emotions into vivid and lasting images. In this regard, the adage proves true, a picture speaks a thousand words. Consequently, biblical authors, whenever possible, engender graphic images in their reader's minds to create depth and meaning in their compositions. A Hebrew poet's skill is

---

1. We have already seen an example of this where chiasmus, a structural feature, is used to enhance a merism.

usually reflected in his ability to transpose abstract notions such as protection, love, fear, and anxiety—concepts that are challenging to explain purely with technical language—into concrete images with which his readers are familiar. To use a contemporary example, if I sought to communicate to an audience the speed of my new electric vehicle, I could adopt a discourse relying on adjectives such as rapid, quick, nimble, and fleet. A more vivid means of conveying the car's mind-blowing speed, however, would be to claim the car moves like lightning. Using a simple phrase in this way allows me to achieve both a degree of economy with my word usage and at the same time generate a lucid image of speed in my readers' minds.

To be sure, however, poetic imagery does not solely reside in the literary arena of biblical poetry and regularly surfaces in the narrative texts of the Old Testament. Thus, for example, in the middle of a prose text in Genesis, the narrator adopts an image to convey the vast quantities of grain that Joseph, through his divine wisdom, accumulated. To convey the immense quantity, he says, "Thus Joseph stored up grain in great abundance like the sand of the sea, until he stopped measuring it, for it was beyond measure" (Gen 41:49). Although the author employs a poetic image here, a simile, he does so within the context of an unequivocally recognizable prose text. One of the key points of divergence between prose and poetry, therefore, is the variety and frequency of poetic imagery appearing in texts commonly designated as poetic.

The poetic features discussed in this chapter do not oppose the structural features of Hebrew but regularly work together with them to contribute toward a desired effect. Consequently, as one analyzes Hebrew poetry, it is important to ask how the poetic features work together with the structural characteristics illustrated in the previous chapters. In many instances no tangible connection arises, but often poets select specific structural devices to correspond with and enhance a poetic image. It is only on rare occasions that authors adopt poetic imagery specifically to generate structure within a composition.

Perhaps the greatest challenge for the modern reader and exegete is to recreate perfectly and precisely the author's intended image in their own mind. In certain instances, this can be easily attained, particularly if the author adopts an image that has withstood the test of time and relates to an unchangeable object such as the sun or the moon. Unfortunately, however, biblical authors regularly employ images that become distorted in the contemporary reader's mind. Psalm 23:2a, "He makes me lie down in green pastures," illustrates this point. To many Western readers, the phrase "green pastures" conjures images of the rolling meadows of the Cotswolds in England, as opposed to the dryer arid pasturelands of the Judean desert, where David led his sheep. The author's image, in cases like this, although similar to landscapes and scenery conjured up in the minds of those who have never visited the Judean desert, also reflects important differences, and consequently interpretations. Thus, it is important for contemporary readers to take the time to delve deeply into images employed by biblical poets. What follows is a discussion of the main categories of imagery found in Hebrew poetry, including some of the more nuanced techniques, such as synecdoche, metonymy, personification, and symbolism.

7.2 Metaphor

A metaphor, in essence, is a direct comparison between two entities that a writer adopts to connect an abstract concept with a concrete image or idea. Watson functionally schematizes the relationship between both entities as X is like Y with respect to Z. Alternative descriptions appear in the literature that detail these crucial elements. The X element emerges as the tenor, in certain schemas, the Y is the vehicle, and the Z is the ground.[2] Psalm 23 illustrates the relationship between the two domains; v. 1a, a well-known passage, begins, "The LORD is my shepherd. . . ." In this colon, the writer compares the Lord, (X) to a shepherd (Y). That part is unmistakable; however, it remains with the reader to discern and determine Z, the intended transferable attribute(s) between X and Y. In this context, readers are not invited to read the words or phrase literally. God, the creator of the universe and everything in it, constitutes so much more than a mere earthly shepherd who

---

2. Concerning this relationship, Bullinger states, "The two nouns themselves must both be mentioned, and are always to be taken in their absolutely literal sense, or else no one can tell what they mean. The figure lies wholly in the verb, or *copula*, which, in English, must always be expressed, and never understood by *Ellipsis*" (*Figures of Speech*, 735, italics original).

leads flocks, or in this case the psalmist in the desert. The literal meaning of the words adopted by the author fails to reflect his intended message. In this instance, the reader's challenge is to deduce the elements of shepherding and a shepherd's role with respect to his sheep that are relevant and transfer them onto the role God plays in the life of the psalmist. Within the context of the entire psalm, God's capability to provide, protect, and lead individuals constitutes the primary transferable element.

Another example of metaphor appears in Ps 69:2[3]a: "I have sunk in deep mire [יָוֵן מְצוּלָה], and there is no foothold." Here the psalmist compares his troubles and the threats of his enemies (X) to a deep pool of mud or quicksand (Y). Again, it is incumbent upon the reader to determine elements of the vehicle that transfer to the tenor: it would be inaccurate to postulate that the psalmist composed his psalm as he literally sank slowly into a mud pool. For the reader, it is easy to visualize the experience of slipping slowly into a pit of soft mud, desperately seeking a foothold, or root, anything that provides a glimmer of hope. Failing to locate an anchorage of any description results in an assuredly slow death. An experience such as this stimulates a range of negative emotions: fear, anxiety, hopelessness, panic, etc. These emotions transfer to the psalmist's experience. His enemies are plotting against him (v. 4[5]) and as time passes, he suffers attack after attack, verbal assault after verbal assault. Despite his desperate search for something, anything, to mitigate the assaults and provide even a glimmer of hope, he finds nothing. In his eyes, if these onslaughts continue, only death itself awaits him. Poetically, the depth of his feelings, his anguish and despair, are succinctly expressed in his image of a man gradually descending into a bottomless pool of mud.[3]

Because metaphors frequently appear in Hebrew poetry, it proves advantageous to categorize them as part of the analytical process. The two main classifications discussed below are simple metaphors and extended metaphors.[4]

---

3. It is important to identify the three elements of metaphors—tenor, vehicle, and ground—when analyzing poetry, in addition to how they are named in the literature.

4. Metaphors may also exist in series, consecutively. This formation, however, is relatively rare, with Gen 49 being the prime example. For more on the concept, see Watson, *Classical Hebrew Poetry*, 270.

7.2.1 Simple Metaphors

The simplest metaphors appear between one or two cola, where the vehicle and tenor emerge within a couplet. Psalm 119:105 presents an example of this metaphor category:

| נֵר־לְרַגְלִי דְבָרֶךָ | Your word is a lamp to my feet |
| וְאוֹר לִנְתִיבָתִי | and a light to my path. |

Very often the relationship is identifiable with the copula in English syntax.

Verse 105a directly refers the word of God, the tenor in this instance, as a lamp, the vehicle. The image of an individual walking in the dark on rocky terrain presents one potentially overarching theme for the verse. In this context, the psalmist projects an image of guidance and leading.[5] The second colon, adopting synonymous parallelism, reinforces the image of guidance and leading with the statement "and a light to my path." Therefore, the word of God, in the present verse, functions as a metaphorical and non-literal source of illumination for the psalmist as he walks the path of life. The subject matter of God's word, implied from the first colon, is not literally a lamp or a light. At no point does the psalmist argue that ancient Torah scrolls possessed the capacity to glow in the dark, enabling their carriers to walk safely at night on rocky terrain. Rather, he posits that the same way the light of a lamp provides illumination for a dangerous and uneven path at night, by following the precepts of God's word, obeying his instruction, the psalmist can avoid the hidden pitfalls that lie ahead of him as he walks the path of life. Because the image of light with respect to guidance remains restricted to two cola, without further development in v. 106, it is classified as a simple metaphor.

Another example of a simple metaphor emerges in Ps 84:11[12]a:

| כִּי שֶׁמֶשׁ וּמָגֵן יְהוָה אֱלֹהִים | For the Lord God is a sun and a shield. |

The psalmist, in this brief colon, explicitly refers to God, the tenor, with two vehicles, שֶׁמֶשׁ, a sun, and מָגֵן, a shield. Since God is not literally being

---

5. A similar example is shown in Prov 6:23. See also Ryken et al., *Dictionary of Biblical Imagery*, 486.

called the sun, it symbolizes the psalmist's appreciation of God as a source of life and lifegiving strength, along with other blessings. Echoes of this sentiment reverberate in the following colon, which declares that the Lord bestows grace and glory, not withholding any good thing from those who walk uprightly.[6] The shield, on the other hand, represents protection and a defense against those external forces that threaten to take the life and blessing that the creator provides.[7] As with the first example, the metaphor remains confined to a single verse.[8]

7.2.2 Extended Metaphors

In some instances, poets develop metaphors, protracting them beyond a single verse. These lengthier images are called extended metaphors. An example of an extended metaphor appears in Ezekiel's condemnation of Judah in Ezek 23:32–34:

כֹּה אָמַר אֲדֹנָי יְהוִה	³²Thus says the Lord Lord,
כּוֹס אֲחוֹתֵךְ תִּשְׁתִּי	"You will drink your sister's cup,
הָעֲמֻקָּה וְהָרְחָבָה	which is deep and wide.
תִּהְיֶה לִצְחֹק וּלְלַעַג	You will be laughed at and held in derision;
מַרְבָּה לְהָכִיל׃	it contains much.
שִׁכָּרוֹן וְיָגוֹן תִּמָּלֵאִי	³³You will be filled with drunkenness and sorrow,
כּוֹס שַׁמָּה וּשְׁמָמָה	the cup of horror and desolation,
כּוֹס אֲחוֹתֵךְ שֹׁמְרוֹן׃	the cup of your sister Samaria.
וְשָׁתִית אוֹתָהּ וּמָצִית	³⁴You will drink it and drain it.
וְאֶת־חֲרָשֶׂיהָ תְּגָרֵמִי	Then you will gnaw its fragments
וְשָׁדַיִךְ תְּנַתֵּקִי	and tear your breasts;
כִּי אֲנִי דִבַּרְתִּי נְאֻם אֲדֹנָי יְהוִה׃	for I have spoken," declares the Lord Lord.

---

6. See Ryken et al., *Dictionary of Biblical Imagery*, 827. Notably, the image or symbol of the sun is not confined to a single interpretation in biblical literature or in the broader ancient Near Eastern context. As part of the analysis process, exegetes must consider how their proposed interpretation of an image integrates with the overall context of the poetic unit.

7. See 2 Sam 22:31, and Ryken et al., *Dictionary of Biblical Imagery*, 785.

8. For further examples, see Pss 39:5; 94:22; and 95:1.

Here the poet employs the metaphor of the cup, where the significance lies not in the object but in the contents. Although the cup metaphor carries with it a slew of possibilities[9]—such as love, comfort, strength, and fellowship—the present context heavily implies that the author references the cup of God's wrath. Unlike the previous examples, however, the image is not confined to a single colon. Instead, the writer develops it over several cola, detailing the nature and effects of drinking its contents. From this one cup, depicted as the cup of Judah's sister, the inhabitants of Judah will experience embarrassment from their neighbors, metaphorically drunk and sorrowful. As part of God's judgment, the contents further induce anguish and pain. The metaphor of the cup and its vile contents, introduced in v. 32, develops over an extended series of cola to paint a vivid picture of sorrow, pain, and desolation for Judah's inhabitants.

Another extended metaphor surfaces in Mic 3:2–3:

שֹׂנְאֵי טוֹב וְאֹהֲבֵי רָעָה	²You who hate good and love evil,
גֹּזְלֵי עוֹרָם מֵעֲלֵיהֶם	who tear off their skin from them
וּשְׁאֵרָם מֵעַל עַצְמוֹתָם:	and their flesh from their bones,
וַאֲשֶׁר אָכְלוּ שְׁאֵר עַמִּי	³who eat the flesh of my people,
וְעוֹרָם מֵעֲלֵיהֶם הִפְשִׁיטוּ	strip off their skin from them,
וְאֶת־עַצְמֹתֵיהֶם פִּצֵּחוּ	break their bones
וּפָרְשׂוּ כַּאֲשֶׁר בַּסִּיר	and chop them up as for the pot
וּכְבָשָׂר בְּתוֹךְ קַלָּחַת	and as meat in a kettle.

The metaphor appearing in Micah transfers the characteristics of a cannibal, an individual hungry for human flesh, to the leaders of Judah who prey on those marginalized in society. These rulers are not literally eating the flesh of God's people, but the psalmist compares their behavior and attitudes to the heartless cruelty and wanton comportment of voracious cannibals. The detailed depiction of a ravenous cannibal conveys to the reader a vivid image of heartless and selfish cruelty.[10] It should be noted that both instances of extended metaphor discussed above reflect examples of hypocatastasis, an

---

9. See Ryken et al., *Dictionary of Biblical Imagery*, 186.
10. For other examples of extended metaphors, consider Pss 23; 76; and Ezek 29:3–5.

implied comparison (see below). At no point do the authors explicitly connect the vehicle with the tenor. Ezekiel refrains from explicitly stating that the cup *is* the Lord's punishment; similarly, Micah eschews the explicit declaration that Judah's leaders are cannibals. In both instances, despite avoiding the specific connection, the primary ground, shared attributes, are apparent to the reader.

7.3 Simile

In essence, the simile functions in the same way as the metaphor: both techniques compare two ideas, and technically both still exhibit the tenor and the vehicle for conveying an image. The primary difference, however, between the two poetic features concerns the comparative particle כְּ that the simile adopts in its association of tenor and vehicle. English Bible translations primarily translate the particle with "as" or "like." With respect to their intensity, it is possible to understand the metaphor as brazenly declaring that one entity *is* another entity, but the simile as gently stating that one entity is *like* or *resembles* another. In this way, it is possible to view the simile as a moderate version of the metaphor. Psalm 38:13[14] provides an example of a simile:

וַאֲנִי כְחֵרֵשׁ לֹא אֶשְׁמָע
וּכְאִלֵּם לֹא יִפְתַּח־פִּיו

But I, *like* a deaf man, do not hear;
and *like* a mute man not opening his mouth.
(emphasis added)

Here the psalmist conveys his vulnerability to the persistent threats of his enemies. For the depiction of his suffering, he employs the simile of being "*like* a deaf man ... *like* a mute man."[11] In this instance, as with most similes, the particle כְּ, "like," functions practically, aiding the reader in properly identifying the psalmist's words as an image and not a literal statement. By portraying himself as deaf, the psalmist is unable to hear his enemy approaching to attack him, and in this respect, he is more vulnerable than if he maintained his hearing faculties. Similarly, by portraying himself as mute, the psalmist underscores his incapacity to verbally defend against the false

---

11. As a metaphor, this would read, "I am a deaf man ... I am a mute man."

accusations and taunts. Together, these metaphorical disabilities coalesce to present a profound sense of helplessness and vulnerability.

Another simple example of simile appears in Ps 123:2:

הִנֵּה כְעֵינֵי עֲבָדִים אֶל־יַד אֲדוֹנֵיהֶם	Behold, as the eyes of servants to the hand of their master,
כְּעֵינֵי שִׁפְחָה אֶל־יַד גְּבִרְתָּהּ	as the eyes of a maidservant to the hand of her mistress,
כֵּן עֵינֵינוּ אֶל־יְהוָה אֱלֹהֵינוּ עַד שֶׁיְּחָנֵּנוּ׃	so our eyes to the Lord our God, till he has mercy upon us.

In this verse, the psalmist employs synonymous parallelism to strengthen the analogy created by the simile. To express his community's disheartening inactivity as they wait for recognition from God, the poet creates the simile, "*as* the eyes of servants . . . *as* the eyes of a maidservant." This concrete imagery of servants waiting on their master's signal mirrors the intense attention with which the psalmist's community waits for God to notice their lowly estate and alleviate their suffering. The example here further demonstrates a common alternative for translating the particle כְּ, instead of "like," seen earlier, the translators opt for "as," creating a preferable translation.[12]

As with metaphors, poets may extend similes over a few verses. Consider Hosea's prophecy of retribution in Hos 13:7–8:

וָאֱהִי לָהֶם כְּמוֹ־שָׁחַל	[7]So I will be like a lion to them;
כְּנָמֵר עַל־דֶּרֶךְ אָשׁוּר׃	Like a leopard I will lie in wait by the wayside.
אֶפְגְּשֵׁם כְּדֹב שַׁכּוּל	[8]I will encounter them like a bear robbed of her cubs,
וְאֶקְרַע סְגוֹר לִבָּם	And I will tear open their chests;
וְאֹכְלֵם שָׁם כְּלָבִיא	there I will also devour them like a lioness,
חַיַּת הַשָּׂדֶה תְּבַקְּעֵם׃	as a wild beast would tear them.

---

12. In numerous instances, across the versions, translators appear to use either "as" or "like" in their interpretation of the particle. As an example, regarding Ps 38:4, the NIV reads "For my iniquities are gone over my head; *As* a heavy burden" (emphasis added); whereas, the NIV 2011 reads, "My guilt has overwhelmed me *like* a burden too heavy to bear" (emphasis added). Each translation has opted for a different translation for the particle כְּ. See also Pss 10:9; 11:1; and 17:12 for further examples of this translational variation.

Overall, the image of an anger-fueled attack against Ephraim is evoked through the depiction of wild animals driven by hunger or protective instincts as they attack their intended target. Each of the vehicals represents a ferocious beast on the verge of striking. They are linked by the author's repeated use of simile, as illustrated in phrases such as "*like* a lion ... *like* a leopard ... *like* a bear ... *like* a lioness."[13]

7.4 Hypocatastasis

Occasionally, writers activate metaphors by directly associating the tenor and the vehicle. In the previous examples, the metaphors were explicit, with both the vehicle and the tenor mentioned and linked by a copula, schematically represented as "X is Y," where X is the tenor and Y is the vehicle. Hypocatastasis, on the other hand, occurs when an author refers directly to the vehicle without using the copula. An example appears in Amos 4:1a:

שִׁמְעוּ הַדָּבָר הַזֶּה פָּרוֹת　　Hear this word, you cows of Bashan who
הַבָּשָׁן אֲשֶׁר בְּהַר שֹׁמְרוֹן　　are on the mountain of Samaria. (NASB)

Here in v. 4a, the author compares the women of Samaria to the sleek, fat cows raised in Bashan on the hills of Samaria. Instead of explicitly stating that the *women* of Samaria are like the cows of Bashan, the author directly addresses them as cows of Bashan, invoking similarities such as indolence and being overindulged[14] and uncaring. Although the author employs a metaphor—since his words are not intended to be taken literally—he does not explicitly identify the tenor, the Samarian women; instead, he only references the vehicle, the cows. By solely referencing the vehicle in this way, the author creates hypocatastasis.

Another example appears in Ps 22:16[17]a:

---

13. Overall, the book of Hosea is replete with similes; for further study, see Hos 1:20; 2:3; 4:16; 5:10, 12, 14; 6:3; 7:4, 6, 7, 11, 16; 8:1; 9:4; and 11:10.

14. For this damning assessment, see McComiskey, *The Minor Prophets*, 1:392.

| כִּי סְבָבוּנִי כְּלָבִים | For dogs have surrounded me; |
| עֲדַת מְרֵעִים הִקִּיפוּנִי | a band of evildoers has encompassed me. |

With the words in v. 16a, the psalmist is not expressing a literal situation where he is surrounded by voracious canines. Instead, he adopts metaphorical language to equate his enemies to dogs encircling him, thereby conveying a powerful and threatening image to the reader. Rather than explicitly stating "my enemies are dogs," including the tenor and vehicle, he directly refers to the enemies as dogs, without the tenor. While the tenor remains somewhat obscured in this initial colon, the subsequent colon clarifies the connection, "A band of evildoers has encompassed me." Applying our understanding of synonymous parallelism to this verse allows us to draw a direct correlation between the enemies and dogs. This use of hypocatastasis intensifies the metaphorical language. Hypocatastasis is a more direct and vivid form of metaphor compared to the examples discussed previously because it directly names the vehicle without explicitly mentioning the tenor, thereby heightening the emotional impact and immediacy of the imagery.[15]

7.5 Metonymy

Metonymy can be understood as a form of substitute naming, or the exchanging of a noun. It appears when an author writes one word, most often a noun, but intends another that is related to it. Today, in Western society, various cultures use metonymy daily. In the United Kingdom, for example, the word Hoover frequently refers to a vacuum cleaner. In this instance, the name of a company that manufactures vacuum cleaners, Hoover, substitutes for the name of the machine itself. Similarly, in the United States, the word bullpen describes the area in a baseball field where relief pitchers warm up. Furthermore, bullpen can also represent a collection of relief pitchers, the players themselves. In both cases, one word adopts a different meaning, usually reflecting a broader concept. Similarly, Hebrew poetry utilizes this concept in a variety of contexts. An example of this poetic technique appears in Ps 7:3[4]:

---

15. For other examples of this phenomenon, see Ps 95:1; Jer 4:7; and Joel 4:13.

יְהוָה אֱלֹהַי אִם־עָשִׂיתִי זֹאת   O Lord my God, if I have done this,
אִם־יֶשׁ־עָוֶל בְּכַפָּי   if there is injustice in my hands.

In this example, the psalmist, seeking justification from God, asks if any injustice has been found in his *hands*. The writer does not intend the reader to understand "hands" in a literal sense but rather as a metonymy representing the works and deeds he has performed—the works of his hands. In this way, his hands symbolize his actions and behavior. It is important to note the functional relationship between the metonymy and what it represents: human hands perform the intentions of the heart, and thus, in the psalmist's poetic imagination, they become representative of injustice. This metonymy emphasizes the connection between physical body parts and moral responsibility.

Another example appears in Ps 78:46:

וַיִּתֵּן לֶחָסִיל יְבוּלָם   He gave also their crops to the grasshopper
וִיגִיעָם לָאַרְבֶּה׃   and their labor to the locust.

This verse provides part of a detailed description of the plagues that God sent against the Egyptians and their devastating effects. The verse under examination here depicts the plague of locusts and the havoc they unleashed against the Egyptians. The psalmist elevates God's role in the events, stating that he gave the labor of the Egyptians over to the locust for consumption. The Hebrew word יְגִיעַ means "labor" or "work," but the intended meaning is the produce or results of work. God did not deliver the Egyptian's physical work to the locust, but the results of their efforts: plowing and sowing.[16] Again, with this example, one should note the connection between the metonymy and its reflected concept. The ideas of work and produce directly relate to each other because one produces the other.[17]

---

16. The KJV in this instance preserves the more literal translation of the word יְגִיעַ, "labor," whereas later translations take an extra step by explicating the metonymy. The ESV translates "fruit of their labor," the NASB similarly states "the product of their labor." The NIV goes one step further by interpreting "their produce," and it leaves out any notion of the Egyptian's labor, which is the primary meaning of יְגִיעַ.

17. For further examples of metonymy, see Ps 5:9 (tongue); Prov 14:18 (lips); and Mic 6:9 (city). See also Bullinger, *Figures of Speech*, 538–40; and Ryken, *Literary Forms*, 125–26.

7.6 Synecdoche

A poetic feature closely related to metonymy is synecdoche. It is, admittedly, slightly inaccurate to refer to synecdoche as a separate technique, and one should perhaps understand it as a nuanced aspect of metonymy. Synecdoche is a figure of speech where one part of an entity is used to represent the whole entity. An example from Prov 1:16 demonstrates the feature:

| כִּי רַגְלֵיהֶם לָרַע יָרוּצוּ | For their feet run to evil |
| וִימַהֲרוּ לִשְׁפָּךְ־דָּם | and they hasten to shed blood. |

This verse warns the reader against participating in the plans and activities of wicked men. The author depicts their feet [רַגְלֵיהֶם] as running toward evil. The poetic feature at work here, though resembling a metonymy, is synecdoche. One small part of a larger entity, the feet, represents the whole person. In this case, the feet symbolize the whole body's movement toward evil. Another example appears in Ps 44:6[7]:

| כִּי לֹא בְקַשְׁתִּי אֶבְטָח | For I do not trust in my bow |
| וְחַרְבִּי לֹא תוֹשִׁיעֵנִי: | nor will my sword save me. |

The synecdoche in Psalm 44 revolves around the terms קֶשֶׁת ("bow") and חֶרֶב ("sword"). These words symbolize more than their literal meanings within the text. The word "bow" in the psalmist's perspective symbolizes all weapons of warfare that may offer an advantage in combat, whether from distance or close quarters. The second colon reiterates this notion but employs the word "sword."[18] The psalmist's concern extends beyond the bow and sword to encompass any weapon. Therefore, although only the bow and

---

18. Students are advised to take care when identifying and discussing synecdoche because the broad semantic plane of Hebrew words may cause confusion with the narrower semantic planes of English words. Take for example the possible synecdoche in Ps 136:25, "Who gives לֶחֶם to all flesh." The Hebrew word לֶחֶם can be translated simply as "bread," creating an apparent synecdoche reflecting all kinds of food. On the other hand, the broader meaning of לֶחֶם may also include all kinds of food as evidenced in Gen 43:31; Lev 8:31; 1 Kgs 17:6; Job 42:11; Ps 132:15; Isa 30:23; 44:15; and Jer 41:1. Consequently, considerable care must be adopted in the identification of this poetic feature.

sword are mentioned, they serve as replacements for other weapons such as spears, slings shots, arrows, knives, and additional armaments.[19]

7.7 Personification

Within the overarching framework of metaphor lies the poetic device of personification. Personification is a form of biblical imagery in which poets attribute human behaviors or emotions to inanimate objects or abstract concepts.[20] By employing this literary technique, biblical authors seek to animate otherwise intangible or abstract ideas, thereby making them more relatable and comprehensible for the reader. A simple example appears in Isa 55:12:

כִּי־בְשִׂמְחָה תֵצֵאוּ	For you will go out with joy
וּבְשָׁלוֹם תּוּבָלוּן	and be led forth with peace;
הֶהָרִים וְהַגְּבָעוֹת יִפְצְחוּ לִפְנֵיכֶם רִנָּה	the mountains and the hills will break forth into shouts of joy before you,
וְכָל־עֲצֵי הַשָּׂדֶה יִמְחֲאוּ־כָף׃	and all the trees of the field will clap their hands.

When describing the rewards for repentance, Isaiah prophesies the jubilation and joy that will come to his community and all creation around them. The mountains, usually inanimate, stationary, and silent formations in creation erupt with shouts of joy. Moreover, the trees awaken and start clapping their hands in jubilation. The prophet personifies, attributes human behavior to, what are generally considered lifeless objects. In doing so, he generates

---

19. For further examples of this feature, see Pss 32:4 (fathers representing all individuals in earlier generations); and 72:15 (gold representing all precious gifts). See also Ryken et al., *Dictionary of Biblical Imagery*, 191; and Bullinger, *Figures of Speech*, 538, who aptly describes this feature as a "change of noun."

20. Technically, this feature is called prosopopoeia, as noted by Bullinger, *Figures of Speech*, 862. Among other poetic features, and perhaps more pertinent to this discussion, personification is not limited to poetic texts in the Bible. To be sure, it is reasonable to speculate that personification is quite prominent in Hebrew prose, as demonstrated by texts such as Gen 4:10: "The voice of your brother's blood is crying to Me from the ground."

a vivid image in the reader's mind that conveys the sense of pure unbounded joy that will come to his community.

Personification can be categorized into two distinct types based on the nature of the subject matter.[21] The first category involves physical inanimate objects to which poets attribute human behaviors. These tangible objects, such as water, mountains, trees, and land, are transformed by the writer into active entities that exhibit human-like actions and qualities. This technique allows the poet to bring these visible and touchable elements to life, imbuing them with a dynamic presence that mirrors human characteristics.[22] An example can be seen in Joel 1:10:

שֻׁדַּד שָׂדֶה	The field is ruined,
אָבְלָה אֲדָמָה	the land mourns;
כִּי שֻׁדַּד דָּגָן	for the grain is ruined,
הוֹבִישׁ תִּירוֹשׁ	the new wine dries up,
אֻמְלַל יִצְהָר׃	fresh oil fails.

Within this account of impending destruction precipitated by a famine, the prophet suggests that the land *mourns*. The land, a physical entity, visible and touchable, in this instance adopts the characteristics of a person, weeping for the loss of a friend or family member. As part of Joel's oracle, the land weeps and mourns for the lack of produce that will come.

Another example involving a physical subject appears in Song 1:6a:

אַל־תִּרְאוּנִי שֶׁאֲנִי שְׁחַרְחֹרֶת	Do not stare at me because I am swarthy,
שֶׁשֱּׁזָפַתְנִי הַשָּׁמֶשׁ	For the sun has burned me [שֶׁזָּפַתְנִי].
	(NASB)

---

21. The division into two categories is quite rudimentary but suitable for the present context. It is possible to subdivide these categories further, as Bullinger does in his work on biblical imagery (*Figures of Speech*, 538–628). He further differentiates personifications based on the classifications of objects attributed with human traits and behavior. Accordingly, he identifies six classifications: (1) members of the human body, (2) animals, (3) products of the earth, (4) abstract entities, (5) kingdoms, countries, and states, and (6) human and divine actions behaving as people.

22. Schökel, *A Manual*, 123, recognizes this distinction, however, he refers to this class of personification as "animation."

In v. 6, the Shulammite describes her appearance to the daughters of Jerusalem, saying that she is dark, because of the sun burning her. This verse demonstrates an instance in which the NASB translators have perhaps obscured a Hebrew image for the sake of a facile English translation. The Hebrew text underlying the depiction of the sun having burned the Shulammite's skin, שֶׁשֱּׁזָפַתְנִי הַשָּׁמֶשׁ, is better rendered "the sun has gazed upon me."[23] The depiction of the sun, an inanimate and visible object, gazing or looking at the Shulammite, darkening her skin as a result, constitutes a personification—the sun acting like a person and *gazing* at someone.

The second type of personification involves the attribution of human behavior to abstract, invisible, and untouchable ideas. Poets portray concepts and virtues, such as love, peace, and wisdom, as adopting the behavior and actions of people. Two examples of this poetic technique demonstrate its usage. The first is Prov 8:1:

| הֲלֹא־חָכְמָה תִקְרָא | Does not wisdom call, |
| וּתְבוּנָה תִּתֵּן קוֹלָהּ | and understanding lift up her voice? |

The author of Proverbs dedicates an entire chapter to depicting the presence and interaction of wisdom with people as they perform their daily activities. To paint this picture vividly, in the verse above he personifies wisdom as a woman who opens her mouth to speak with anyone willing to listen. The virtue of wisdom cannot be touched or directly seen—it comprises an abstract phenomenon—and yet the author portrays it with the behavioral attributes of a person. The second example of this kind of personification is Isa 59:12a:

| כִּי־רַבּוּ פְשָׁעֵינוּ נֶגְדֶּךָ | For our transgressions are multiplied before you, |
| וְחַטֹּאותֵינוּ עָנְתָה בָּנוּ | and our sins testify against us; |

---

23. The verb שָׁזַף means to gaze as witnessed in Job 20:9 and 28:7. Accordingly, the ESV and KJV preserve this more literal rendition.

This verse recalls the words of a community rejected and abandoned by the God they once served. As a result of their rebellious behavior, Isaiah's audience not only distances themselves from God, but they also struggle to cope with their guilt. When describing their current predicament, they personify their transgressions. Their sins adopt the character of a human witness who testifies before a judge against them, revealing their shortcomings. Although the concept of sin is abstract and untouchable, Isaiah clothes it with human behavior, presenting sin as person speaking against the forsaken community.

When analyzing personification, readers should first place it into one of the categories above.[24] After this initial analysis, it is useful to search other Old Testament texts to see if the same entity under investigation is attributed with the same characteristics. (Do mountains always dance, for example, or do they perform other actions?) In doing so, one can identify and discuss innovative aspects of a poet's work if the attributes assigned to a specific entity are unique. Similarly, if both the entity and attributes are shared with other biblical texts, a further investigation into textual borrowing is advised.

7.8 Anthropomorphism

Anthropomorphism is a poetic technique that resembles personification because the attributes of one entity are transferred and applied to another entity of a different genus. With personification, poets transpose the traits or characteristics of humans to inanimate objects or abstract entities; with anthropomorphism, the characteristics of humans are transposed to God, attributing him with physical body parts. God is a spirit, an incorporeal entity whose nature, character, and even physical appearance is far beyond anything humans can comprehend.[25] As a result of God's indescribable nature and spiritual form, biblical poets are forced to adopt human language

---

24. Or attempt to place it into one of Bullinger's categories mentioned earlier.
25. God's incorporeal nature appears to contradict any notion of his physical appearance or him being visible at all; however, Scripture undoubtedly recognizes these two images of God. Passages such as 1 Kgs 22:19 suggest God can be seen (see also Isa 6:1, Ezek 1:1 and Amos 9:1). On the other hand, scripture also affirms the opposite, that nobody can see God, as seen in John 1:18 and 1 Tim 6:16.

to describe him, enabling the reader to construct a more visual and tangible image in their minds. When biblical authors ascribe human physical features to God, features that can be seen and touched, they create an anthropomorphism. An example appears in Ps 33:18:

הִנֵּה עֵין יְהוָה אֶל־יְרֵאָיו	Behold, the eye of the LORD is on those who fear him,
לַמְיַחֲלִים לְחַסְדּוֹ:	on those who hope for his lovingkindness.

Here the psalmist highlights God's omniscience and constant vigilance over his people by employing anthropomorphism, stating that "the eye of the LORD is on those who fear him." Although God does not possess physical features like a human or any other creature, such as eyes, nose, or mouth, the psalmist attributes these features to him to emphasize and animate a particular aspect of his divine nature. This literary device tangibly helps readers relate to and understand God's attentive and protective presence.

Another example appears in Isa 59:1:

הֵן לֹא־קָצְרָה יַד־יְהוָה	Behold, the LORD's hand is not shortened
מֵהוֹשִׁיעַ	that it cannot save;
וְלֹא־כָבְדָה אָזְנוֹ	nor is his ear so dull
מִשְּׁמוֹעַ:	that it cannot hear.

In this verse, Isaiah comforts his listeners by accentuating God's ability to hear and recognize the exiles' desperate situation and to respond by delivering them from it. To achieve this, Isaiah utilizes two anthropomorphisms in synonymously parallel couplets. The poet mentions God's *hand* to symbolize his power to redeem his people. Similarly, his ear is used as a symbol of his attentiveness and cognizance of the exiles' destitution.

When analyzing anthropomorphisms, it is not enough to simply identify them; one must also consider how the poet utilizes the image and specifically which aspect of God's character or ability is represented. To demonstrate this, consider the use of the hand as an anthropomorphism in the following texts.

כִּי־חִצֶּיךָ נִחֲתוּ בִי וַתִּנְחַת עָלַי יָדֶךָ׃	For your arrows have sunk deep into me, and your hand has pressed down on me. (Ps 38:2[3])
אֲשֶׁר בְּיָדוֹ מֶחְקְרֵי־אָרֶץ וְתוֹעֲפוֹת הָרִים לוֹ׃	In whose hand are the depths of the earth, the peaks of the mountains are his also. (Ps 95:4)
פּוֹתֵחַ אֶת־יָדֶךָ וּמַשְׂבִּיעַ לְכָל־חַי רָצוֹן	You open your hand and satisfy the desire of every living thing. (Ps 145:16)

In Ps 38:2[3] the speaker suffers from an undisclosed physical ailment, a vehicle through which the Lord himself oppresses the sufferer. In recognition of this, the psalmist employs the imagery of the hand of God as the agent of his pain, pressing down upon him, inflicting suffering. The anthropomorphism in this context is framed negatively because God's hand constitutes an agent of pain and affliction.[26] The same anthropomorphic figure appears in Ps 95, where it adopts the guise of a metaphysical location. In this context, the psalmist ascribes God's hand as the place where, even though unseen, the whole of the created world rests. The imagery in this context is one of possession and ownership. Further in Ps 104, the poet adopts the same anthropomorphism, the hand of God, but with a nuance that differs from the previous appearances. The author of Psalm 104 does not recognize the hand of God as an instrument of affliction or as a symbol of possession. Instead, he implements the anthropomorphism as an instrument of provision. God's hand represents a provision of food for all his creation, man and beast. From these examples, it is first notable that the image of the hand appears in both positive and negative frameworks. Furthermore, the comparison between the three verses above demonstrates that further investigation and analysis is advised after initially discovering an anthropomorphism.

---

26. See also Ps 39:10.

7.9 Anthropopathism

Anthropomorphism, as previously discussed, involves attributing human physical attributes to God, who is inherently spirit. In this context, the human characteristics are those that can be physically seen or touched: for instance, a hand, an arm, or an eye. However, another category of imagery exists where less tangible human attributes, specifically those pertaining to emotions and feelings, are ascribed to God. This technique, analogous to anthropomorphism, is termed anthropopathism.[27] While anthropomorphism attributes physical characteristics to the divine, anthropopathism imputes human emotions and feelings to God. Both literary devices serve to make the divine more relatable and comprehensible to human readers by adopting familiar human characteristics and experiences. Consider Ps 106:45 below:

| וַיִּזְכֹּר לָהֶם בְּרִיתוֹ | And he remembered his covenant for their sake, |
| וַיִּנָּחֵם כְּרֹב חֲסָדָו | And relented according to the abundance of his lovingkindness. |

To communicate God's merciful response to the Israelites after they rebelled against his word by failing to respond appropriately to his grace and favor, the psalmist employs two anthropopathisms. The first portrays God as *remembering* his covenant, suggesting he can forget, as humans do. Then, in v. 45b, the psalmist portrays God relenting, נָחַם, translated as "repented" in older literal English translations.[28] The act of repenting—changing one's mind and reversing one's direction of thought and intent—primarily relates to humanity. It represents an intrinsically human behavioral pattern because people consistently make mistakes that need correction via altered behavior.[29] To help his readers understand God's actions, the psalmist ascribes the human behavioral pattern of repentance to the divine. Note especially that a behavior or feeling is imparted to God, as opposed to a human physical and palpable characteristic. Consider Ps 95:11:

---

27. An instance of the convergence of these two forms is evident in Eakins, "Anthropomorphisms in Isaiah 40–55." Within his classification system, he categorizes both body parts and emotions as subcategories of anthropomorphism.
28. See the KJV, for example.
29. This imagery of God appears quite frequently, as seen Joel 2:13 and Amos 7:3.

אֲשֶׁר־נִשְׁבַּעְתִּי בְאַפִּי	Therefore I swore in my anger,
אִם־יְבֹאוּן אֶל־מְנוּחָתִי׃	surely they shall not enter into My rest.

This hymn of praise ends with a stern warning to those reciting the psalm, presumably entering the temple precincts and into the Lord's presence. The final words of the psalm itself are directly from God, and he exhorts the listeners not to doubt his presence among them like the desert generation. Concerning that generation, God swore in his *anger* that they would not enter his rest, the promised land, because of their unbelief. In Ps 95, the poet portrays God expressing anger, generating an anthropopathism, an emotion typically expressed by humans that is attributed to God. To create a poetic effect, drawing the reader closer to the divine, the author depicts the motivation behind God's actions in words that the human audience can better understand.

7.10 Hyperbole

In essence, hyperbole is a form of exaggeration or extreme characterization that authors employ to construct vivid imagery.[30] As with most semantic poetic techniques, hyperbole engenders an economy of expression while concurrently illuminating themes and ideas. In certain respects, hyperbole can be considered a type of metaphor, or at least falls under the broader category of metaphor, although it is not identical to metaphor. Hyperbole tends to push the boundaries of figurative comparison beyond belief and is more inclined to distorting the truth.[31] Ryken rightly avers that the purpose of hyperbole in the poet's arsenal is not to convey literal truth but emotional truth,[32] how an individual or group feels. Consider Jer 15:8:

עָצְמוּ־לִי אַלְמְנֹתָו	Their widows will be more numerous before me

---

30. It is difficult to overstate how the poetic features listed in this section synergize with the structural features in part 3. For instance, hyperbole may be employed in the second half of a bicolon to amplify the degree of intensification between the parallel cola.
31. See Preminger and Brogan, *Encyclopedia of Poetry and Poetics*, 648.
32. See Ryken, *Literary Forms*, 105.

מֵח֣וֹל יַמִּ֑ים	than the sand of the seas;
הֵבֵ֨אתִי לָהֶ֥ם עַל־אֵ֛ם בָּח֖וּר	I will bring against them, against the mother of a young man,
שֹׁדֵ֣ד בַּֽצָּהֳרָ֑יִם	a destroyer at noonday;
הִפַּ֤לְתִּי עָלֶ֙יהָ֙ פִּתְאֹ֔ם	I will suddenly bring down on her
עִ֖יר וּבֶהָלֽוֹת׃	anguish and dismay.

In the verse above, God details how he will vent his anger against the inhabitants of Jerusalem, punishing them. As part of this extended description, he determines to make their widows more numerous than the sand of the seas (lines 1–2). The literal quantity mentioned here, the sand of the seas, overtly outnumbers the inhabitants of all Israel, let alone the inhabitants of Jerusalem. Consequently, this overinflated figure, the sand of the seas, in the present context represents an instance of hyperbole, highlighting the extraordinary number of men who will ultimately lose their lives.

Another example appears in Ps 69:4[5]a:

רַבּ֤וּ מִשַּׂעֲר֣וֹת רֹאשִׁי֮ שֹׂנְאַ֪י חִ֫נָּ֥ם	Those who hate me without a cause are more than the hairs of my head.

In the psalmist's distress, he portrays those who hate him without cause as being "more than the hairs of my head." The poet adopts this expression, an example of hyperbole, to accentuate his sense of feeling outnumbered and the futility of his situation.[33] In most cases, it is not difficult to identify hyperbolic expressions, but like metaphor, certain instances arise in which exegetes disagree on whether it is present. Consider the following in Ps 119:164:

שֶׁ֣בַע בַּ֭יּוֹם הִלַּלְתִּ֑יךָ	Seven times a day I praise you,
עַ֝֗ל מִשְׁפְּטֵ֥י צִדְקֶֽךָ׃	because of your righteous ordinances.

The psalmist claims that he prays seven times a day in response to the righteous ordinances of the Lord. Poetically, the number seven can be

---

33. For other examples of hyperbole, consider Eccl 6:6; Isa 5:15; Amos 6:9; and Nah 3:15.

interpreted as a symbolic and hyperbolic figure representing a general concept of "many" or "constantly" or even "perfectly."[34] His praise, with this understanding, is perfect and constant. However, a more literal exegete could interpret the figure seven as an actual reference to the seven watches of the day. Thus, the psalmist establishes a determined pattern of prayer seven times each day. The boundary between figurative and literal language, in this instance, especially if it is isolated from its historical context, potentially complicates the interpretation.[35]

Overall, classifying types of hyperbole for further analysis is challenging. However, two potential categories may prove beneficial: numerical and nonnumerical.[36] Another set of possible classifications includes military contexts[37] and humorous or sarcastic backdrops.[38] Although these tentative groups are not mutually exclusive, they can assist the exegete in analyzing instances of hyperbole.

Questions for Consideration: Is the poetic device an anthropomorphism or anthropopathism? Is the context in which is it being used positive or negative? Does it have the same nuance in any other poetic text? Is the imagery active, stative, or passive? How commonly is the image in the text used elsewhere in the Bible? What aspect of God's character does the image represent? Is the use of the image unique in any way?

Further Reading: Berlin, "Motif and Creativity"; Bullinger, *Figures of Speech*; Schökel, *A Manual*; Hernández, "Metaphor and the Study of Job"; Kirk, "Agur's Beastly Ethics"; Law, "Hyperbole in Mythological Comparisons"; McClish, "Recognizing and Interpreting Synecdoche"; Montefiore, "A Tentative Catalogue"; Ryken, *Literary Forms*; Ryken, et al., *Dictionary of Biblical Imagery*.

---

34. See Ryken et al., *Dictionary of Biblical Imagery*, 774–75.
35. Job 1:3 is another example of an interpretation that exists between the literal and symbolic realms.
36. These categories I derive from Watson, *Classical Hebrew Poetry*, 316–21, esp. 319.
37. Watson, *Classical Hebrew Poetry*, 319, recognizes this phenomenon, citing Hab 1:6–11 and Ezek 24:6.
38. See Ryken, *Literary Forms*, 105.

8

Playing with Words

Although biblical Hebrew poetry staunchly resists rhyme as a primary building block of poetic form, unlike English poetry, Hebrew poets actively and cleverly manipulated the meanings and sounds of words in various contexts. Broadly speaking, this manipulation is called wordplay, an overarching category encompassing various subcategories. Unfortunately, identifying this poetic feature is highly nuanced, and no consensus currently exists regarding the exact categorization of different types of wordplay in the Bible. Consequently, the following discussion on the different types of wordplay in Hebrew poetry should not be considered exhaustive and complete.

Detecting wordplay in Hebrew poetry presents numerous challenges, necessitating caution from exegetes when determining its presence in biblical texts. One significant challenge in identifying wordplay arises from the nature of Semitic languages, particularly Hebrew. The triliteral root system inherent to these languages results in frequent repetition and pseudo-wordplays within Hebrew poetry. Despite these challenges, however, one can still discern instances where Hebrew poets undoubtedly employ a wide variety of wordplays in biblical texts.

8.1 Paronomasia

Paronomasia, often referred to as a play on words or a pun, is a literary device where poets exploit the similarity in sound or morphology between two different words by placing them in close proximity within a verse. This technique not only enhances the aesthetic quality of the poem but also adds layers of meaning and wit. To fully appreciate the various forms of paronomasia, it is instructive to examine a range of illustrative examples. Let us first consider Ps 15:3a, which juxtaposes two different words with similar morphology:

לֹא־רָגַל עַל־לְשֹׁנוֹ	He does not slander with his tongue,
לֹא־עָשָׂה לְרֵעֵהוּ רָעָה	nor does evil to his neighbor.

Psalm 15:3a is part of a longer list of qualifications delineated by the psalmist to identify those deemed worthy of entering the presence of the Lord, likely within the temple. One such qualification specifies that a person must refrain from slandering with their tongue and from doing "evil to his neighbor." Notably, the psalmist's word choice in the phrase "evil to his neighbor" in Hebrew deliberately underscores the morphological resemblance between two words. The Hebrew word רֵעֵהוּ, "his neighbor," contains three letters—*resh*, *ayin*, and *he*—that repeat in the subsequent word, רָעָה, "evil." The juxtaposition of these words is unlikely to be accidental for two reasons. First, as a pair the two words are relatively rare. Second, a variety of other words could have been chosen to reflect the idea of a friend or associate, such as אָח, "brother," or עָמִית ("friend, associate"), or even חָבֵר ("friend/companion"), which appears in Prov 28:24. While the two words selected by the author of Psalm 15 do not exhibit a semantic connection, their morphological similarity is striking and purposeful. A similar example appears in Ps 28:5:

כִּי לֹא יָבִינוּ אֶל־פְּעֻלֹּת יְהוָה	Because they do not regard the works of the Lord
וְאֶל־מַעֲשֵׂה יָדָיו	nor the deeds of his hands,
יֶהֶרְסֵם וְלֹא יִבְנֵם׃	he will tear them down and not build them up.

In these cola, the psalmist presents a simple cause-and-effect statement: because evildoers do not recognize God's hand in creation, he will bring them down. The play on words, in this example, connects the phrase לֹא יָבִינוּ, "they do not regard," with the words לֹא יִבְנֵם, "not build them up." In both instances the words chosen contain the sequence of letters *yod*, *bet*, and *nun*, in that order (see Fig. 15). Further drawing the reader's attention to this play on words is the addition of the particle of negation, לֹא, appearing before them.[1]

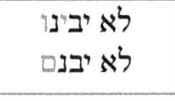

FIGURE 15

8.1.1 Same Word Different Meaning

Another type of paronomasia occurs when an author intentionally adopts one word or root in a short excerpt with two different meanings. This technique, which leverages the broad polysemy of the Hebrew language, appears in Prov 24:10:

| הִתְרַפִּיתָ בְּיוֹם צָרָה | If you are slack in the day of *distress*, |
| צַר כֹּחֶכָה | your strength is limited. (emphasis added) |

In this aphorism, the writer reveals the key to understanding the true strength of an individual. Regardless of how you assess your inner fortitude, it is only when you are tested that you gain a true appreciation of that measure. To teach this lesson, the writer employs two senses of the root צרר: first as a noun in the word צָרָה with the meaning of distress, and then as an adjective in the word צַר, which translates to "limited" in this context. The same root appears in both contexts but the translation and meaning differ in each case, revealing the author's clever exploitation of a Hebrew word's polysemy.

Isaiah 58:10 provides another example:

וְתָפֵק לָרָעֵב נַפְשֶׁךָ	And if you give *yourself* to the hungry
וְנֶפֶשׁ נַעֲנָה תַּשְׂבִּיעַ	and satisfy the *desire* of the afflicted,
וְזָרַח בַּחֹשֶׁךְ אוֹרֶךָ	then your light will rise in darkness
וַאֲפֵלָתְךָ כַּצָּהֳרָיִם:	and your gloom will become like midday.
	(emphasis added)

---

1. Further examples appear in Job 29:6; Pss 18:13; 129:5–6; Isa 16:10; and 63:2.

Here the prophet signifies a pathway to blessing through self-sacrifice, and to achieve this he plays on two meanings of the word נֶפֶשׁ. First, it connotes "self" in the word נַפְשְׁךָ, "yourself," and then the same root appears in the word נֶפֶשׁ, signifying "desire" in the second line. The Hebrew word order juxtaposes the two words, drawing sharper attention to the wordplay. Reading the first two lines while preserving the word order yields the translation, "If you give to the hungry *yourself*, and the *desire* of the afflicted you satisfy."[2]

8.1.2 Same Word for Reversed Contexts

Another class of paronomasia, like the one just discussed, occurs when poets reuse the same word but in two contrasting contexts. Rather than simply rendering alternative meanings, within this modified usage, the same word signifies opposing meanings in the same text segment. Consider Eccl 10:4 (NASB, emphasis added):

אִם־רוּחַ הַמּוֹשֵׁל תַּעֲלֶה עָלֶיךָ	If the ruler's temper rises against you,
מְקוֹמְךָ אַל־תַּנַּח	do not *abandon* your position,
כִּי מַרְפֵּא יַנִּיחַ חֲטָאִים גְּדוֹלִים׃	because composure *allays* great offenses.

In this maxim from Ecclesiastes that instructs on behavior before dignitaries, the author twice adopts the same root, נוח, but in opposing contexts. First, it carries the sense of abandonment, a negative context, leaving one's guard post at the first sign of trouble. Then, it appears in a positive context, still as a verb but with the meaning of allay or mitigate. In reference to one's composure, the verb functions to laud the act of ameliorating the anger of one's ruler. In a relatively short text, the author employs the same root with both positive and negative meanings. Another example of the phenomenon appears in Jer 34:17 (emphasis added):

לָכֵן כֹּה־אָמַר יְהוָה	Therefore thus says the LORD,
אַתֶּם לֹא־שְׁמַעְתֶּם אֵלַי	"You have not obeyed me
לִקְרֹא דְרוֹר	by proclaiming *release*

---

2. Wordplay using polysemy overlaps with the earlier structural feature of Janus parallelism; see Paul, "Polysemous Pivotal Punctuation."

אִישׁ לְאָחִיו וְאִישׁ לְרֵעֵהוּ	each man to his brother and each man to his neighbor.
הִנְנִי קֹרֵא לָכֶם דְּרוֹר	Behold, I am proclaiming a *release* to you,"
נְאֻם־יְהוָה	declares the Lord,
אֶל־הַחֶרֶב אֶל־הַדֶּבֶר וְאֶל־הָרָעָב	"to the sword, to the pestilence and to the famine;
וְנָתַתִּי אֶתְכֶם לְזַוֲעָה לְכֹל מַמְלְכוֹת הָאָרֶץ	and I will make you a terror to all the kingdoms of the earth."

After King Zedekiah reneges on his promise to release slaves in honor of the Sabbath Year, Jeremiah conveys to him a chastising word from the Lord. Because Zedekiah failed to grant a *release* [דְּרוֹר] to the slaves, God was going to essentially grant a release to Zedekiah, and the people of Judah, releasing them to judgment: the sword, pestilence, and famine. In this way, the writer adopts a single word, דְּרוֹר, placing it in two related but contrasting contexts. It is, therefore, important, when analyzing texts to note root repetitions, even if a root only appears twice in an extended text.[3]

8.2 Alliteration

Alliteration forms another type of wordplay, where poets repeat consonants sounds and sounds at the beginning of words and in relatively close succession.[4] For the present volume, alliteration is considered in its wider sense, one that is not confined to word-initial repetition of consonants. Although it serves as one of the most frequent types of wordplay in the Old Testament, care must be exercised in its identification because of the Hebrew language's natural sound, syntax, and grammar. Instances arise in which poets select

---

3. Repetition of the same word in this context hints toward the biblical principle of measure for measure. The author selects the same word in describing Zedekiah's sin as he does with Zedekiah's punishment. He is effectively being punished in the same way that he sinned. For more on the principle of measure for measure, see Shemesh, "Measure for Measure."

4. A degree of overlap exists between alliteration and assonance, the repetition of vowel sounds. Often the recurring consonantal elements are repeated together with a specific vowel. For a further discussion on alliteration, with particular regard to its relationship with assonance, see Watson, *Classical Hebrew Poetry*, 225–29.

and arrange words out of necessity, creating alliteration without specific intent. Caution is advised when interpreting the meaning of instances like this lest exegetes ascribe significance to certain verses or phrases where none was intended. Naturally, no fixed rules exist for consistently identifying alliteration with certainty; therefore, it is good practice, when possible, to adduce additional supporting data when assessing the presence of alliteration. One undisputable appearance of the poetic technique appears in Job 5:8:

| אוּלָם אֲנִי אֶדְרֹשׁ אֶל־אֵל | But as for me, I would seek God, |
| וְאֶל־אֱלֹהִים אָשִׂים דִּבְרָתִי׃ | and I would place my cause before God. |

In his opening discourse, Eliphaz, one of Job's professed friends, advises Job on how he would behave in Job's situation: He would directly appeal to God, pleading his case before the divine. In v. 8 the poet expresses his intention with an extended instance of alliteration, where eight out of the nine words in the couplet begin with the Hebrew letter *aleph*. The intense repetition in this verse speaks against an arrangement formed through happenstance; therefore, the alignment of the words likely resulted from a purposeful arrangement to achieve a poetic effect.

Another highly probable instance of alliteration appears in Ps 122:6:

| שַׁאֲלוּ שְׁלוֹם יְרוּשָׁלָ͏ִם | Pray for the peace of Jerusalem: |
| יִשְׁלָיוּ אֹהֲבָיִךְ | may they prosper who love you. |

Midway through this song exalting the holy city, Zion, the psalmist exhorts his hearers to pray for the peace of Jerusalem. Within this verse, four of the five words contain the letters *shin* and *lamed*, creating the alliterative sequence. Again, the frequency of this letter combination presents a substantial obstacle to denying that the author intentionally implemented alliteration. Furthermore, in this specific instance, it is possible to see that the alliteration continues into the following verse.

יְהִי־שָׁלוֹם בְּחֵילֵךְ	May peace be within your walls,
שַׁלְוָה בְּאַרְמְנוֹתָיִךְ׃	and prosperity within your palaces.
	(Ps 122:7)

In this continuation, the letters *shin* and *lamed* continue repeating, spanning vv. 6–7, with the words שָׁלוֹם, "peace," repeated from the previous verse, and שָׁלוֹם, "prosperity." The appearance of these two words corroborates the conclusion that the author intended to utilize this feature.[5]

In certain instances, alliterated forms have been fossilized, creating established expressions that were subsequently reused by biblical authors. One such instance appears in the expression עָפָר וָאֵפֶר, "dust and ashes,"[6] which appears as a word pair in Gen 18:27; Job 30:19; and 42:6.[7]

8.3 Rhyme

In limited situations, but still worth noting, the repetition of similar sounds occurs at the end of word clusters, creating an end rhyme.[8] Although this type of rhyme frequently surfaces in English poetry, it is not a prominent feature in the Hebrew Bible. When attempting to identify rhyme in Hebrew poetry, exegetes must exercise caution to avoid confusing intentional rhyme with Hebrew pluralized endings of the same gender and other natural Hebrew constructs. As an example, the words מַיִם רַבִּים, "great waters," in Ps 32:6 fails to achieve the designation of poetic end rhyme because it reflects a standard syntactic form sequence in biblical Hebrew for n.-adj. combinations. Notwithstanding this potential pitfall, the poetic feature of end rhyme does represent an extant phenomenon,[9] and concrete examples, although somewhat challenging to isolate, can be identified. One example appears in Isa 62:3a:

| וְהָיִיתְ עֲטֶרֶת תִּפְאֶרֶת | You will be a crown of beauty |
| בְּיַד־יְהוָה | in the hand of the Lord. |

---

5. For another example of a distributed alliteration, see Judg 5:4, within the Song of Deborah.
6. Some of the letters are not the same but they carry an equivalent value when establishing alliteration. See Casanowicz, "Paronomasia," 107–08.
7. For further examples of regular alliteration, consider Pss 21:6; 45:4; 104:1; 111:3; Job 40:10; and Isa 24:6.
8. This could be more accurately described as the *perception* of rhyme.
9. Various scholars who focus on poetics recognize this poetic feature and cite examples. See, for example, Schökel, *A Manual*, 22–26; Watson, *Classical Hebrew Poetry*, 231–33; and Casanowicz, "Paronomasia," 112.

In v. 63a Isaiah prophecies to the returned remnant of Israel words of consolation, hope, promise, and encouragement. He depicts his people as a crown of beauty in the hand of the Lord, and in doing so, utilizes end rhyme to accentuate the words. By adopting end rhyme Isaiah masterfully constructs a beautiful phrase, ʿateret tiferet, to exemplify a beautiful concept, "a crown of beauty."[10]

Another example appears in Hos 8:7:

כִּי רוּחַ יִזְרָעוּ	For they sow the wind
וְסוּפָתָה יִקְצֹרוּ	and they reap the whirlwind.
קָמָה אֵין־לוֹ צֶמַח	The standing grain has no heads;
בְּלִי יַעֲשֶׂה־קֶּמַח	it yields no grain.
אוּלַי יַעֲשֶׂה	Should it yield,
זָרִים יִבְלָעֻהוּ׃	strangers would swallow it up.

As part of an oracle of indictment and judgment against the Northern Kingdom of Israel, v. 7 graphically conveys destruction wrought against the crops and the expected harvest. Within these words, the prophet includes the expression "the standing grain has no heads [צֶמַח]; / it yields no grain [קֶמַח]." Quite intentionally, it appears that the prophet here introduces the rhyming pair *tsemakh* and *qemakh* to highlight the lack of grain production.[11] One could further argue that the poet adopts rhyme here to generate a disrupted rhythm, drawing attention to the final couplet. Both end words in the opening couplet close with an extended [u] sound, *yizraʿu* and *yiqtsoru*, and the following couplets similarly rhyme, as mentioned above. When considering the three couplets together, one notices a rhythm generated in the first four lines that the poet disrupts in the final couplet.[12]

To highlight the relevance of rhyme in Hebrew poetry, a final example deserves citation, Prov 5:15:

---

10. See Casanowicz, "Paronomasia," 112, for this example. Ideally, the more syllables that rhyme at the end of the word, the stronger the argument for alliteration.

11. Casanowicz cites further examples of end rhyme in Exod 28:30; Ps 18:8; and Isa 24:4, ("Paronomasia," 125 and 130).

12. At this point, one can only speculate why the final couplet ends this way, but it could be to form a climactic end to the strophe.

שְׁתֵה־מַיִם מִבּוֹרֶךָ   Drink water from your own cistern
וְנֹזְלִים מִתּוֹךְ בְּאֵרֶךָ:   And flowing water from your own well.

Verse 15 reflects a euphemism that encourages a monogamous and self-controlled disposition. At the end of each colon, the poet employs two words that generate an end rhyme, *mibboreka* and *be'ereka*. In doing so, he creates a word pair based on a phonological overlap in addition to a semantic overlap. Berlin refers to this concept as a sound pair, as opposed to a regular word pair.[13] In instances like this, the sound pair's formation serves as a device that contributes to the poetic couplet's cohesion.

8.3.1 Assonance

At this point, the poetic feature of assonance deserves mention because it falls under the broader definition of rhyme. Assonance, which contributes to the formation of rhyme, is the term used to describe the repetition of sounds, vowels, and/or consonants, as opposed to syllabic units. As with rhyme, exegetes are advised to adopt immense caution when determining instances of intentional assonance because of the developments in the Hebrew language's pronunciation. Hebrew was originally written purely with consonants, and the vowels were not inserted in written form until ca. the seventh century CE, at the earliest. Consequently, a degree of dispute arises concerning how certain vowel signs should be pronounced.[14] The matter is further complicated when the question of dialects within the Hebrew language is considered.[15]

Notwithstanding the potential complications, one cannot refute the

---

13. Berlin has done some excellent work on this feature of poetics and cites numerous examples of the phenomenon. See Berlin, *Biblical Parallelism*, 103–26.

14. See Casanowicz, "Paronomasia," 112. Furthermore, even today, the *qamets* in Modern Hebrew has at least two different pronunciations among Ashkenazi and Sephardic Jews.

15. The words of Holladay should be taken into consideration here: "Any modern conventional Hebrew pronunciation, or the Masoretic vocalization, may mislead us as to the pronunciation of Hebrew in a time as remote as that of David" ("Form and Word-Play," 57). Rendsburg has conducted extensive research on the northern dialects of the Hebrew language. Assuming that a distinct dialect of Hebrew was spoken in the north, an instance of assonance that is valid for a northern speaker may prove invalid for a southern speaker. For more on the phenomenon of Northern (or Israelian) Hebrew, see Rendsburg, "A Comprehensive Guide to Israelian Hebrew"; and more recently, "Israelian Hebrew in the Book of Amos," 717–40. It must be noted, however that the notion of a northern dialect has been challenged by Schniedewind and Sivan in "The Elijah-Elisha Narratives."

presence of assonance in Hebrew poetry. One potential location for the poetic device appears in Ps 16:6:

חֲבָלִים נָֽפְלוּ־לִי בַּנְּעִמִים	The lines have fallen to me in pleasant places;
אַף־נַחֲלָת שָֽׁפְרָה עָלָֽי׃	Indeed, my heritage is beautiful to me.

As the psalmist begins to contemplate God's goodness to him, he affirms that his heritage, what he has received from God's hand, is a beautiful thing. The second colon ends here with an apparent repetition of five consecutive [a] vowels, which reflects an intentional implementation by the author: *nakhalat shaprah 'alay*.

Another example appears in Jer 49:1c:

מַדּוּעַ יָרַשׁ מַלְכָּם אֶת־גָּד	Why *then* has Malcam taken possession of Gad
וְעַמּוֹ בְּעָרָיו יָשָֽׁב׃	And his people settled in its cities? (NASB)

At the start of this indictment oracle against the Ammonites, God condemns Ammon's treatment of Gad, relocating them to foreign cities. In v. 1c, it is difficult to ignore the repetition of the [a] class vowels. Although the author has not exclusively restricted himself to this vowel class, the [a] vowels undoubtedly dominate the couplet.[16] Even in the two examples cited above, however, one could argue that the appearance of the [a] vowels simply results from writing Hebrew poetry, without any intention of highlighting a sound pattern.

8.4 Anadiplosis

Another type of wordplay employed by Hebrew poets is anadiplosis,[17] which strictly speaking describes instances where a poet repeats the last word or

---

16. See Gaines, *The Poetic Priestly Source*, 50.
17. Anadiplosis falls under the broader heading of a type of epanastrophe. Frequently in the literature, these two terms are used interchangeably, although strictly speaking, despite their overlap, epanastrophe can emphasize a broader circular or connective repetition pattern beyond immediate sequential repetition described above. An example of which would be a speech where the phrase "I have a dream" is inserted after several key points are made.

phrase of one sentence or clause at the beginning of the following clause. We have already seen examples of this strict definition in the discussion of the terraced pattern. Broadly speaking, anadiplosis can also describe the sequencing of consonants in the last syllable of a word to match the opening syllables in the following word. Only a few instances appear in Hebrew poetry, but the phenomenon still deserves mention. A simple example appears in Ps 132:18:

| אוֹיְבָיו אַלְבִּישׁ בֹּשֶׁת | His enemies I will clothe with shame, |
| וְעָלָיו יָצִיץ נִזְרוֹ: | But upon him his crown shall shine. |

Here in a climactic verse depicting the final defeat of David's enemies and the exaltation of his kingship, the poet proclaims that David's enemies will be clothed with shame.

To express this thought, the psalmist implements the Hebrew words אַלְבִּישׁ בֹּשֶׁת, *'albish boshet*. Ignoring the vowels—the extended [i] and the long [o]—the last two consonants of the first word, *bet* and *shin*, repeat at the start of the following word.[18] As with the earlier examples of repetition, caution is advised when identifying this form because certain instances are undoubtedly generated through happenstance.[19]

8.5 Proper Noun Wordplays

Frequently in Hebrew poetry, writers employ wordplays through a careful deployment of proper nouns—place names, people groups, and even personal names. This kind of wordplay most often finds expression in prophetic material, usually indictment prophecies and judgment oracles against the nations, and/or Israel's enemies. A distinct example of this type of wordplay appears in Zeph 2:4:

---

18. Casanowicz, "Paronomasia," 113, cites another example in Eccl 3:18, which is not written in poetry, unlike other significant portions of the book.

19. For more on this poetic device, see Casanowicz, "Paronomasia," 112.

כִּי עַזָּה עֲזוּבָה תִהְיֶה	For Gaza will be abandoned
וְאַשְׁקְלוֹן לִשְׁמָמָה	and Ashkelon a desolation;
אַשְׁדּוֹד בַּצָּהֳרַיִם יְגָרְשׁוּהָ	ashdod will be driven out at noon
וְעֶקְרוֹן תֵּעָקֵר:	and Ekron will be uprooted.

Here words of castigation are leveled against the land of the Philistines, specifically the main Philistine cities Ashkelon, Ashdod, and Ekron. The first wordplay appears in judgment against Gaza, despite the English spelling of the city name. The prophet proclaims that Gaza will be abandoned, עַזָּה עֲזוּבָה, which transliterates to 'azzah 'azuvah, playing on the Hebrew letters *ayin*, *zayin*, and *he*, which constitutes a direct play on the two words, linking the punishment with the city. In the same verse, a similar play occurs with the prophecy against Ekron. Line four above states that Ekron will be uprooted, עֶקְרוֹן תֵּעָקֵר, which transliterates to 'eqron te'aqer, playing on the Hebrew letters *ayin*, *qoph*, and *resh*.

Sometimes wordplays of this kind present no problems in their identification, as in the examples just cited, but at other times the exegete will need to devote a little more thought to tease out levels of irony the poet may have planted within the text. One such instance arises in the words of Hos 9:16 below:

הֻכָּה אֶפְרַיִם	Ephraim is stricken,
שָׁרְשָׁם יָבֵשׁ	their root is dried up,
פְּרִי בְּלִי־יַעֲשׂוּן	they will bear no fruit.
גַּם כִּי יֵלֵדוּן	Even though they bear children,
וְהֵמַתִּי מַחֲמַדֵּי בִטְנָם	I will slay the precious ones of their womb.

In this verse, the prophet pronounces words against Ephraim, which in the present context reflects the whole of the Northern Kingdom. A surface reading of the text simply suggests that the north will be cut off and annihilated, but the meaning of the name Ephraim adds another layer of understanding. The name Ephraim originates from Gen 41:52, when Joseph names his second son. Joseph names the child Ephraim, meaning "twice fruitful," which in the context of Genesis reflects a wordplay because God made Joseph fruitful, הִפְרַנִי, in the land of his affliction.

Following from Genesis, the idea of fruitfulness plays into Hosea's judgment prophecy. Instead of making fruitful—as God had done to Joseph, and as the name Ephraim implies—God was about to impoverish Ephraim to punish them. Ephraim was a child who symbolized God's blessing to Joseph through the womb, but that same blessing through the womb of Ephraim is being cursed. Ephraim, the Northern Kingdom, is condemned to bearing no fruit, and even that which they can produce is destined for destruction.[20]

Wordplay often represents one of the most challenging poetic techniques to identify in Hebrew poetry. It demands not only a robust knowledge of biblical Hebrew but also the ability to distinguish intentional instances from nonintentional ones, where authors may sequence words without purposeful poetic intent. Alliteration and assonance, for instance, are particularly susceptible to misidentification. However, three heuristic guidelines can facilitate the detection of wordplay. First, consider whether the author could have composed the verse differently. Anomalies such as slightly awkward phrases or rare words might indicate intentional wordplay. Second, evaluate whether the author employs wordplay as a poetic device elsewhere in the composition. The presence of multiple instances of wordplay increases the likelihood of intentional usage. Therefore, all suspected instances should be noted. If only one questionable instance remains after analysis, it is more likely a coincidental arrangement. Third, assess whether the wordplay appears in a particularly impactful segment of the poet's message. Biblical authors are more inclined to use wordplay to emphasize key points or highlight specific sections of their compositions. Although these guidelines are not infallible, they can significantly enhance and refine the exegetical process.

One can determine three potential functions of wordplay that Hebrew poets appear to adopt. First, it may contribute toward sustaining the reader's interest and attention in a textual unit. In this way, returning to our house construction analogy, wordplay carries out the role of vivid paint colors applied to a newly constructed house. It is not primarily a functional addition but serves a useful and necessary role in generating aesthetic appeal to the exterior of the house and the interior rooms, thus contributing toward an

---

20. These appear frequently in poetry and prose. For further examples, see Isa 63:1–2; Ezek 39:11; Jer 48:2; Hos 12:4; and the cluster in Mic 1:10–16.

individual identity for the house. Second, wordplay may contribute toward a degree of emphasis in a text, highlighting a memorable point or action. Doron explains that wordplay can "impress the reader and inculcate certain truths in a striking manner."[21] In this context, one often finds wordplay at the end of a stanza, or text, in a place where an author desires to emphasize a specific and valuable truth, raising it to the reader's attention. Third, wordplay may be used to demonstrate and highlight a dramatic reversal of circumstances or outcome in a scene. This particular use predominantly surfaces in wordplays involving the replication of a root or word, where one word is strategically used twice in two opposite contexts. In this way, wordplay often implements the poetic device of measure for measure.[22]

8.6 Irony

Irony is a poetic feature in which uniquely chosen words conceal a hidden nuance or meaning that readers are required to extract through inference. Weber succinctly characterizes it as "an element of covertness by concealing the meaning in its opposite."[23] In spoken, face-to-face communication, vocal intonation and subtle physical movements aid in conveying senses of irony. In written poetic texts, however, those cues remain inaccessible; thus the burden of identification falls upon the reader. As an unsatisfactory consequence, irony in biblical poetry presents various challenges in its identification. In English literature along with biblical poetry, three different types of irony exist, with perhaps the most common type being verbal irony.

8.6.1 Verbal Irony

Verbal irony arises when an author or speaker within a text says one thing but undoubtedly intends the opposite meaning of what is said. As an example, consider these words in Job 12:1–2:

---

21. Doron, "Paronomasia in the Prophecies to the Nations," 41.
22. This is a common biblical principle that has a variety of expressions. For more on the concept and its outworking in the book of Samuel, see Shemesh, "Measure for Measure."
23. See Weber, "Mockery and Irony in the Psalms," 178. Weber is one of the few scholars who has attempted to identify irony in the Psalter.

וַיַּעַן אִיּוֹב וַיֹּאמַר:	¹Then Job responded,
אָמְנָם כִּי אַתֶּם־עָם	²"Truly then you are the people,
וְעִמָּכֶם תָּמוּת חָכְמָה:	and with you wisdom will die!"

In this passage Job initiates another round of verbal defense against the accusations of his so-called friends, who relentlessly accuse him of concealing wrongdoing, which they believe explains his suffering.[24] Opening his defense in ch. 12, he sarcastically and ironically jabs at all three of his friends, suggesting that they hold the keys to all wisdom and after they die wisdom will be no more. These represent the words spoken by Job, but he does not intend their literal meaning. In this text, the author implements verbal irony to convey Job's sentiment: his friends are not as wise as they think.

Another example of this type of irony appears in Amos 4:4–5:

בֹּאוּ בֵית־אֵל וּפִשְׁעוּ	⁴Enter Bethel and transgress;
הַגִּלְגָּל הַרְבּוּ לִפְשֹׁעַ	in Gilgal multiply transgression!
וְהָבִיאוּ לַבֹּקֶר זִבְחֵיכֶם	Bring your sacrifices every morning,
לִשְׁלֹשֶׁת יָמִים מַעְשְׂרֹתֵיכֶם:	your tithes every three days.
וְקַטֵּר מֵחָמֵץ תּוֹדָה	⁵Offer a thank offering also from that which is leavened,
וְקִרְאוּ נְדָבוֹת הַשְׁמִיעוּ	and proclaim freewill offerings, make them known.
כִּי כֵן אֲהַבְתֶּם בְּנֵי יִשְׂרָאֵל	For so you love to do, you sons of Israel,
נְאֻם אֲדֹנָי יְהוִה:	declares the Lord LORD.

Amos levels these harsh and scathing words against the inhabitants of Israel's Northern Kingdom. Due to their excessive affluence, they had abandoned God but maintained a pretense of religiosity through extravagant feasts and celebrations. In doing so, they assumed they were pleasing God and living in obedience to him. God, however, speaks through the prophet words of condemnation and disapproval and adopts verbal irony to achieve his desired effect. With these words, vv. 4–5, God is not actually encouraging

---

24. The book of Job is exceptionally well crafted, infused with double entendre and irony throughout. To explore this further, see Meshel, "Whose Job Is This?."

them to continue with their futile rituals. Even though God desires that they cease such practices, a literal reading of the ironic words adopted in the text conveys the opposite message. Thus, the text conceals a subtle meaning under the guise of the words used.[25]

8.6.2 Dramatic Irony

Dramatic irony constitutes another strain of this poetic device. In British stage tradition, dramatic irony most famously surfaces in pantomimes, when the audience can clearly see potential humorous dangers that are about to befall an unwitting character on stage. Although the threat is painfully obvious to the audience, the endangered character remains blissfully ignorant. Likewise, in biblical poetry, dramatic irony surfaces when the reader is privy to hidden knowledge or a concealed perspective that the threatened character fails to see. The overall context of the book of Job presents an apprehensible example of dramatic irony. At the beginning of the story, the author reveals to the reader an interaction that transpires in heaven. God and Satan participate in what could be described as a divine wager, unfortunately resulting in Job's suffering, despite his righteousness. The prologue informs the reader of the circumstances that evoke Job's suffering, but Job himself and his three so-called friends remain oblivious.

Another instance of dramatic irony in poetry occurs in Judg 5:28–30, within the song of Deborah:

בְּעַד הַחַלּוֹן נִשְׁקְפָה וַתְּיַבֵּב	[28]Out of the window she looked and lamented,
אֵם סִיסְרָא בְּעַד הָאֶשְׁנָב	the mother of Sisera through the lattice,
מַדּוּעַ בֹּשֵׁשׁ רִכְבּוֹ לָבוֹא	"Why does his chariot delay in coming?
מַדּוּעַ אֶחֱרוּ פַּעֲמֵי מַרְכְּבוֹתָיו׃	Why do the hoofbeats of his chariots tarry?"
חַכְמוֹת שָׂרוֹתֶיהָ תַּעֲנֶינָּה	[29]Her wise princesses would answer her,
אַף־הִיא תָּשִׁיב אֲמָרֶיהָ לָהּ׃	indeed she repeats her words to herself,
הֲלֹא יִמְצְאוּ	[30]"Are they not finding,
יְחַלְּקוּ שָׁלָל	are they not dividing the spoil?

---

25. See also, Deut 32:37–38.

רַחַם רַחֲמָתַיִם לְרֹאשׁ גֶּבֶר	A maiden, two maidens for every warrior;
שְׁלַל צְבָעִים לְסִיסְרָא	to Sisera a spoil of dyed work,
שְׁלַל צְבָעִים רִקְמָה	a spoil of dyed work embroidered,
צֶבַע רִקְמָתַיִם לְצַוְּארֵי שָׁלָל:	dyed work of double embroidery on the neck of the spoiler?"

This brilliantly crafted text presents the reader with the viewpoint of Sisera's mother, who waits anxiously for her son to return from battling a coalition of Israelite tribes. As she tensely waits, her mind races through the endless possibilities of what could be delaying his return home. Unfortunately, her thoughts veer toward a positive hypothetical outcome of victory and the necessity of dividing up the excess of spoil captured from the Israelite tribes. In her mind, Sisera is delayed because of his responsibility to distribute the wealth of the enemy among his men. This scenario reflects *her* perspective of events as a character within the story. The reader, on the other hand, is privy to a different perspective, as the narrator has revealed to the reader what has really happened to Sisera: he is delayed because he lies dead in a pool of blood resulting from a fatal tent peg plunged into his temple by Jael. The poet conceals this knowledge from the characters in the story but reveals it to the reader for their amusement.

Although dramatic irony exists in the Psalter, it is far more nuanced and difficult to identify. One instance appears in Ps 105:18–19, during the recitation of the Joseph narrative:

עִנּוּ בַכֶּבֶל רַגְלָיו בַּרְזֶל	¹⁸They afflicted his feet with fetters,
בָּאָה נַפְשׁוֹ:	he himself was laid in irons;
עַד־עֵת בֹּא־דְבָרוֹ	¹⁹until the time that his word came to pass,
אִמְרַת יְהוָה צְרָפָתְהוּ	the word of the LORD tested him.

Verses 18–19 recount Joseph's imprisonment by the Egyptians, when they placed him in chains before his incarceration. Joseph's perspective at this time must have been one of bewilderment, perhaps, and most certainly despair at the chain of events that led him there. Although he remains innocent of any crime, he is humbled in prison. The second couplet above,

however, reveals a fresh perspective to the reader. From the reader's viewpoint, another divine process is active in Joseph's life, part of a divine plan to test, forge, and shape Joseph into an instrument for the Lord's purposes. The reader is thus privy to information that remains hidden to the characters in the text, creating dramatic irony.[26]

8.6.3 Irony of Situation

The irony of situation represents the third type of irony, and it is perhaps more nuanced than the two types of irony discussed above. Situational irony occurs when an author alerts the reader to an extreme incongruity or discrepancy between two situations or conveys a dramatic reversal of fortunes. Outside the world of biblical literature, situational irony occurs in the lives of everyday people. Think of a potential situation where a man, brimming with good intention, buys a puppy for a nephew or niece only to discover that the child contracts a severe allergic reaction to the dog two weeks after they receive it. A dramatic change, a stark and unexpected reversal transpires, with damaging results stemming from good intentions.

Biblically, an example of dramatic irony surfaces in Ps 106:13–15:

מִהֲרוּ שָׁכְחוּ מַעֲשָׂיו	¹³They quickly forgot his works;
לֹא־חִכּוּ לַעֲצָתוֹ׃	they did not wait for his counsel,
וַיִּתְאַוּוּ תַאֲוָה בַּמִּדְבָּר	¹⁴but craved intensely in the wilderness,
וַיְנַסּוּ־אֵל בִּישִׁימוֹן׃	and tempted God in the desert.
וַיִּתֵּן לָהֶם שֶׁאֱלָתָם	¹⁵So he gave them their request,
וַיְשַׁלַּח רָזוֹן בְּנַפְשָׁם׃	but sent a wasting disease among them.

Psalm 106 recounts numerous rebellious acts that the Israelites perpetrated against God during their desert sojourn. In vv. 13–15, the psalmist recalls their request for meat when they grew sick of eating manna every day. The dramatic change arises when God grants them what they craved, resulting in a short-lived period of relief, but at the same time through the meat they craved, he punished them with a wasting disease. The same divine act

---

26. For more on this, and further examples of dramatic irony in Ps 105, see Ceresko, "A Poetic Analysis of Ps 105."

that granted the Israelites a modicum of joy simultaneously unleashes against them grief and discomfort.

Irony in Hebrew poetry, and in all its various forms, serves a variety of functions. On a general level, it creates a degree of amusement for the audience, causing them to chuckle or to smile as they read through the poet's work. As a result of this potential amusement, readers are more likely to engage more deeply with the text as they anticipate instances of irony or humorous witticisms in each subsequent section. Once readers identify irony, the discovery indirectly strokes their ego to a degree, helping them feel that that they are "in the know" because the essential nature of irony limits certain readers from grasping the subtleties of this poetic feature. Thus, identifying irony bolsters the ego, even if just a little. Another function of irony is to highlight a specific point or message, creating a dramatic effect that draws the reader's attention to a particular place in the poetic text.

Naturally, exegetes are advised to proceed with care when determining the function of irony. If someone suspects that an author has adopted irony for emphasis, they should ideally provide further justification for their final conclusions. In many cases, it is obvious when poets implement this poetic device. However, at times, one cannot state with absolute certainty that an author intended it, which may lead to the trap of reading irony into situations where it was never intended. It is therefore advisable, when performing exegetical work on poetry, to explicate unequivocally to your readers your level of certainty concerning the identification of this poetic feature.[27]

Questions for Consideration: What types of wordplay does the author use? What type of irony is in the text? What effect does irony have on the reader? Does the irony contribute toward an emphatic statement?

Further Reading: Casanowicz, "Paronomasia"; Ceresko, "A Poetic Analysis of Ps 105"; Doron, "Paronomasia in the Prophecies to the Nations" Grossberg, "Multiple Meaning"; Holladay, "Form and Word-Play"; Kennedy "Isaiah 57:5–6: Tombs in the Rocks"; Meshel, "Whose Job Is This?"; Weber, "Mockery and Irony in the Psalms."

---

27. For more, see Ryken, et al., *Dictionary of Biblical Imagery*, 726.

9

Assorted Techniques

What follows is a discussion of another "mixed bag" of poetic techniques that do not fall cleanly under the headings of wordplay and imagery. Despite their failure to fall into these categories, each of the following poetic forms is important in its own right and frequently appears in biblical texts.

9.1 Merismus

Merismus occurs when an author draws upon a word pair, involving two words at either extreme of a specific entity, to represent the complete entity.[1] In this sense, merismus can be viewed as a type of metonym, a part representing the whole. For the most part, however, what distinguishes merismus from metonym is that two parts of the whole are generally involved, and that these two parts reflect polar opposites.[2] Ideally, exegetes are advised to observe two rules when identifying this poetic feature. First, ancient poets only use word pairs that represent natural opposites—such as heaven and earth, and day and night—to generate this feature. Second, not all opposite word pairs reflect merismus. The following verses from Hosea and Psalms illustrate the second point.

---

1. The phenomenon of merismus possibly developed from an abbreviated form of the longer prosaic expression "from [מִן] . . . to [לְ/עַד]." Job 10:19, for example, demonstrates the full prose expression, "I should have been as though I had not been, / Carried from womb [מִבֶּטֶן] to tomb [לַקֶּבֶר]". Expressions like this apparently abbreviated as time passed and reduced to the polar opposites currently found in merismus. For more on the development of this feature, see Honeyman, "Merismus in Biblical Hebrew."

2. Naturally, there is also a relationship here between synecdoche and merismus because both fall under the umbrella of metonymy. Once again, however, it is the two polar opposites that create the best distinguishing factor between these poetic techniques.

אֶתֶּן־לְךָ מֶלֶךְ בְּאַפִּי	I gave you a king in my anger
וְאֶקַּח בְּעֶבְרָתִי	and took him away in my wrath. (Hos 13:11)

כַּסְפּוֹ לֹא־נָתַן בְּנֶשֶׁךְ	He does not put out his money at interest,
וְשֹׁחַד עַל־נָקִי לֹא לָקָח	nor does he take a bribe against the innocent. (Ps 15:5a)

In both Hosea and Psalms above, the authors employ the words נָתַן, "give," and לָקַח, "take," which form a known word pair in biblical Hebrew,[3] and they reflect opposite meanings—the opposite of giving is taking away. That said, the word pair's appearance in Hos 13:11 fails to reflect an instance of merismus. Hosea in this context adopts the word pair to describe sequential actions, and he is not attempting to represent the concept of a whole or entirety. He depicts God acting in anger, first by giving Israel a king and then by removing the king. These actions are sequential and represent expressions of divine wrath. The appearance of the same verbs in Ps 15:5a, however, are representative of merismus. The psalmist is not attempting to describe an individual who first avoids "putting out [נָתַן]" his money for interest and subsequently refrains from "taking [לָקַח]" a bribe. Instead, the author draws on the word pair to imply that the righteous man is wholly innocent in his financial transactions. The two words, "give" and "take," combine to represent a larger entity, a whole. Ordinarily, merismus reflects the use of two nouns, which may appear in the same colon, unified with a conjunctive *waw*. Consider the following example from Ps 1:2b:

וּבְתוֹרָתוֹ יֶהְגֶּה יוֹמָם וָלָיְלָה׃	And on his law he meditates day and night.

The psalmist, in his depiction of a righteous man, portrays him meditating on the law of the Lord "day and night [יוֹמָם וָלָיְלָה]." By adopting this wording, the author is not implying that the righteous man meditates once in the day and then again once at night but that he meditates continually. The merismic opposites, יוֹמָם וָלָיְלָה, "day and night," in this context, reflect the

---

3. See for example Job 1:21; and 35:7.

notion of totality, nonstop meditation. Note too that the word pair in v. 2b appears in a single colon, joined by the *waw* conjunction. Jeremiah 31:13a presents another example:

| אָז תִּשְׂמַח בְּתוּלָה בְּמָחוֹל | Then the virgin will rejoice in the dance, |
| בַּחֻרִים וּזְקֵנִים יַחְדָּו | and the young men and the old, together. |

In Jeremiah's oracle of hope he portrays a jubilant scene of rejoicing when God will transform Israel's mourning to joy. To convey the deep sense of unrestricted jubilation, Jeremiah says that "the young men and the old [בַּחֻרִים וּזְקֵנִים]" together will dance. The intention here is not to suggest that only teenagers and pensioners partake in the celebration, but that all men are involved in rejoicing, from the young men *to* the old, including all in between. As in the previous example, Jer 31:13a separates the word pair with a simple conjunctive *waw*.[4] Psalm 77:2[3]a presents the reader with a slightly different sequencing of the word pair:

| בְּיוֹם צָרָתִי אֲדֹנָי דָּרָשְׁתִּי | In the day of my trouble I sought the Lord; |
| יָדִי לַיְלָה נִגְּרָה וְלֹא תָפוּג | In the night my hand was stretched out without weariness. |

Psalm 77 depicts an individual's distress as he desperately seeks God's face for any semblance of mercy and relief from his suffering. In v. 2[3]a, above, the psalmist, like the author of Psalm 1, employs the polar word pair יוֹם, "day," and לַיְלָה, "night." Within the lament's context, the author undoubtedly adopts these words as a merism, where they signify a totality with respect to time. In his suffering, the psalmist entreats the Lord all the time, constantly in the day and in the night. The major difference in the use of the word pair in Ps 77:2[3]a, however, pertains to its splitting of the word pair over two cola to express the same totality.[5] Another example of a merism split between cola appears in Ps 95:5:

---

4. See also, Ps 55:10.

5. See also, Ps 139:2: "You know when I sit down and when I rise up; / you understand my thought from afar."

| אֲשֶׁר־לוֹ הַיָּם וְהוּא עָשָׂהוּ | The sea is his, for it was he who made it, |
| וְיַבֶּשֶׁת יָדָיו יָצָרוּ׃ | and the dry land his hands formed. |

The word pair, or merism, in this example is יָם, "sea," and יַבֶּשֶׁת, "dry land," which is no stranger to Hebrew poetry. Together, the psalmist in v. 5 presents the reader with an image of God creating the whole earth. Like Ps 77:2[3]a, each part of the polar opposite word pair appears in successive cola, arranged with synonymous parallelism. Often in Hebrew poetry, however, merismus appears within chiastic couplets—almost as though ancient poets understood that chiastic structures somehow accentuated the appearance of polar opposite word pairs.[6] Consider Ps 78:14 below (emphases added):

| וַיַּנְחֵם בֶּעָנָן יוֹמָם | Then he led them with the **cloud** by *day* |
| וְכָל־הַלַּיְלָה בְּאוֹר אֵשׁ | and all the *night* with a **light of fire**. |

This verse forms part of the psalmist's description of God, in his mercy, leading the Israelites through the desert. God led them constantly, and the psalmist emphasizes this consistency with a merism enfolded within a chiastic pattern. The word pair expressing the merism is יוֹמָם, "[by] day," and לַיְלָה, "night." Here, however, the word sequence surfaces as part of a chiastic arrangement, a—b // b'—a', where the merism reflects the "b" portion of the equation.

At various points, psalmists adopt more than two words to create a merism, producing a merismic list. In these instances, the principle of "the part representing the totality" remains true, and the main point of deviation stems from the number of elements that comprise the parts. Instead of two words, psalmists can utilize three or more. Consider Ps 98:7–8 (emphasis added):

יִרְעַם הַיָּם וּמְלֹאוֹ	[7]Let the *sea* roar and all it contains,
תֵּבֵל וְיֹשְׁבֵי בָהּ׃	the *world* and those who dwell in it.
נְהָרוֹת יִמְחֲאוּ־כָף	[8]Let the *rivers* clap their hands,
יַחַד הָרִים יְרַנֵּנוּ׃	let the *mountains* sing together for joy.

---

6. For more on this, see Ceresko, "The Function of Chiasmus," 7; and Watson, *Classical Hebrew Poetry*, 205.

Within these verses, the psalmist exhorts all creation to rejoice with great jubilation before the Lord. To convey the sense of unrestrained jubilation, instead of simply employing two words to enumerate the totality of creation, he creates a representative list, or what is better described as a merismic list of created elements. He selects הַיָּם, "the sea," תֵּבֵל, "the world,"[7] נְהָרוֹת, "the rivers," and הָרִים, "the mountains." This list is still considered an abbreviation of a larger concept or entitiy. Unlike synecdoche, where one word, a part, is used to represent a whole, with merismus (and the merismic list) two or more parts are used to represent a totality.

Another example of a merismic list appears in Ps 135:6:

כֹּל אֲשֶׁר־חָפֵץ יְהוָה עָשָׂה	Whatever the Lord pleases, he does,
בַּשָּׁמַיִם וּבָאָרֶץ בַּיַּמִּים וְכָל־תְּהוֹמוֹת	in heaven and in earth, in the seas and in all deeps.

In v. 6 the psalmist portrays the created world as God's cosmic playground, where he acts as he pleases, doing what he likes, when he likes, and in any place he chooses. There are no boundaries in the created order that restrict God's jurisdiction. To represent this notion, the psalmist carefully selects four items to represent the entirety. The words שָׁמַיִם, "heaven," אֶרֶץ, "earth," יַמִּים, "seas," and תְּהוֹמוֹת, "deeps" were selected by the author to represent all creation.[8]

When it comes to analyzing merismus, naturally the first task is identifying what type of merismus appears in the investigated text. Does it use nouns or verbs, is the word pair split over two cola or joined by the *waw* conjunction within a single colon, are only two words involved or is it a merismic list? Once this is established, a second stage of inquiry involves a search to see where else the same word pair surfaces in biblical literature as a merismus. By performing an investigation like this, it is possible to determine whether the author simply draws from an established lexicon of poetics or if he demonstrates innovation in his adaptation of poetic norms.

---

7. Simply as a reminder that structural and poetic features usually coalesce, note that the word here for "world" is primarily found in poetic texts.

8. Further examples of a merismic list appear in Pss 8:7–8 and 148:12.

Revealing this information contributes to the exegete's knowledge of a biblical poet's writing style.

9.2 Delayed Identification

The poetic technique of delayed identification, although frequent in Hebrew poetry, has failed to garner much attention among biblical scholars. Delayed identification, also called delayed explication, occurs when the name of a subject remains concealed until after its actions are described, later than grammatically usual. As is the case with many of the poetic features discussed, and perhaps even more so, English translators are particularly susceptible to mitigating the effect of this poetic technique during the translation process from Hebrew to English, with the result that it is often overlooked. A simple example of the feature appears in Isa 13:5:

בָּאִים מֵאֶרֶץ מֶרְחָק	They are coming from a far country,
מִקְצֵה הַשָּׁמָיִם	From the farthest horizons,
יְהוָה וּכְלֵי זַעְמוֹ	The Lord and His instruments of indignation,
לְחַבֵּל כָּל־הָאָרֶץ׃	To destroy the whole land. (NASB)

Isaiah 13:5 reflects the sharp end of a judgment oracle against the land of Babylon. The verse opens with the depiction of an unknown threat that is referenced by the third-person personal pronoun "they." The author delays revealing the pronoun's referent until the third colon: "the Lord and His instruments of indignation." Grammatically, one naturally expects the identity of the Lord and his instruments to appear first, followed by a subsequent reference to them with the 3mp pronoun or pronominal form. However, the author in this instance delays the full identification until the third colon in the verse and opens the verse with an implied pronoun. In this instance, the delay of the revealed subject is well preserved in the English translation (NASB). Consider another example in Ps 105:17:

שָׁלַח לִפְנֵיהֶם אִישׁ	He sent before them a man,
לְעֶבֶד נִמְכַּר יוֹסֵף׃	who was sold as a slave, Joseph.

Here in v. 17, the psalmist conceals the fact that it is Joseph who is God's instrument for saving Jacob's family. It is not until the last line of the verse that the identity of the person sent by God is revealed. As reflected in the more sequentially literal translation above, the name Joseph does not appear until the final word in the Hebrew verse. The name, and hence full revelation of the individual, more logically belongs at the end of the first colon, replacing אִישׁ; thus, the psalmist delays the central character's identification. The examples discussed thus far purely relate to bicola, but this feature similarly exists in larger contexts. Consider the whole of Ps 114 below:

בְּצֵאת יִשְׂרָאֵל מִמִּצְרָיִם	¹When Israel went forth from Egypt,
בֵּית יַעֲקֹב מֵעַם לֹעֵז׃	the house of Jacob from a people of strange language,
הָיְתָה יְהוּדָה לְקָדְשׁוֹ	²Judah became his sanctuary,
יִשְׂרָאֵל מַמְשְׁלוֹתָיו׃	Israel, his dominion.
הַיָּם רָאָה וַיָּנֹס	³The sea looked and fled;
הַיַּרְדֵּן יִסֹּב לְאָחוֹר׃	the Jordan turned back.
הֶהָרִים רָקְדוּ כְאֵילִים	⁴The mountains skipped like rams,
גְּבָעוֹת כִּבְנֵי־צֹאן׃	the hills like lambs.
מַה־לְּךָ הַיָּם כִּי תָנוּס	⁵What ails you, O sea, that you flee?
הַיַּרְדֵּן תִּסֹּב לְאָחוֹר׃	O Jordan, that you turn back?
הֶהָרִים תִּרְקְדוּ כְאֵילִים	⁶O mountains, that you skip like rams?
גְּבָעוֹת כִּבְנֵי־צֹאן׃	O hills, like lambs?
מִלִּפְנֵי אָדוֹן חוּלִי אָרֶץ	⁷Tremble, O earth, before the Lord,
מִלִּפְנֵי אֱלוֹהַּ יַעֲקֹב׃	before the God of Jacob,
הַהֹפְכִי הַצּוּר אֲגַם־מָיִם	⁸who turned the rock into a pool of water,
חַלָּמִישׁ לְמַעְיְנוֹ־מָיִם׃	the flint into a fountain of water.

Reading through Ps 114, one can detect hints of an entity that disrupts the normal course of events. In the first two verses, this entity emancipates Israel from a land of people with strange speech, and once freed, they simply become the property of an unidentified "him." In the following four verses, mountains and hills are metaphorically reported as quaking in response to this same unnamed entity, whose identity remains concealed from the reader. The insertion of vv. 5–6, which in essence repeat the actions depicted in

vv. 3–4 in question form, delays the revelation of the entity's identification. Thus, the psalmist prolongs the final revelation until v. 7 where he reveals who it was that made Judah his sanctuary (v. 2) and caused creation to quake (vv. 3–5)—it was the Lord, the God of Jacob. Thus, the poet delays the final identification of the subject not for a single verse, but over six verses in the psalm and reveals it in the seventh.[9]

Concerning the function of this poetic feature, it is probably best to agree with Watson's assessment that Hebrew poets adopt delayed identification to stimulate a degree of suspense, a quality that especially manifests itself in the context of the longer poetic unit above. More importantly, the inclusion of this feature improves reader engagement. It helps readers remain connected to the plot and flow of the poetic unit. Returning to our developed analogy of poetry as a journey, delayed identification functions like the driver or guide telling the passengers about a magnificent mystery site that is guaranteed to take their breath away. In doing so, they know that something good lurks on the horizon, but they do not know exactly what it is. By enticing the passengers in this way, the guide encourages them to remain engaged in the journey. In the same way, by placing the actions of the main subject in a text first, and delaying the revelation of the subject's identity, ancient Hebrew poets generate a heighted sense of anticipation, attracting reader engagement throughout the flow of the poetic unit.

9.3 Hendiadys

Hendiadys, from a Greek word meaning "one through two," is a poetic technique whereby a poet brings two words together to form a single concept or meaning. The two components lose their individual identities and become a new semantic entity, encompassing a more complex idea. Hendiadys frequently appears in the Hebrew Bible, and exegetes are advised to be constantly looking for it when reading and interpreting biblical texts. In most cases, biblical writers combine two nouns, with a conjunctive *waw* inserted between them, to create the fresh concept. Consider Ps 55:5[6] below:

---

9. For further examples see, Pss 112:6; 129:5; Isa 28:26; and Jer 5:30–31.

יִרְאָה וָרַעַד יָבֹא בִי	Fear and trembling come upon me,
וַתְּכַסֵּנִי פַּלָּצוּת:	and horror overwhelms me.

As part of the psalmist's portrayal of his fear, he exclaims that יִרְאָה וָרַעַד, "fear and trembling," have come upon him. Reading this phrase as an instance of hendiadys rejects the idea of two separate feelings befalling the song writer, both "fear" and "trembling." Instead, one new sensation grips him, a fearful trembling, a specific type of fear that necessarily generates an involuntary response of trembling. Because the parallel element in the second colon, "horror" is singular, reading "fearful trembling" as a singular concept improves balance between the cola.

Another example of hendiadys appears in the lament of Ps 43:1:

שָׁפְטֵנִי אֱלֹהִים וְרִיבָה רִיבִי מִגּוֹי לֹא־חָסִיד	Vindicate me, O God, and defend my cause against an ungodly nation,
מֵאִישׁ־מִרְמָה וְעַוְלָה תְפַלְּטֵנִי:	from the deceitful and unjust man deliver me!

The psalmist suffers at the hands of evildoers and pleads for God to undertake his cause against them. In the first line he depicts them as an ungodly people, but in the second line they are referred to as the deceitful and unjust man. Reading the plain sense of v. 1b renders two characteristics of the ungodly man: he is מִרְמָה, "deceitful," and עַוְלָה, "unjust." However, as a hendiadys these words are better interpreted as a single concept, the deceitfully unjust man. Although *waw* conjunctive usually appears between the nouns, there are times when, as expected with poetry, the authors omit it.[10]

Consider the following in Ps 42:5[6]b:

---

10. Unfortunately, hendiadys is seldom reflected in English translations of the Old Testament. Consequently, even the most recognized example in Gen 1:2, תֹהוּ וָבֹהוּ, is still expressed in two words in the English editions. Thus, for example, we see, "formless and void" (NASB); "without shape and empty" (NET); "formless and empty" (NIV 2011); "without form and void" (KJV). Despite these renditions, scholarly consensus recognizes this expression as an example of hendiadys. See, for example, Williams, *Hebrew Grammar*, §72 (who also cites "blackest darkness" in Job 10:21 and "devastating violence" in Jer 6:7, which are not reflected in EVs); Speiser, *Genesis*, 5; and Lillas, *Hendiadys in the Hebrew Bible*, 371. When analyzing and describing Hebrew Poetry, it is, therefore, advisable to mention instances of hendiadys even if it is not reflected in the English translations.

הוֹחִילִי לֵאלֹהִים כִּי־עוֹד אוֹדֶנּוּ   Hope in God, for I shall again praise Him
יְשׁוּעוֹת פָּנָיו: *For* the help of His presence. (NASB)

To revive his hope, the psalmist utters words of hope and encouragement directly to his own soul, telling himself to hope in God once again. The psalmist yearns for a time when he can look back, post-crisis, and express gratitude for the divine assistance he received. The NASB translates the final words of the verse as a construct expression "the help of His presence," and although this reflects an adequate translation, reading it as a hendiadys, "his helping presence," more accurately reflects the poet's intentions. In this example, contrasting the earlier examples, the two nouns are not separated by the *waw* conjunction.

Although the examples cited thus far contain nouns, other parts of speech may be represented. Psalmists, for example, can sequence verbs to formulate hendiadys. Psalm 112:9 provides an example:

פִּזַּר נָתַן לָאֶבְיוֹנִים   He has given freely to the poor,
צִדְקָתוֹ עֹמֶדֶת לָעַד   His righteousness endures forever;
קַרְנוֹ תָּרוּם בְּכָבוֹד: His horn will be exalted in honor. (NASB)

As part of the psalmist's depiction of the gracious man, Ps 112:9 says in the NASB that he gives freely to the poor.[11] In this instance, the translators interpreted two consecutive verbs together, reading them as hendiadys. The Hebrew states that the gracious man פִּזַּר, "scatters," and נָתַן, "gives," to the poor, adopting two related but independent verbs. Together, however, they form a single more complex entity, "giving freely," demonstrating that the same principles for creating hendiadys with nouns also hold true for verbs.[12]

Although biblical Hebrew authors frequently utilize hendiadys, identifying this poet device presents its fair share of challenges. Hendiadys is ordinarily formed by the juxtaposition of two nouns separated by a conjunctive *waw*; however, not all nouns sequenced this way constitute hendiadys.

---

11. English translations remain divided on how to translate this verse; however, this is one instance where some have recognized the hendiadys. The NASB opted to translate the hendiadys and include a footnote pointing to the literal meaning, along with the NIV; more literal translations like the KJV and ESV opt to reflect both verbs, "scatter" and "give," separately.

12. See also Pss 42:3; 73:19; and 106:13.

Take Joel 3:16 for example: "The LORD roars from Zion / and utters his voice from Jerusalem, / and the heavens and the earth [שָׁמַיִם וָאָרֶץ] tremble." It would be incorrect to interpret the juxtaposition of "heaven and earth" as an instance of hendiadys, even though they follow the sequencing discussed above.[13] Therefore, exegetes must, when possible, identify contextual features that support the identification of hendiadys.[14] Two practical heuristics are identified below using Ps 55:5[6] as an example:

יִרְאָה וָרַעַד יָבֹא בִי	Fear and trembling come upon me,
וַתְּכַסֵּנִי פַּלָּצוּת:	and horror has overwhelmed me.

In v. 5a the two nouns comprising the hendiadys, יִרְאָה וָרַעַד, "fear and trembling," are governed by the verb יָבֹא, "come upon," a singular, imperfect verb. The governing verb being singular suggests that even though two nouns appear, they should be understood as a single entity, perhaps something along the lines of "fearful trembling." Additionally, the syntactically chiastic sequencing of the verse, a—b // b'—a' (n.—v. // v.—n.), deserves consideration. The corresponding "a" elements of this sequence are significant because the first instance, reflected by two nouns in hendiadys (fear and trembling), correlates with a singular noun, פַּלָּצוּת, "horror," in the second colon. Identifying these characteristics, therefore, substantiates the case for the two nouns in colon A reflecting a single concept, producing hendiadys.

A third means of identifying hendiadys arises when a poet fails to repeat a common agent in his description. Consider Ps 42:4[5] below:

אֵלֶּה אֶזְכְּרָה	These things I remember
וְאֶשְׁפְּכָה עָלַי נַפְשִׁי	and I pour out my soul within me.
כִּי אֶעֱבֹר בַּסָּךְ אֶדַּדֵּם	For I used to go along with the throng
	and lead them in procession
עַד־בֵּית אֱלֹהִים	to the house of God,
בְּקוֹל־רִנָּה וְתוֹדָה הָמוֹן חוֹגֵג	with the voice of joy and thanksgiving,
	a multitude keeping festival.

---

13. It is more accurate in this instance to understand this combination as a merism, two parts representing a whole.

14. The basis for these contextual clues appears in Watson, *Classical Hebrew Poetry*, 325–26.

In the fifth line above, because the poet fails to repeat the initial governing noun קוֹל—which would produce a theoretical line, בְּקוֹל־רִנָּה וְקוֹל תּוֹדָה, "with the voice of joy and voice of thanksgiving"—the context indicates that the noun sequencing reflects hendiadys, "with the voice of joyful thanksgiving."

The three heuristics discussed above serve as guidelines for identifying this poetic feature, though they are not infallible. Ultimately, the identification and determination of hendiadys, as well as other poetic features, should be approached with common sense and an appreciation for poetic creativity.

The purpose of hendiadys is to generate new and complex ideas from older, conventional elements, thereby revealing the creative profile of a biblical author. When analyzing instances of hendiadys in a text, it is valuable to examine whether the word combination occurs elsewhere in the Bible or if the poet has crafted a novel expression for their composition. Additionally, one should observe whether the poet consistently employs this poetic technique throughout their work or uses it in a single, isolated instance. Another significant point of analysis concerns whether the poet selects common words for creating hendiadys or incorporates rarer words to form a more intricate and complex expression. By scrutinizing the author's use of hendiadys, one may uncover aspects of his creativity and ingenuity in his application of Hebrew poetics.

9.4 Rhetorical Question

In essence, a rhetorical question is a question posed by a writer or speaker within a poem, for which an answer or immediate response is not expected. Syntactically, these questions resemble normal Hebrew interrogative statements, employing the same interrogative particles and pronouns used to create the questions, such as the interrogative הֲ and standard interrogative pronouns like מָה, "how," and מִי, "who." Pragmatically, however, these questions are less about acquiring information from another party and more about expressing feelings and establishing a point. A simple example appears in Amos 6:12a:

Assorted Techniques

הַיְרֻצוּן בַּסֶּלַע סוּסִים	Do horses run on rocks?
אִם־יַחֲרוֹשׁ בַּבְּקָרִים	Or does one plow there with oxen?

Here the author, Amos, poses questions to inhabitants of the Northern Kingdom. He asks two questions to which the answer for both is "no." In asking these questions, the prophet is not expecting a response from his audience; the answer to the question is known to all parties involved. Although the interrogative הֲ appears in its expected position in biblical Hebrew, creating an interrogative clause, its function differs: the clause is not designed to facilitate a direct inquiry.

The rhetorical question above represents an example of a question in which the assumed answer is "no," but cases also exist in which the implied answer is "yes." Consider Ps 94:9 below:

הֲנֹטַע אֹזֶן הֲלֹא יִשְׁמָע	He who planted the ear, does he not hear?
אִם־יֹצֵר עַיִן הֲלֹא יַבִּיט׃	He who formed the eye, does he not see?

Here the psalmist addresses the senseless ones among his people and attempts to arouse them to the understanding that nothing remains hidden from God and that he will uncover their deeds. To achieve this, he poses two rhetorical questions that both imply the answer "yes." Because God planted both the ears and the eyes, he is more than capable of noticing their deeds and bringing them to judgment.

Despite the clarity in the above instances, often in Hebrew poetry the implied answer is neither yes nor no. In the individual lament of Ps 10:1 below, the psalmist questions God's presence in his life:

לָמָה יְהוָה תַּעֲמֹד בְּרָחוֹק	Why, O LORD, do you stand far away,?
תַּעְלִים לְעִתּוֹת בַּצָּרָה	Why do you hide yourself in times of trouble?

In this psalm, the author questions God for being distant and even hidden from him while he suffers unrighteously. Syntactically, the verse employs the usual interrogative pronoun לָמָה, "why," to pose the question. However, this is not a question the psalmist realistically expects God to answer.

Neither does the question warrant a "yes" or "no" answer. In this instance, the words constitute a statement more than a question. The psalmist is not attempting to query God regarding his whereabouts; rather, he is emphatically articulating his present condition: he feels alone and deeply desires his God to fight against his enemies. The psalmist could have simply declared that he feels alone in his suffering. Instead, he questions God's whereabouts, implying that his sole advocate has abandoned him, purposefully avoiding the situation.[15]

Quite frequently, rhetorical questions surface in clusters, grouped together in more than one couplet. Usually in these instances, the poet inculcates the same point through repeated questions. An example appears in Ps 88:10–12[11–13]:

הֲלַמֵּתִים תַּעֲשֶׂה־פֶּלֶא	[10]Will you perform wonders for the dead?
אִם־רְפָאִים יָקוּמוּ ׀ יוֹדוּךָ	Will the departed spirits rise and praise you?
סֶלָה׃	Selah.
הַיְסֻפַּר בַּקֶּבֶר חַסְדֶּךָ	[11]Will your lovingkindness be declared in the grave,
אֱמוּנָתְךָ בָּאֲבַדּוֹן׃	your faithfulness in Abaddon?
הֲיִוָּדַע בַּחֹשֶׁךְ פִּלְאֶךָ	[12]Will your wonders be made known in the darkness?
וְצִדְקָתְךָ בְּאֶרֶץ נְשִׁיָּה׃	And your righteousness in the land of forgetfulness?

In this example, the psalmist appears to be walking the fine line between life and death from an undisclosed physical ailment. In this state of fear, psychological distress, and desperation, he protests to God. As part of his plea, he formulates an argument for why God should be compelled to reach out

---

15. In situations like this, modern exegetes may readily adopt a rigid theological stance, arguing God's omnipresence as evidence for his proximity to the psalmist. However, such an approach, particularly within the framework of Hebrew poetry, fundamentally misses the point. Engaging with poetry necessitates a full immersion into the experience, where we align ourselves with the subjects and their distress, adopting their perspective and seeing the world through their eyes at their time. Therefore, statements emanating from the sufferer's heart must be interpreted from his perspective: in his suffering, he perceives God as distant and finds no indication of his presence.

and deliver him. The argument hinges on his prayers and ability to proclaim God's goodness and kindness to others. The psalmist argues that should he die, he would cease praising God and declaring his goodness to those around him. To drive home this point, the psalmist resorts to a series of rhetorical questions that fundamentally express the same sentiment: If you let me die, I cannot proclaim your righteousness to others. Each question appearing in the excerpt above demands a single response, "no." However, by repeating the rhetorical questions, in different forms, no less than six times, the psalmist emphasizes his cause, presenting a more persuasive case to God.[16]

9.4.1 Functions

Regarding the functions of the rhetorical questions, a variety of nuanced theories have been proposed. Due to present space constraints, however, only the more salient ideas are presented below.[17] Rhetorical questions may appear at the opening of either entire psalms or poetic speeches or stanzas within a psalm. Psalm 74:1 opens with the following words:

| לָמָה אֱלֹהִים זָנַחְתָּ לָנֶצַח | O God, why have you rejected us forever? |
| יֶעְשַׁן אַפְּךָ בְּצֹאן מַרְעִיתֶךָ׃ | Why does your anger smoke against the sheep of your pasture? |

These words open a community lament, pleading for divine assistance. The rhetorical questions at the opening of the psalm express the petitioners' feelings, accentuating their complaint. At the start of the composition, these questions lay the foundation for what is to come: a detailed description of the community's suffering at the hands of foreign nations. Adopting rhetorical questions at this point generates a powerful opening to a compelling lament.[18] Rhetorical questions are not only used to open poetic units but also to close them. Consider Psalm 77:7–9[8–10] below:

---

16. For further examples of clustering rhetorical questions, see Pss 13:1–2; 85:5–6; 94:9; and perhaps the most renowned concentration in God's response to Job, in Job 38–41.

17. For a more detailed exploration of the nuances of meaning afforded by this poetic feature, see Schökel, *A Manual*, 150–52; and Watson, *Classical Hebrew Poetry*, 338–42.

18. Other examples of rhetorical questions opening poetic units appear in Pss 2:1; 82:2; and 115:2.

הַלְעוֹלָמִים יִזְנַח ׀ אֲדֹנָי	7[8]Will the Lord reject forever?
וְלֹא־יֹסִיף לִרְצוֹת עוֹד:	And will he never be favorable again?
הֶאָפֵס לָנֶצַח חַסְדּוֹ	8[9]Has his lovingkindness ceased forever?
גָּמַר אֹמֶר לְדֹר וָדֹר:	Has his promise come to an end forever?
הֲשָׁכַח חַנּוֹת אֵל	9[10]Has God forgotten to be gracious,
אִם־קָפַץ בְּאַף רַחֲמָיו	Or has he in anger withdrawn his compassion?
סֶלָה:	Selah.

In this composition, the psalmist spends the first half of his lament detailing his misery before the Lord. To close off this deep expression of despair, he resorts to a series of rhetorical questions suggesting to the reader the possibility of God ceasing his lovingkindness. Each of the questions, although different, assumes the same answer, "no." These questions form a turning point in the composition, transitioning the psalmist from despair to hope.[19]

In addition to the above uses, the rhetorical question generates a degree of dramatic effect and more importantly draws audiences' attention and involvement into the world of the poet. When posing the rhetorical questions, the explicit answer never appears in the biblical text. Rather, the poet relies on the audience to hear and understand the question, arrive at the appropriate conclusion, and then apply that conclusion to the context of the biblical text. The processing of the question demands a degree of audience participation and involvement in the affairs of the text's author. It is like a painter who leaves a space in a crucial part of a masterpiece and invites the viewer to complete the gap, thus participating in the work.

Certain biblical poets adopt the rhetorical question to create emphasis in their work. Rhetorical questions effectively draw distinct attention to crucial parts of a poetic text, generating a kind of literary shouting to ensure that readers pay due attention to specific parts of the composition's message. Clustering rhetorical questions, as discussed above, reinforces the emphatic nuance of this particular poetic enhancement.[20]

---

19. This function of the rhetorical question is not used for opening sections. Another example appears in Job 40:27, as cited by Watson, *Classical Hebrew Poetry*, 339.

20. For more on the rhetorical question, see Gordis, "Rhetorical Use of Interrogative Questions"; Moshavi, "A Positive Rhetorical Question"; and Watson, "הֲ: A Rhetorical Question."

9.5 Oxymoron

An oxymoron is a figure of speech in which poets conjoin two words or expressions that are semantically incompatible. At first, such expressions appear foolish and incomprehensible, but they are ultimately designed to convey complex images through the reader's deeper contemplation of the words spoken. This figure of speech often occurs in everyday English language, where people use expressions such as "you need to be *cruel to be kind*." Cruelty is usually considered the opposite of kindness, thus, juxtaposing the two words in this way does not make immediate sense. What is intended here, however, is that an element of an apparently cruel act, in the short term, can produce a longer-term substantial kindness.[21] For the most part, this poetic feature appears relatively rarely in Scripture and is predominantly confined to wisdom and prophetic poetry.[22] An example appears in Job 22:6:

כִּי־תַחְבֹּל אַחֶיךָ חִנָּם	For you have taken pledges of your brothers without cause,
וּבִגְדֵי עֲרוּמִּים תַּפְשִׁיט:	and stripped men naked.

Here Eliphaz, one of Job's presumed friends, levels a slanderous accusation against Job, where the English translation above states that he "stripped men naked." Underlying the translation, however, is the expression בִּגְדֵי עֲרוּמִּים תַּפְשִׁית, which more literally translates to, "You have stripped the clothes of the naked." The incompatibility presented here is that naked people do not have clothes, so for them to be stripped is ostensibly nonsensical. The poet, in this instance, adopts a powerful image that implies a heightened degree of uncompassionate cruelty. Eliphaz, in essence, suggests that Job had in the past stripped what little clothing poor people owned from them. The expression "stripping the naked of clothes," therefore, falls into the realms of hyperbole, but in this instance additionally forges an oxymoron.

---

21. A succinct breakdown of the cognitive theory behind this figure of speech appears in Ruiz, "Paradox and Oxymoron Revisited."
22. Wisdom literature in Scripture generally does more than simply teach and impart wisdom to its readers. A closer examination reveals that its phrases and syntactic constructions require a degree of wisdom and contemplation to comprehend and apply fully. Recognizing this characteristic of the genre explains why oxymorons predominantly appear in this body of literature.

Another example of this poetic technique surfaces in Prov 25:15:

בְּאֹרֶךְ אַפַּיִם יְפֻתֶּה קָצִין   With patience a ruler may be persuaded
וְלָשׁוֹן רַכָּה תִּשְׁבָּר־גָּרֶם׃   and a soft tongue breaks the bone.

The verse above contains two aphorisms that laud the potential power of calm and patient speech. To emphasize this point, the author adopts an oxymoron in the second colon, suggesting that a *soft* tongue possesses power to *break bone*. Bringing together the softness of the tongue with the solidity and rigidness of bone, the poet unites two semantically incompatible elements into a single expression. The colon makes a figurative point: the gentle use of the tongue, speaking calmly and positively, can ameliorate a potentially catastrophic verbal altercation.[23]

The inclusion of oxymoron in biblical poetry primarily serves to increase the reader's engagement and connectivity to poetic texts. The attraction generated by this rare feature is twofold. First, it creates an added degree of entertainment, stemming from the humor arising from ostensibly impossible images. Second, it draws the reader into deeper thought and contemplation concerning the meaning of the expression. Readers seldom grasp the significance of oxymoronic expressions instantly upon reading them. Oxymorons demand a little more thought and contemplation to comprehend fully the intentions of the poet. Their addition to Hebrew poetry, especially wisdom poetry, contributes an invaluable tool that is crucial to creating richness of biblical poetic form.

9.6 Apostrophe

Apostrophe is a figure of speech in which an author addresses an inanimate object, an abstract concept, or an absent individual or entity as though it were present and capable of listening. The nature of this absent entity varies in different contexts. It can be an idea, an abstract quality, a dead person,

---

23. For further examples, see Prov 11:24; 28:19; Isa 58:10; Jer 22:19. See also Bullinger, *Figures of Speech*, 818.

a place, or an inanimate object.[24] In most cases, the author or poet turns to address the entity as though it is present, able to hear, and even respond to his words. One example of this phenomenon appears in Joel 2:22:

אַל־תִּירְאוּ בַּהֲמוֹת שָׂדַי	Do not fear, beasts of the field,
כִּי דָשְׁאוּ נְאוֹת מִדְבָּר	for the pastures of the wilderness have turned green,
כִּי־עֵץ נָשָׂא פִרְיוֹ	for the tree has borne its fruit,
תְּאֵנָה וָגֶפֶן נָתְנוּ חֵילָם׃	the fig tree and the vine have yielded in full.

In this verse, the prophet looks forward to a time of blessing and restoration that will come to his community and to his land, which had been devastated by famine. In his proclamation, the prophet addresses the beasts of the field, telling them not to fear, as though they were present before him and could respond to the good news he proclaimed. By addressing an absent entity the poet creates an instance of apostrophe.

Another example appears in the words of 2 Sam 1:21:[25]

הָרֵי בַגִּלְבֹּעַ	O mountains of Gilboa,
אַל־טַל וְאַל־מָטָר עֲלֵיכֶם וּשְׂדֵי תְרוּמֹת	let not dew or rain be on you, nor fields of offerings;
כִּי שָׁם נִגְעַל מָגֵן גִּבּוֹרִים	for there the shield of the mighty was defiled,
מָגֵן שָׁאוּל בְּלִי מָשִׁיחַ בַּשָּׁמֶן׃	the shield of Saul, not anointed with oil.

Here David mourns deeply for the death of Saul after the Philistines kill him and his sons on Mt. Gilboa. In his grief, David directly addresses the mountains of Gilboa, requesting that they cease producing fruit as a sign of mourning. For David, the death of Saul and his family creates a catastrophe so horrific that even the hills and mountains—every element of creation that witnessed his death—are obliged to participate in mourning.[26]

---

24. Bullinger, *Figures of Speech*, 903, attempts to categorize the different types; however, some of his examples are somewhat unclear.

25. Although most of the book of Samuel is written in Hebrew prose, brief sections, such as the lamentation in 2 Sam 1:19–27, appear in poetry.

26. For further examples, see Deut 32:1; Pss 2:11; 6:8[9]; 42:5[6]; 77:16[17]; 103:2; 148:3; Jer 2:12; 15:10; 47:6; Mic 6:2.

In addition to constituting another means of poetic expression employed by poets, apostrophe may serve to determine the opening of a new stanza or strophe. Longer instances of apostrophe, such as the one appearing in Joel 2:21–22, form complete literary units. In Joel, the prophet directly addresses the land and the beasts, prophesying their physical restoration. The apostrophe in this instance delimits a contained textual unit within the broader poetic framework. Although apostrophe does not always function structurally, exegetes are advised to note the possibility.

9.7 Epanalepsis

Epanalepsis—stemming from the Greek, meaning "taking up again"—is a figure of speech where a word (or words) at the beginning of a clause or sentence repeats at the end of the clause/sentence (i.e., is taken up again). The English expression, "The king is dead, long live the king," exemplifies the technique. Even though the repeated elements may not be positioned exactly at the extremities of the clause or verse, a substantial number of words should appear in between. An example of the technique appears in Ps 148:11:

| מַלְכֵי־אֶרֶץ וְכָל־לְאֻמִּים | Kings of the earth and all peoples; |
| שָׂרִים וְכָל־שֹׁפְטֵי אָרֶץ | princes and all judges of the earth; |

As part of a merismic expression, v. 11 encompasses the notion of a totality of rulers. The psalmist, in this instance, adopts the word אֶרֶץ, "earth," to reiterate and exaggerate the number of rulers called to praise God. The psalmist employs the word אֶרֶץ at the start of the verse (second word in Hebrew) and again at the end.

Another example of the technique appears in Prov 16:25:

| יֵשׁ דֶּרֶךְ יָשָׁר לִפְנֵי־אִישׁ | There is a way which seems right to a man, |
| וְאַחֲרִיתָהּ דַּרְכֵי־מָוֶת | but its end is the way of death. |

In v. 25 the sage cautions his audience on how they assess their behavior and its subsequent results. To establish unity in the verse, he repeats the word דֶּרֶךְ, "way," at the beginning and the end of the verse—the second word from the start and the second-to-last word at the end.[27]

9.8 Repetition

In Hebrew poetry, repetition surfaces in a broad variety of packages, some of which have been discussed above with poetic techniques such as rhyme and structural features like the terraced pattern and refrain. The present section, however, addresses the repetition of individual words, or Hebrew roots, that appear throughout an extended text. In the world of biblical narrative, scholars label repetition of this nature with the term *leitwörter*.[28] Similar to its prominence in biblical narrative, repetition of words and roots in Hebrew poetry constitutes a crucial thread within the poetic fabric. It is difficult to overstate the importance of identifying repeated keywords when interpreting a poetic text. Unfortunately, due to the nature of Bible translation, English versions frequently obscure root and keyword repetition in attempts to smooth out the translation. This is accomplished by generating synonyms to avoid excessive repetition of the same word, which is considered poor style in English writing.

A good example of repetition in Hebrew appears in Ps 121:1–8:

---

27. Some overlap exists between this poetic feature and inclusion, so exegetes are advised to exercise care when determining their appearance in a text. I have mentioned it as a separate feature because it is often treated as such in the literature. See Bullinger, *Figures of Speech*, 206; Cuddon, *Literary Terms*, 239; Wansbrough, "Hebrew Verse." For more on epanalepsis, see Ryken, *Literary Forms*, 77; and Loewenstamm, "The Expanded Colon," who includes staircase parallelism among his examples because as a structure the second colon picks up from the first and develops it. Among the examples he cites are Exod 15:6; Pss 29:1; 92:2; Prov 31:4; Song 4:8; Hab 3:8 (see p. 294).

28. Martin Buber first coinded this phrase and describes it as "a linguistic word or root repeated significantly within a text or a sequence of texts or an anthology of texts. The significance of these repetitions is the single meaning of the texts which becomes clear. The repetition does not have to be of the very same word; on the contrary, it can be the root of the word which is repeated, and different words can themselves often reinforce the overall dynamic effect of the repetition." (this translation of Buber's original work is by Kalimi, *Reshaping*, 356). Alter describes these repeated words (or ideas) as a means of driving home the thematic emphasis of a poem (*The Art of Biblical Poetry*, 144).

אֶשָּׂא עֵינַי אֶל־הֶהָרִים	¹I will lift up my eyes to the mountains;
מֵאַיִן יָבֹא עֶזְרִי׃	From where shall my help come?
עֶזְרִי מֵעִם יְהוָה	²My help *comes* from the LORD,
עֹשֵׂה שָׁמַיִם וָאָרֶץ׃	Who made heaven and earth.
אַל־יִתֵּן לַמּוֹט רַגְלֶךָ	³He will not allow your foot to slip;
אַל־יָנוּם שֹׁמְרֶךָ׃	He who **keeps** you will not slumber.
הִנֵּה לֹא־יָנוּם וְלֹא יִישָׁן	⁴Behold, he will neither slumber nor sleep²⁹
שׁוֹמֵר יִשְׂרָאֵל׃	He who **keeps** Israel.
יְהוָה שֹׁמְרֶךָ	⁵The LORD is your **keeper**;
יְהוָה צִלְּךָ עַל־יַד יְמִינֶךָ׃	The LORD is your shade on your right hand.
יוֹמָם הַשֶּׁמֶשׁ לֹא־יַכֶּכָּה	⁶The sun will not smite you by day,
וְיָרֵחַ בַּלָּיְלָה׃	Nor the moon by night.
יְהוָה יִשְׁמָרְךָ מִכָּל־רָע	⁷The LORD will **protect** you from all evil;
יִשְׁמֹר אֶת־נַפְשֶׁךָ׃	He will **keep** your soul.
יְהוָה יִשְׁמָר־צֵאתְךָ וּבוֹאֶךָ	⁸The LORD will **guard** your going out and your coming in
מֵעַתָּה וְעַד־עוֹלָם׃	From this time forth and forever.
	(NASB, emphasis added)

In the psalm above, the psalmist has clearly employed repetition in the organization of his composition. Six times in this relatively short composition we find the root שָׁמַר (shaded above), meaning "to watch." The notion of watching, therefore, constitutes a crucial backbone of the psalm, and it is essential for exegetes to recognize this kind of repetition. Turning to the English translation, it is noteworthy that despite the literal approach to the translation of Scripture by the NASB, there are two occasions in which the translators have obscured the Hebrew text to enhance the English translation. In v. 7 the Hebrew word יִשְׁמָרְךָ is translated as "protect you," even though the same root is translated "keep" in vv. 3, 4, and 5. Similarly, in the final verse, the same root is rendered as "guard" rather than "keep." Additionally, it is worth noting the concentration of the name of the LORD, the Tetragrammaton, in the last four lines. It appears four times, and in three of those instances surfaces before the root שמר, firmly establishing it as the

---

29. This line and the next one have been adjusted slightly to align with the Hebrew text.

subject of the verb. This additional repetition in the psalm underscores the portrayal of the Lord as Israel's protector.

Another striking instance of repetition appears in Ps 148, where the root הלל, meaning "to praise," is prominently featured throughout the composition. From the opening verse to the conclusion, this root serves as a persistent exhortation to all creation to offer praise and speak majestic words of adulation to God. The pervasive use of הלל underscores the psalm's thematic focus on universal worship, inviting all beings to engage in a continuous chorus of divine glorification.

The idea of repetition extends further, especially in the realms of biblical poetry. More than just repeated words or roots, poets adopt collections of related words to assist in propagating their message. Consider, for example, Ps 90, a lament. The table below presents the repeated theme and where the phrases appear in the psalm.

Verse	Hebrew	English
1	בְּדֹר וָדֹר	in all generations
2	מֵעוֹלָם עַד עוֹלָם	from everlasting to everlasting
4	אֶלֶף שָׁנִים	a thousand years
4	כְּיוֹם אֶתְמוֹל	like yesterday
4	אַשְׁמוּרָה בַלָּיְלָה	a watch in the night
5	בַּבֹּקֶר	in the morning
6	בַּבֹּקֶר ... לָעֶרֶב	in the morning ... toward evening
9	כָל יָמֵינוּ ... שְׁנֵינוּ	all our days ... our years
10	יְמֵי שְׁנוֹתֵינוּ	the days of our life
10	שִׁבְעִים שָׁנָה ... שְׁמוֹנִים שָׁנָה	Seventy years ... eighty years
12	יָמֵינוּ	our days
14	בַּבֹּקֶר ... יָמֵינוּ	in the morning ... all our days
15	כִּימוֹת ... שְׁנוֹת	according to the days ... years

Scattered throughout the composition are myriads of words depicting measurements of time. The inclusion of the semantic motif contributes toward the psalmist's main point, his community's case for why God must deliver them: because man's lifespan, his *time* on earth, is so short, why should God extend his anger toward them any longer, filling their short lifespan with misery? Because instances like this constitute semantic repetition, as opposed to lexical, they are readily visible from English translations.

The examples of repetition discussed above represent extreme cases where the biblical text voluntarily surrenders evidence of the poetic technique. However, not all examples are so simple to uncover, and repetition often presents itself in far more subtle guises that necessitate additional teasing out by the exegete. The important thing to remember is that if a reader suspects an instance of word/root or semantic repetition, they should further demonstrate its alignment with the composition's central theme.

Regarding the repetition discussed above, one can determine at least three purposes for its existence in a poetic text. First, it may function to reveal and emphasize the central message of the text in which it occurs, either throughout a whole psalm or in a section from a prophetic or sapiential text. Second, a repeated word or root may segregate a stanza within a larger poetic text. While surveying individual poetic units, it is possible to identify a unified stanza of five to eight verses, for example, that contains a repeated word, root, or semantically related words. It is possible for Hebrew poets to employ repetition purely to define and shape an important stanza within a larger composition. Third, repetition sometimes surfaces throughout a text to generate a unifying theme that links ostensibly diverse stanzas together. In this way, the theme serves as a literary chord woven into the fabric of the psalm that holds the patchwork elements, stanzas in this case, together. In any event, the proper identification of word/root and semantic repetition is crucial to uncovering the meaning of a poetic text.

9.9 Biblical Allusion

Biblical allusion occurs when an author intentionally references an earlier literary source that is familiar to his audience.[30] For an allusion to succeed,

---

30. The concept of allusion is not exclusive to Hebrew poetry; in fact, it is quite prevalent in

certain literary conditions must be present. First, a recognized literary tradition—a written source text with origins that precede the poet's work—must exist.[31] Thus, a poet cannot allude to a text that has not been written—Samuel cannot allude to events in the book of Esther.[32] Second, the source text should be relatively popular and not an obscure reference known only to a few. For the allusion to succeed, it should be recognizable by a relatively wide audience.[33] Third, a distinctive literary element within the poet's work connects his work to his source text. The distinctive element could be represented by a single word, or a phrase, or a sequence of events connecting the poet's source to his own composition—this connective literary element is commonly called a marker.[34] The marker's form in the source text varies from text to text. Sometimes it constitutes a brief and direct citation appearing in precisely the form from which it was appropriated. In other instances, the marker adopts the guise of a vague reference in the poet's work, one that tenuously attaches to the literary source. In these situations, the source text may constitute multiple chapters in the Hebrew Bible. When authors connect to source material in this fashion, it is more challenging to narrow the allusion to a specific text within a broader event, such as the creation of the world or the flood story. Fourth, when a literary nexus is identified, exegetes are required to tease out and describe the nature of the connection between

---

narrative. It is mentioned here because it remains an invaluable tool for Hebrew poets and because the study of allusion in poetic texts, particularly the psalms, has been largely overlooked by contemporary scholarship.

31. In theory, an oral tradition could be at play, but that idea falls beyond the purview of the present work because oral traditions are much more difficult to establish. Additionally, there is a wealth of literary sources that can be identified as potential source texts in the Hebrew Bible.

32. The source text does not necessarily need to be biblical; an author can allude to any other well-known text from the ancient Near East. However, it is crucial that the text predates the author's work, and that the audience is familiar with it. As an example, words from the book of Ecclesiastes can allude to the Gilgamesh Epic. See, e.g., Samet, "The Gilgamesh Epic." For the sake of simplicity, however, focus will remain on earlier biblical written sources.

33. To be sure, some scholars validate this type of literary connection, even to the point of calling it allusion. In strict terms, however, this kind of connection is better designated as intertextuality. When scholars operate under these governing principles, they freely forget any issues concerning the dates of the two connected texts. The present volume does not espouse this type of literary connection.

34. This term is commonly used in biblical studies, and it was certainly popularized in Sommer, *A Prophet Reads Scripture*, 11. See also Leonard, "Inner-Biblical Interpretation and Intertextuality," 97–142, for a more detailed discussion on the nature of the potential connections between texts. I present above only a brief introduction to the topic, enough to get students who are unfamiliar with the idea started.

the two texts. Or to put it more succinctly, how has the poet adopted and/or adapted his source text for his composition? Naturally, this angle of analysis presents the exegete with an open-ended question; so, for an initial investigation into this area, it is advisable to begin with the most basic reason for allusion: economy of expression. By alluding to an earlier source, biblical poets conjure up in the minds of their audience any number of powerful and pertinent images via brief words and expressions. Once they call up the image, the author is then free to interact with it creatively in his own composition. Often, it is possible to identify instances from a source text where an author, in the process of alluding to an earlier text, appends his own interpretation of events into his source or strives to present or even manipulate them according to the literary themes in his composition.

Regarding the more expansive instances of allusion, the question of selection rises to analytical prominence, and each exegete is advised to ask the crucial question: To which elements in the source text is the poet alluding? If, for example, a poet alludes to the exodus tradition, it is important to identify the segments of the broader literary tradition to which he refers and ask why he focuses on these specific textual locations. Because of the necessity of asking and answering this question, it is important for the exegete to identify the source text and become familiar with it, because only then can one understand how the poet interprets and intertwines that material into his work.

Comparing Ps 105 with Ps 106 exemplifies how two authors adopt from a common source but adapt the material for their individual purposes. Both compositions assuredly allude to the exodus tradition—Israel's redemption story, beginning in the book of Exodus and depicting their deliverance from slavery in Egypt, contentious desert sojourn, and entry into the promised land. Although both draw from the same literary well, they undoubtedly deviated in motivation for doing so. The author of Ps 105, who composes a song of praise and celebration, restricts his source selection to positive images of the exodus, events highlighting God's victory over creation and any force or people who threatened his people. The author conveniently overlooks any negative act of rebellion perpetrated by the Israelites and their leaders. On the other hand, the author of Ps 106 composes a lament, and although he concentrates on the same tradition, he primarily selects incidents from Israel's past that specifically highlight their numerous and most egregious rebellions against God. The author draws from the same literary tradition but selects material relevant to his reworked composition. Analyzing these two psalms exemplifies well the value and necessity of discerning a poet's purpose for alluding to another text.

To understand the concept of allusion better, consider the following two examples. The first is a citation from Ps 106:9–12:

וַיִּגְעַר בְּיַם־סוּף וַיֶּחֱרָב	⁹He rebuked the Sea of Reeds and it dried up,
וַיּוֹלִיכֵם בַּתְּהֹמוֹת כַּמִּדְבָּר:	and he led them through the deeps, as through the wilderness.
וַיּוֹשִׁיעֵם מִיַּד שׂוֹנֵא	¹⁰So he saved them from the hand of the one who hated them,
וַיִּגְאָלֵם מִיַּד אוֹיֵב:	and redeemed them from the hand of the enemy.
וַיְכַסּוּ־מַיִם צָרֵיהֶם	¹¹The waters covered their adversaries;
אֶחָד מֵהֶם לֹא נוֹתָר:	not one of them remained.
וַיַּאֲמִינוּ בִדְבָרָיו	¹²Then they believed his words;
יָשִׁירוּ תְּהִלָּתוֹ:	they sang his praise.

These verses allude to a critical turning point in the exodus story: the waters of the Sea of Reeds crushing the Egyptian army as they pursued Israel. The psalmist selects just four verses to reflect events recorded in Exod 14–15. Numerous words in the psalmist's account connect to his source in Exodus, among the more notable are: יַם־סוּף, "Sea of Reeds" (Exod 15:4, 22), אוֹיֵב, "enemy" (Exod 15:6, 15:9), וַיְכַסּוּ־מַיִם, "the waters covered" (Exod 14:28), יָשִׁירוּ, "they sang" (Exod 15:1, 21), תְּהִלָּה, "praise" (Exod 15:11). Combined, these words create a marker, connecting the reader to a specific location in the book of Exodus, the section describing Israel crossing the Sea of Reeds, the Egyptians being overwhelmed by the sea, and Israel's response of praise to the mighty deeds of God.

One could examine the interaction, or connection, between the psalm and source text in various ways,[35] but the present discussion limits itself

---

35. For an overview of potential interactions between a text and its source, see Leonard, "Inner-Biblical Interpretation and Intertextuality," 123–27.

to two of the more obvious points of comparison. The first concerns the question of lexical economy. In alluding to the two chapters in exodus, the psalmist conjures up images of a much larger text into his reader's mind through the recollective power of four verses. Undoubtedly, the psalmist's original audience knew well the story of the exodus, and all that transpired, especially the crossing of the Sea of Reeds. Therefore, by conscientiously selecting a few pertinent words, the psalmist exercises an economy of expression to evoke a vivid and expanded image in his audience's mind.

The second concerns the poetic transformation of the source text. In choosing specific words and expressions for his allusion, the psalmist not only guides the reader to his source, but he also further embellishes his reading of the source with words added to the original account. Thus, expressions in Ps 106, such as וַיִּגְעַר, "he rebuked [the Sea of Reeds]," and וַיַּאֲמִינוּ בִדְבָרָיו, "They believed his words," remain absent from the source but embellish the psalmist's version of events.[36] Consequently, it is important to remember that although biblical allusion primarily functions to point the reader to an earlier text, identifying the literary nexus only represents the initial stage of appreciating the connection and adaptations that transpire when poets use biblical allusion.

The connection to the exodus account constitutes a relatively blatant instance of allusion, but exegetes are more likely to stumble upon more subtle examples, such as that in Ps 31:13[14], and its connection to Jer 20:10. Consider the table below:

Psalm 31:13[14]	Jer 20:10
כִּי שָׁמַעְתִּי דִּבַּת רַבִּים מָגוֹר מִסָּבִיב בְּהִוָּסְדָם יַחַד עָלַי לָקַחַת נַפְשִׁי זָמָמוּ׃	כִּי שָׁמַעְתִּי דִּבַּת רַבִּים מָגוֹר מִסָּבִיב הַגִּידוּ וְנַגִּידֶנּוּ כֹּל אֱנוֹשׁ שְׁלוֹמִי שֹׁמְרֵי צַלְעִי אוּלַי יְפֻתֶּה וְנוּכְלָה לוֹ וְנִקְחָה נִקְמָתֵנוּ מִמֶּנּוּ׃

---

36. In a sense, these words can be interpreted as hyperbole because they slightly exaggerate the recounting of the source in Exodus. Such embellishment or transformation is common in biblical allusion.

Psalm 31:13[14]	Jer 20:10
For I have heard the whispering of many, "Terror is on every side!" While they took counsel together against me, they schemed to take away my life. (emphasis added)	**For I have heard the whispering of many, "Terror on every side!** Denounce him; yes, let us denounce him!" All my trusted friends, watching for my fall, say: "Perhaps he will be deceived, so that we may prevail against him and take our revenge on him." (emphasis added)

The bolded sections above generate the marker linking the two texts together. Because the words shared between the two fail to appear elsewhere in biblical literature, the marker increases its effectiveness. Usually, it is best to establish unique markers to avoid situations where a psalmist's wording may connect to two or more possible texts. In the example above, the psalmist composes an individual lament, conveying to his readers the unfathomable depths of his sufferings, fear, and psychological trauma. In typical lament fashion, the author supplies no evidence regarding the identity of the psalmist's enemies, or the precise intentions of those who threaten his well-being. For Jeremiah, the notion of suffering under psychological torment and fear is far more pronounced. Jeremiah speaks of his fear and anxiety when he recognizes that all his friends are betraying him, turning on him, and waiting for him to fall. His profound despair, in a manner similar to Job, drives him to the point of cursing the day of his birth (20:15). Through the allusion to Jeremiah,[37] the psalmist weaves the acute sense of despair, fear, grief, and loss from his source text and into the fabric of his own composition. The magnitude of Jeremiah's pain and fear is economically transferred to the poet's work through the repetition of a few purposefully selected words.

---

37. The assumption here that the psalmist draws from Jeremiah primarily rests on the eclectic fabric of Ps 31, which seems to draw from various other locations in Scripture, especially Ps 71. See Emanuel, *Intertextual Commentary*, 140–44.

A few words of warning deserve mention regarding the identification of biblical allusion. It is important that exegetes separate biblical allusion from the phenomenon of textual duplication. Throughout the Hebrew Bible, numerous instances arise, especially in the psalms, where identical poetic traditions appear in two earlier collections of sacred writings that biblical editors amalgamate into larger collections, which are subsequently crystallized as part of the biblical canon. Such a process results in duplicate compositions or text segments in the Old Testament. A prominent example of this process appears in Pss 14 and 53. Although slight differences exist between the two compositions, it would be incorrect to define their relationship as a biblical allusion. Concerning these psalms, it is more accurate to understand them as alternative versions of the same composition. It is possible to analyze the two psalms armed with a series of questions like those employed for examining biblical allusion. The relationship between the two psalms differs, however, and it is incorrect to posit that the author of Ps 53 alludes to Ps 14, or vice versa. Other examples of textual duplication appear in Ps 18 and 2 Sam 22; Ps 108:1–6 and Ps 57:7–11; and Ps 108:6–13 and Ps 60:5–12.

9.9.1 Functions

As previously discussed, the primary function of allusion (at least in this stage of analysis) is to economically connect the reader to an earlier text. Rather than recounting vast swaths of citations from his source, a Hebrew poet carefully selects words from an earlier text, creating a marker that conjures up images of an earlier tradition into his audience's mind. Once that connection is established, a world of opportunities exists with respect to how the psalmist can interact with his source. Space restricts the explication of all the various nuances of possible intertextual connections,[38] but one function deserves further explanation. In certain instances, psalmists allude to earlier sources to shed additional light (or simply cast their opinion) onto their source text. A simple example appears in Ps 105:17:

---

38. For more on the topic of inner-biblical interpretation and allusion with specific regard to poetic texts, see Emanuel, *From Bards to Biblical Exegetes*; Emanuel, *Intertextual Commentary*; Emanuel, "An Unrecognized Voice"; Leonard, "Identifying Inner-Biblical Allusions"; Sommer, *A Prophet Reads Scripture*; and Williamson, "Isaiah 62:4."

שָׁלַח לִפְנֵיהֶם אִישׁ	He sent before them a man,
לְעֶבֶד נִמְכַּר יוֹסֵף:	Joseph, who was sold as a slave.

In this succinct verse, the author of Ps 105, with an economy of words, alludes to the events narrated in Gen 37, which details Joseph's brothers selling him into slavery, leading to his eventual arrival in Egypt. The author of Genesis fails to mention God in his depiction of Joseph's brothers' vindictive actions toward him. There is no recollection of a divine hand guiding the actions of the malicious siblings. When the psalmist recounts this same account, however, he inserts the influence of a divine hand shaping and guiding the brothers' actions. Furthermore, the primary agents of the slave sale, Joseph's brothers, fail to surface in the psalmist's rendition. Instead, Joseph's going down to Egypt is portrayed purely as a divinely initiated act. This kind of alteration amounts to a reinterpretation of the originally recorded events, a recitation by the psalmist that both reduces the negative memory of Joseph's brothers and highlights the magnificent work of God in Israel's history.

Questions for Consideration: How often does the author employ hendiadys? Does he create new forms of hendiadys or borrow known forms? Where does the rhetorical question appear in the text? Does it appear at the beginning, as an introduction? Does it appear at the end, summarizing a central message? Is it clustered with other rhetorical questions, and if so, do they all say the same thing, or make the same point? Does the question anticipate a "yes" or "no" answer? Is there a change of topic before or after the rhetorical question? What effect did the delayed identification have on you as a reader? Does the author use this device elsewhere in the text? What structural technique is used with the delayed identification? What parts of speech are used in the merismus—verbs, nouns, adjectives, etc.? What verse structure does the merismus appear in—parallelism, chiasmus, terraced pattern, etc.? Is merismus common in the text? What kind of merismus is it—extended or limited? Is the word pair in the merismus used elsewhere? What words, roots, and/or themes are repeated in the text under investigation? How does the repetition relate to the overall message of the text? Does the author allude to other texts in the Bible? Does the author allude to a general event or a specific text in Scripture? How does the target text relate to the source?

Further Reading: Emanuel, "An Unrecognized Voice"; Emanuel, *Intertextual Commentary*; Emanuel, "The Elevation of God"; Gordis, "Rhetorical Use of Interrogative Questions"; HKuntz, Hendiadys"; Leonard, "Identifying Inner-Biblical Allusions"; Leonard, "Inner Biblical Interpretation and Intertextuality"; Meek, "Intertextuality, Inner-Biblical Exegesis"; Moshavi, "A Positive Rhetorical Question"; Schnittjer and Harmon, *The Bible's Use of the Bible*, Sommer, *A Prophet Reads Scripture*; Watson, "הֲ: A Rhetorical Question"; Williamson, "Isaiah 62:4".

PART 5

Putting It All Together

10

Guidelines for Poetic Analysis

This chapter aims to synthesize much of the preceding discussion to demonstrate its application within a broader system of exegesis and analysis. What follows is an outline of the steps necessary to transition from reading to exegesis and analysis.[1] It is crucial to note that this outline is not intended to be infallible or complete by any stretch of the imagination. There is no guarantee that adhering to the following procedure will consistently yield perfect results. Personal preference also plays a significant role in methodological analysis, and some may find it beneficial to alter the order of the steps presented below. For instance, some may prefer to identify poetic features before addressing structural poetics. It would be challenging, if not impossible, for me, or any author, to present an unequivocally correct procedure for approaching poetic analysis. An outline for the proposed guidelines is as follows:

1. Text Selection
2. Reading the Text
3. Initial Translation
4. Concordance Work
5. Initial Stanza Division
6. Structural Features
7. Poetics

---

1. Numerous attempts have been made to develop a process for poetic analysis. What I present here is a synthesis of existing material and my own experience. For other methods, see Fokkelman, *Reading Biblical Poetry*, 207–9; and Wendland, *Analyzing the Psalms*, 204–9, although he exclusively deals with the Psalter. For a broader and more technical method, it is worth consulting Weiss, *The Bible from Within*, who provides a detailed method of total interpretation from the smallest units of a text (i.e., words) to understanding the whole composition.

8. Revision
9. Big Picture
10. Textual Associations
11. Commentary Consultation

Before any technical procedural work begins, an important and potentially contentious issue must be addressed: is it preferable to consult commentaries first, or early in the investigative process, or is it better to conduct one's own analysis initially? To be sure, numerous benefits can be derived from reading commentaries and academic papers on a particular text early in the exegetical process. Often, such material can quickly help establish the main themes and questions that arise from the text. One could argue that more time could then be devoted to addressing and refining one's work by spending more concentrated effort focusing on the main issues that arise from the text. This reflects one approach to poetic analysis. However, for the purposes of the present volume, and in keeping with its goals of aiding students in transitioning from an introductory grammar to poetic analysis, I do not recommend surveying and researching secondary and tertiary sources as a first course of action. In my experience, students who adopt this approach quickly become engrossed in the opinions and ideas of other scholars and tend to view the texts through the eyes of their favorite exegetes. Another pitfall of this approach is that it tends to lead students to produce exegetical and analytical papers that are essentially a florilegium or patchwork of analyses drawn from contemporary scholarship. In both instances, the crucial ingredient is missing: the student's individual thoughts and ideas about a text and their personal engagement with that text.

Therefore, as a general principle, I advocate for students to engage directly with the text initially, allowing their own insights and interpretations to develop before consulting secondary sources. This method ensures a more original and personally meaningful engagement with the material, fostering a deeper and more nuanced understanding of Hebrew poetry.

That said, the astute reader will quickly recognize that some degree of secondary source material must be consulted in any preliminary work of exegesis, and this is a fact I must concede. It is unimaginable, after all, that a student could begin even the initial stages of creating their own translation without the use of dictionaries, grammars, and encyclopedias. Fundamental tools such as these are essential and foundational to all exegetical work at the early stages of investigation. Notwithstanding such necessities, my continual advice, based on personal observation and experience, is that consultation with academic books, especially commentaries, and articles that discuss your texts is best kept to a minimum during the early stages of investigation. This approach allows students to form their own interpretations and insights before being influenced by the perspectives of other scholars, thereby fostering a more original and personal engagement with the text.

Another important consideration that all exegetes must address early on is the purpose and overall objective of their study. Naturally, the reasons can be varied for tackling a poetic analysis of a Hebrew text. Some may be completing a paper for a second-year course in biblical Hebrew, while others may be attempting to write a more detailed seminar paper involving poetry. The specific fields within poetry can also guide a student's motivations. The poetic text under investigation may form part of a broader study of prophetic literature, or wisdom literature, or it may be included as part of a paper addressing issues of redactional criticism. Potentially, the student may be involved in the study of psalms or poetry embedded in narrative. The main point here is that once an exegete knows and understands the specific focus of their research, they can incorporate additional questions relevant to their particular area of study into the process outlined below. This clarity of purpose allows for a more directed and nuanced approach to the text, enhancing the overall quality and depth of the exegetical work.

Before detailing the stages of the proposed exegetical process, one last point deserves mention: the tentative nature of exegetical work. One of the more seductive traps in poetic analysis is to become enamored with an early and premature conclusion or idea about a particular composition. It cannot be emphasized enough how crucial it is to maintain an open mind throughout the process of poetic analysis. Completing one stage of analysis does not signify a lock and a seal on that aspect of investigation. Students should avoid becoming deeply emotionally attached to any decisions made during the investigative process. For instance, if a student opts to translate a verb in a particular way, with a particular tense or mood, early on during the third stage of the process, this does not mean that they must adhere to that decision indefinitely. As they continue to work on their text, they may discover a more accurate or nuanced translation. Refining one's work is a natural and essential part of the exegetical journey, and it should not be frowned upon as a methodological shortcoming. Embracing an iterative process allows for more comprehensive and insightful analysis, ultimately leading to a richer understanding of the text.

10.1 Text Selection

The initial step in the exegetical process involves the student selecting a text, and where necessary establishing the boundaries of the text they wish to analyze. Naturally, in certain instances an instructor may determine their poetic unit, leaving the student or exegete without a choice.[2] For this early stage it is recommended to begin with relatively short texts, ranging from three to eight verses, and it is advisable to select texts from the Psalter because prophetic literature, such as Isaiah and Ezekiel, can be more challenging to interpret. Similarly, wisdom literature, especially the book of Proverbs, presents its own subtle challenges and complications (see appendix 2). The poetry of Job, for example, is viewed by many to have extremely ancient origins and contains an extremely high number of *hapax legomena*, posing unique challenges to students. That said, even among the compositions in the Psalter, certain texts pose specific problems that can confound first-time exegetes. Even shorter texts, such as Ps 82, for example, may not be suitable for second-year Hebrew students. Additionally, well-known poetic passages in the Bible, such as Pss 1; 23; 51; and Isa 40, should be approached with caution. Although these passages are worthy of detailed analysis, a student's likely familiarity with these texts makes it difficult for them to avoid eisegesis, that is, reading their preconceived notions *into* the biblical text. While avoiding such passages is suggested as a guideline, there is no inherent issue with analyzing the poetry found within them.

An important part of the selection process involves delimiting the beginning and ending of the text under investigation. For the psalms—another

---

2. Usually, it is easier for instructors to assign students specific texts rather than letting students select texts for themselves. Instructors generally have a better understanding of what constitutes a suitable text.

reason why I would recommend them early on—this delimitation process is relatively straightforward because each psalm generally constitutes an independent unit. However, even within the Psalter, caution is required due to texts such as Ps 10. One might assume that the composition begins at Ps 10:1, but further investigation raises questions concerning this starting point. A significant amount of scholarship posits that this composition was erroneously divided in the MT[3] and that it should be part of the longer composition comprising Pss 9 and 10, as reflected in the LXX. Therefore, I do not recommend Ps 10 as a candidate for research because the necessity to determine an acceptable demarcation point adds an additional layer of complication that could unduly burden students.[4]

When dealing with prophetic texts and wisdom texts, it is necessary to determine where the text begins and ends. In certain cases, this task is straightforward, and it is easy to identify with certainty the start and end of a short oracle or topic. However, in other cases, distinguishing these division points demands more extensive groundwork. Once textual boundaries are defined, it is then important to read and understand the surrounding context and the major topics addressed in the framing text. This should not demand an excessive amount of time and resources, but it is worthwhile taking notes on the key components of the immediate context. This guideline applies to all poetic texts. If the poetry is embedded in narrative, the narrative portions should be examined. Similarly, if a psalm is under investigation, its neighbors should be reviewed to identify any potential lexical or thematic connections.[5]

10.2 Reading the Text

Once the boundaries of the text are established, the first task is to read the text both in your native language and in the original language, preferably

---

3. Numerous scholars attest to this probability, including Alter, *The Book of Psalms*, 25; Brueggemann and Bellinger, *Psalms*, 63; Emanuel, *Intertextual Commentary*, 59–60; and Kraus, *Psalms 1–59: A Commentary*, 191.

4. Naturally, however, if the point of the assignment is to determine shared poetic forms between these compositions, then a vastly different situation presents itself.

5. The thematic connection between psalms is an often-neglected area of research. See Emanuel, *Intertextual Commentary*, 2–9, for more on this topic.

in the original language first. This step can be daunting to some second-year students who may not have mastered all the vocabulary in their text. However, even without knowing all the meanings of the words in a particular poetic text, several insights can still be gleaned.

One key aspect to observe is the repetition of sound—not rhyme, as one would expect in English, but repeated sequences of letters and roots. As discussed extensively in this volume, English translations frequently obscure multiple occurrences of a single root in their attempts to alleviate the apparent monotony of Hebrew repetition. In addition to repeated words or roots, one should note recurrent themes during this initial reading. Themes may be identified through the repetition of words that share the same semantic field. In such cases, the poet may adopt synonyms within the composition to emphasize a particular point.

It is also important to note the line length and identify any abnormally long verses or cola that disrupt the natural rhythm of the text. Similarly, conspicuously short cola should be noted. In general, at this stage anything that stands out as being abnormal deserves noting, even if an explanation is not immediately apparent. This could include strange spellings or misspelled words—as with the *qere-ketiv* Masoretic tradition. Additionally, the verbs and their tenses/moods should be noted during this stage of reading. These can later assist in identifying stanza divisions and the overall flow of the text.[6]

10.3 Initial Translation

After the initial reading, it is worthwhile accomplishing your initial translation of the text. This translation may be a very literal rendering of the text under investigation. For this initial translation, Hebrew lexicons,[7] grammars,[8]

---

6. Additionally, one should attempt to identify clause types—commands, statements, descriptions, questions, etc.—to help determine the logical cohesion of a text. For more on this idea, see Patton, *Basics of Hebrew Discourse*, 251–61.

7. Here BDB, although a little dated, still proves beneficial. For a more modern alterative, students should consider *HALOT*.

8. Perhaps the most comprehensive grammar on the market is Joüon, but other good alternatives exist, such as Waltke and O'Connor, *Biblical Hebrew Syntax*. Another resource that should be consulted is Noonan, *Advances in the Study of Biblical Hebrew and Aramaic*.

and Bible dictionaries⁹ should be consulted to establish the meanings of the words and their syntax. During this initial translation phase, students will need to address any text-critical issues that may arise. Time and space prevent presenting a detailed method for addressing all the intricacies of this phase; however, the main objective is to reconstruct the best viable reading of the Hebrew text. This may sound strange, but it is important to remember that even among the English translations there can be differences of opinion regarding the correct translation of the Hebrew text. At a rudimentary level, difficult readings can be identified via the Masoretes' *qere-ketiv*[10] readings and also through a comparison of English versions.[11] More experienced students can also identify textual problems through use of a critical edition of the Bible such as the BHS. Critical editions of the Bible allow exegetes to compare various Hebrew manuscripts with early translations of Scripture.[12]

In addition to settling on a preferable reading of the Hebrew text, it is also useful to identify semantic possibilities—alternative valid readings for specific words in your text. Many Hebrew words have a broad semantic

---

9. Here students should consider something similar to Freedman, *Anchor Yale Bible Dictionary*; *NIDB*; or Strauss and Longman, *Baker Expository Dictionary of Biblical Words*. Obviously, the more comprehensive the dictionary, the better the overall results. At this stage, students must staunchly resist the desire to consult an English dictionary to define a biblical word or concept.

10. Frequently in the Hebrew Bible, words in the main body of a text are written incorrectly by the scribes. This form is called the *ketiv*, the "written" form, from the Aramaic כְּתִיב. These incorrect forms are corrected in the margins, which creates the "read" form, called the *qere*, from Aramaic קְרִי. It is the exegete's responsibility to consult the corrected form in the margins to establish the best reading. For example, in Ps 54:5[7], the main text contains the reading יָשׁוּב, which is unreadable and incorrect. The correct form, יָשִׁיב, according to the Masoretic scribal *qere* tradition, appears in the margin. See Chisholm, *From Exegesis*, 19–29, for further examples.

11. As a general rule of thumb, when comparing translations, the older translations of the Bible (such as the KJV) are corrected by newer literal translations. Comparing 1 Sam 13:1 KJV with the NASB provides an example. However, it is important to remember that identifying these differences highlighted by the later readings is not a foolproof method of revealing the best reading of the Hebrew Bible.

12. These scribal developments contribute to the differences between the Leningrad Codex, the base text for the BHS, and textual witnesses from other scribal traditions. When encountering these discrepancies, exegetes must determine which version to include in their poetic analysis. Consider, for example, in Ps 105:36, whose first colon reads, "He also struck down all the firstborn in their land [בְּאַרְצָם]." The amendment proposed by the Targums and multiple Hebrew manuscripts suggests that the word bracketed above should be changed to בְּמִצְרָיִם. Although this alteration appears logical due to its morphological similarity, it affects the potential for an instance of inclusion between vv. 23–38 by introducing a third appearance of the word "Egypt." Thus, while textual reconstruction may be necessary in certain situations, it is essential to consider how such reconstruction impacts the poetic balance of the overall composition. For a comprehensive approach to this process of textual criticism, see Tov, *Textual Criticism*.

plane, consequently, two or three valid meanings, depending on context. Furthermore, as discussed in the section on wordplay, a Hebrew poet may purposefully intend for more than one meaning to be applicable to his composition. Even though one might be inclined to settle on a single translational option at this stage, it is always worth noting alternatives that could prove a better fit later in your analytical work.

It is crucial to remain objective and avoid becoming emotionally attached to your translation at this stage of the investigation. Its primary purpose is to facilitate your ongoing analysis of the text. The initial translation is a working document, and it is likely that adjustments will be needed later in your investigative work. As you complete your initial translation, it is wise to begin marking repeated words and phrases in your selected text, in the original language. Usually this is best accomplished by color-coding a printout of the original text.

10.4 Concordance Work

After completing the initial translation work, a more detailed concordance study is recommended.[13] At this stage, the goal is to isolate certain keywords and phrases to examine how they are used elsewhere in Scripture. Essentially conducting your own word studies specific to the text you are analyzing will prove beneficial. The objective is to acquire a deeper understanding of the words and phrases in your text. Although it is challenging to create a formula for selecting words and phrases for further examination, students will develop an intuitive sense for this as they analyze more texts.

Once the key words and phrases are isolated, several questions may guide the examination: Is the word or phrase only found in a particular type of literature? Is the word or phrase unique or rare? Does the word or phrase only appear in specific contexts (legal, punitive, theophanic, etc.). At this stage in the investigation, it is beneficial to seek out potential markers that indicate biblical allusion. If a relatively rare word or phrase only appears in one other

---

13. Naturally, the term "concordance" is not limited to a particular book. Today, most concordance work is performed via electronic Bible programs such as BibleWorks, Accordance Bible, and Logos.

location in Scripture, it is likely that biblical allusion is present. Additionally, examining word pairs for uniqueness and contextual occurrence is advisable at this point.

As part of the concordance work, it is essential to identify any specific poetic morphology present in the text. This means referring to ch. 2 of the present volume to identify syntax and morphology unique to poetry.

10.5 Initial Stanza Division

The next stage involves establishing the text's overall structure by dividing it into stanzas via its content. As previously noted, this process can be somewhat subjective. Nevertheless, there are certain clear guidelines to follow. Ideally, the result should reveal a text with stanzas of relatively uniform length. For instance, it would be inadvisable to divide a fourteen-verse poetic text into two stanzas, one consisting of thirteen verses and the other containing a single verse.

Several markers can indicate a change in stanza, signifying the end of one and the beginning of another. Students should look for changes in topic or subject (such as an extended metaphor), speaker, or temporal shift. In a text with more pronounced breaks, these markers become increasingly difficult to overlook.

After establishing the textual divisions, it is essential to analyze how the units relate to each other. Begin by summarizing the contents of each stanza in a sentence and then examine how each stanza connects to the others. Consider various factors such as change in speaker, change in emotion, or a change in person.[14] For example, consider the juncture in Ps 81:5–6[6–7], "He established it for a testimony in Joseph / When he went throughout the land of Egypt. / I heard a language that I did not know: / 'I relieved his shoulder of the burden, / his hands were freed from the basket.'" Verses 5–6[6–7] illustrate a change in voice, shifting from the psalmist to God. This division is reflected in the NASB's interpretation of the stanza divisions.[15]

---

14. See Wendland, *Analyzing the Psalms*, 118, for more information.
15. Similar shifts also occur in Ps 54:4[6] and 60:6[8], among other locations in the Psalter.

It is generally advisable to start with the more obvious breaks in the poetic unit. As you progress through the stanzas, consider various relationships such as continuity, explication, contrast, and restatement. The relationships between stanzas are often like those found between cola.

Remember, stanza relationships may not always be consecutive—do not just examine the relationship between one stanza and its immediate neighbor. In lengthier compositions, chiastic relationships between stanzas may exist, linking, for example, the first stanza to the last. In addition to discussing stanza relationships, it is important to identify any recurring themes or motifs, examining whether a particular theme or word appears in each section to establish unity and continuity throughout the text.

10.6 Structural Features

After a preliminary assessment of the stanza divisions, attention should then shift to the structural poetic features within the text under examination, as outlined in part 3 of the present work. At this stage, it is necessary to divide the verses into individual cola and discuss their relationships. The cola divisions should adhere to the Masoretic cantillation marks and should, therefore, correspond to the divisions found in English translations. A word of caution is warranted at this point. Throughout the discussions in this volume, I have endeavored to present clear examples that illustrate the structural features of Hebrew poetry. However, examples of the various features are frequently not straightforward and may require careful contemplation to determine accurately certain poetic presentations. This complexity is to be expected and should not be considered abnormal.

It is important to remember that at least two phases of examination are necessary here. First, identify one or more structural features relating to each verse. Second, as far as possible, describe the function of that poetic feature; i.e., why the poet adopts that particular form in that specific place. Certain structural features can demarcate the beginning, middle, or end of a poetic unit. Given that a preliminary division of stanzas has been performed, it is now necessary to see where the structural features coincide with the semantic divisions. For this reason, semantic division takes place first, and only after these preliminary divisions are identified should the structural poetic features be considered to further strengthen the evidence for stanza division choices. It is not advisable to divide a text into stanzas based solely on data derived from the structural analysis. Structures such as chiasmus, for example, can be used to indicate the beginning and end of stanzas, but this is not their sole purpose. Therefore, their identification alone cannot serve as proof of a unit division.

10.7 Poetics

After identifying structural features, attention should then turn to the poetics found in the text under examination. This line of investigation relates to part 4 of the present volume. For this phase, it is probably best to first work through the text and simply note which poetic features are present. Undoubtedly, this will be an iterative process, requiring thoughtful consideration to establish exactly what poetics are being used. Students will likely need to review their decisions multiple times before continuing their investigations.

Next, it is important to explain or describe how each poetic feature functions within the psalm and how it relates to the overall message and purpose of the text in question. It is easy to identify a poetic feature and then sit back thinking your work is done, but the identification is only one part of the process. For example, in identifying a metaphor, several further questions should be considered: What structural feature serves as its vehicle? Is it developed throughout the psalm? Is it unique to biblical literature? Is it the only metaphor in the composition? How does it relate to other metaphors in the text? Several other possibilities have been provided in the preceding chapters, but the examples in the present volume should by no means be considered exhaustive.

10.8 Revision

At this point in the analysis, it is prudent to formally review your overall work. Throughout the textual analysis process, revisions are often necessary.

For instance, discovering a particular metaphor midway through a text may prompt you to revise your translation at the beginning or alter a word choice for a variant translation. It can be challenging for students new to this process to adapt to this phase of investigation, as they may find it difficult to go back and change their work. Despite the difficulty, the process of revision is crucial to developing sound exegetical and analytical skills.

Two of the most important aspects of revision will involve your translation and the stanza divisions. As students read more scholarly material and other English translations, they will likely find that their personal translation requires adjustments. Sometimes the change reflects a matter of right and wrong—where an early translation may violate the rules of Hebrew grammar. At other times, however, the difference may simply be a question of nuance or choice. Opting for one translation of a word over another may better reflect a more widespread theme that the psalmist is employing.

There is a natural tendency for newer exegetes to automatically conform their translations to one of the common English versions. While this is not necessarily poor practice, it is not always recommended. My advice is that if you can justify a slightly innovative or unorthodox translation, then you should retain it, detailing the reasons for your decision in a footnote. Another likely area of change concerns the stanza divisions. Like the translation choices, students may find that their divisions clash with those in popular English versions. Again, this is not necessarily a reason to alter your work. The important thing is that students can justify and explain the decisions made in their analysis.

Usually, at this phase, most of the decision-making process concerns individual verses and whether they belong to one stanza or another. There may not necessarily be a single right answer to this question. What is important is to be able to explain any decisions made.

10.9 Big Picture

At some point, it is important to take an overall look at the poetic text with which you are working, much like stepping back after the completion of a house to see what it looks like from a slight distance. As you review the poem, the goal is to make an overall assessment of the composition.[16] This involves reading through the text again and, with your newly acquired knowledge, assessing the following aspects.

First, consider how the text begins and what mood can be assigned to the opening. Is it calm and restful, intense and joyful, somber and desperate, or perhaps filled with anticipation of something dramatic? After reading the first few verses, reflect on how you feel as a reader.

Next, jump to the end of the composition and ask yourself the same question. The conclusion of the text is particularly important, as discussed earlier, because it often serves as an emphatic location, the place where biblical authors are careful about leaving a lasting impression, much like the final taste of a new meal or the last word in an argument

Once you have ascertained the sense and emotion of the composition's close, compare it to the beginning to start understanding the journey that the author is leading. Does he begin in despair and end in hope, or open with joy and end with warning, or open with expectation and end with joy? Does the poet finish where he began, with no discernable change? Returning to the journey motif, as you read through the text, try to discern its pace, where and how it moves, whether it speeds up, moves at a consistent speed, or slows down. As a basic rule, the poem's pace is determinable through structural analysis. Synonymous parallelism in all of its various forms represents slowing down as the reader does not move forward with much new information or direction in poetic expression. The most extreme instance of this is strict parallelism, where words and syntactic elements are repeated from one colon to the next.

Quick forward movement results from synthetic parallelism,[17] with minimal repetition between individual cola, providing larger bites of new information to the reader. The forward process also occurs with changes in subject or stanza, signaling a new direction and a change in lyrical pace. Be on the lookout too for in-between patterns, such as the terraced patterns, which employ a degree of repetition but also include clear forward movement.

---

16. I have inserted this stage of the process here, but logically it could have been completed earlier and simply revised at this point.
17. This may also be known as formal parallelism.

Analyzing the macrostructure of the text in this way is akin to reflecting on a long journey, recalling what you have seen, and the distances you have traveled. This provides a better sense of the text as a whole rather than just as a collection of poetic features and traits.

As a final part of this process, it is always worthwhile attempting to describe the meaning and purpose of the text under investigation. In this description, try to use no more than two sentences, making your description unique to your text, highlighting some of its more important features. It is important to avoid a simple recitation of the text in your own words, so adherence to the sentence limit is crucial. This part of the analysis helps you think about and understand the composition as a complete unit, as it was written and intended to be read.

10.10 Textual Associations

From the overall perspective just taken of the specific text under investigation, continue to broaden your scope by examining how it fits into its broader context and perhaps how it thematically relates to biblical literature as a whole. Understanding how it fits into its immediate context is an extremely important part of the exegetical process, revealing how your defined unit slots into the greater tapestry of an author's or redactor's grand scheme. A good place to begin this analysis is by looking at keywords or themes that connect your text to what comes immediately before or after. Authors frequently use specific words to unite one textual unit to another, generating a sense of continuity and linkage.[18]

Care must also be taken to analyze the logical connections and relationships with the surrounding compositions. Consider how your text relates to what precedes it: Does it build on an argument for the book or major section? Does it exemplify a principle that has just been announced? Does it

---

18. At this point, the process deviates from the stricter realms of poetic interpretation, veering into the field of general hermeneutics and exegesis. Regarding a methodology for understanding and analyzing the broader contextual matters, refer to DeRouchie, *How to Understand and Apply the Old Testament*, 323–43; Duvall and Hays, *Grasping God's Word*; Kaiser, *Toward an Exegetical Theology*, 69–86; and Stuart, *Old Testament Exegesis*.

open a section or topic that is further developed in successive chapters? This type of analysis may ostensibly seem limited to larger prophetic texts, wisdom literature, and Lamentations, but it should also be applied to the Psalter. Assuming the book of Psalms was created from a combination of individual authors and later editors and redactors, it is reasonable to assume that it was not arranged haphazardly but that a logical rationale was employed in the psalms' sequencing.[19]

10.11 Commentary Consultation

At this stage in your investigation, it is important to engage in serious and intense consultation with commentaries and academic articles. Although it has been recommended to minimize consulting secondary sources until after your initial analysis, it is not realistic to expect students to entirely avoid scholarly sources during the entire research process. Methodologically, however, it is best to perform as much of the poetic analysis and translational work as possible independently. After compiling notes on your text—considering how it functions as a poetic unit and forming your own firm opinions—it is then appropriate to extensively engage with secondary academic opinion.

Following this process enables you, even as a student, to engage more efficiently with the scholarly community and dialogue with their ideas and thought processes. A common issue among students is the tendency to treat commentaries merely as sources of information to be collected and cited in research or seminar papers, producing, as noted earlier, a florilegium of old and new ideas about a poetic text rather than a cohesive analysis. By dedicating individual effort to reading and analyzing poetry, you can engage deeply with the views of commentators, understanding their strengths and weaknesses. More importantly, this process allows you to find your own voice, establishing and expressing your views concerning a piece of biblical poetry.

When selecting commentaries, it is essential to recognize the various types available, especially if you have access to a large library. Some

---

[19]. For more on this often-neglected aspect of psalms study, see Emanuel, *Intertextual Commentary*.

commentaries have a strong philological focus, concentrating on the Hebrew language and its relationship to other Semitic languages and texts.[20] Other commentaries adopt a historical perspective, comparing historical events mentioned in the text with known historical and textual traditions of the era. Additionally, homiletical commentaries emphasize practical application and are geared toward preaching and pulpit exposition.[21] These are just a few of the available options, and many commentaries combine two or more approaches. The key consideration at this point is to include a selection from each group of commentaries, assuming access and availability, to gain a comprehensive understanding of your selected text.

Finally, it should be noted that the poetic analysis of a specific text may not be the final destination for your research project. Your research may uncover a rare or even unique feature that requires further expository work. For instance, you might identify a biblical allusion that has not been previously noted by other scholars, or you may discover a special use for a poetic structure that warrants further expansion and analysis. It is essential to approach all poetic analyses with an open mind, treating each text as a new journey and a path to discovery.[22] This mindset will enable you to uncover novel insights and contribute meaningfully to the field of biblical studies.

Further Reading: Chisholm, *From Exegesis to Exposition*, 187–220; Fokkelman, *Reading Biblical Poetry*, 207–09; Muilenburg, "Form Criticism and Beyond"; Patton, Hebrew Discourse, 151–276; Weiss, *The Bible from Within*; Wendland, *Analyzing the Psalms*, 204–35.

---

20. Examples of this type of commentary are: Dahood, *Psalms* (who similarly emphasizes the linguistic connections between the Hebrew of the Psalter and other Semitic languages, especially Ugaritic); and Keil and Delitzsch, *Psalms* (who frequently compare the biblical texts to other Semitic languages in addition to the Greek).

21. See, for example, Henry and Manser, *The New Matthew Henry Commentary*.

22. In addition to commentaries, other books discussing poetics should be consulted. Fokkelman, *Reading Biblical Poetry*, 211–24, for example, could be consulted to compare stanza divisions. In this section of his book, he delimits all the major poetic texts in the Old Testament into stanzas. Similarly, many of the books mentioned throughout the present volume should be consulted, such as Berlin, *Biblical Parallelism*; Schökel, *A Manual*; Watson, *Classical Hebrew Poetry*; and Wendland, *Analyzing the Psalms*.

11

A Worked Example

Having discussed the linguistic, structural, and poetic aspects of biblical Hebrew poetry, it is now time to synthesize these elements by presenting a practical worked example of how the methodology outlined in the previous chapter can be used to analyze a poetic text from the Bible. The text selected for this exercise is Ps 54, chosen for its brevity and the relative scarcity of poetic analysis by scholars on this composition.

In the discussion of the psalm that follows, I have intentionally omitted the inclusion of commentaries and secondary articles on the psalm. My aim is to avoid overcomplicating the analysis with extensive side discussions on how my findings compare with those of other scholars. This methodological choice aligns with procedures outlined in the previous section, where it was advised to conduct an independent analysis prior to consulting scholarly literature. Once your own ideas are well established, you can then investigate how your research interacts with the broader academic discourse. Naturally, however, the use of basic tools such as concordances, lexicons, and theological dictionaries must be consulted to create a basic interpretation of the text.

Where applicable, I have annotated my discussion with footnotes to highlight connections between the analysis of the psalm and the topics covered in the earlier chapters of this primer. Because it is not possible to present the results of each individual stage of the exegetical method, the footnotes will further serve as a guide to connect various parts of the final analalytical work with the stages of the exegetical process. The discussion below consists of two main parts. The first part examines the psalm's overall structure, describing the individual stanzas and their interrelations. The second part offers a more detailed analysis of each stanza and verse, with a particular focus on the poetic features and how they convey meaning within the composition. We begin with an overview of the psalm's layout.

PSALM 54[1]

1a[2]	לַמְנַצֵּחַ בִּנְגִינֹת מַשְׂכִּיל לְדָוִד׃	To the choirmaster, on the *neginot*, a *maskil* of David.	1. Musical and literary context
2a	בְּבוֹא הַזִּיפִים וַיֹּאמְרוּ לְשָׁאוּל	When the Ziphites came and said to Saul,	
2b	הֲלֹא דָוִד מִסְתַּתֵּר עִמָּנוּ׃	"Is not David hiding himself with us?"	
3a	אֱלֹהִים בְּשִׁמְךָ הוֹשִׁיעֵנִי	O God, by your name deliver me,	2. Impassioned plea
3b	וּבִגְבוּרָתְךָ תְדִינֵנִי׃	And by your strength vindicate me.	
4a	אֱלֹהִים שְׁמַע תְּפִלָּתִי	O God, hear my prayer,	
4b	הַאֲזִינָה לְאִמְרֵי־פִי׃	Give ear to the words of my mouth.	
5a	כִּי זָרִים ׀ קָמוּ עָלַי	For arrogant men have risen up against me,	3. Complaint
5b	וְעָרִיצִים בִּקְשׁוּ נַפְשִׁי	And ruthless ones seek my life;	
5c	לֹא שָׂמוּ אֱלֹהִים לְנֶגְדָּם סֶלָה׃	They do not put God before them—Selah.	
6a	הִנֵּה אֱלֹהִים עֹזֵר לִי	Behold, God is my helper;	4. Declaration of Faith
6b	אֲדֹנָי בְּסֹמְכֵי נַפְשִׁי׃	My Lord is the sustainer of my soul.	

---

1. This text was selected (Stage 1) because it was relatively short and also self-contained, so there would be fewer problems determining the boundaries. Laying out the psalm in this way provides a simple overview of the composition's structure and allows each colon to be individually referenced. I have described each stanza in the right column. The working translation provided is my own, and it was written to preserve as much of the original word order and roots as possible. Often, the working translation will change as research and contemplation on the text continues.

2. Here I am adopting the Hebrew verse numbers. In this particular psalm, the English verse numbers differ.

7a	יָשׁוֹב הָרַע לְשֹׁרְרָי	May he return evil to my enemies;	5. Imprecation against enemies
7b	בַּאֲמִתְּךָ הַצְמִיתֵם׃	In your faithfulness, destroy them.	
8a	בִּנְדָבָה אֶזְבְּחָה־לָּךְ	(then) Freely I will sacrifice to you;	6. Assurance of deliverance
8b	אוֹדֶה שִּׁמְךָ יְהוָה	I will give thanks to your name, O Lord,	
8c	כִּי־טוֹב׃	for it is good.	
9a	כִּי מִכָּל־צָרָה הִצִּילָנִי	For he has delivered me from all my distress;	
9b	וּבְאֹיְבַי רָאֲתָה עֵינִי׃	And my eye(s) has (have) seen my enemies.[3]	

11.1 Structure [3]

Psalm 54 begins with an incipit containing two key elements. First, in v. 1a instructions are provided regarding the performance of the composition, along with a designation of the psalm type, identified as a *maskil* (which will be discussed further below). Second, in v. 2, a subtitle specifically links the composition to an event in the life of David, king of Israel. Following this introductory material, the main body of the psalm reflects a chiastic structure composed of five sections.

The opening section of the psalm comprises two verses, vv. 3–4, which

---

3. The present schematic results from reading the text, the initial translation, and stanza divisions (Stages 2, 3, and 5, respectively). Reading the text, Stage 2, does not yield visible results that could be presented as part of this schematic. What is not obvious here is Stage 8 of the process, the revision. The layout and translation above is not my first attempt at translating and dividing the psalm (and it may see further revisions in future). For example, in my initial evaluation of the text, vv. 7–9 formed a single stanza. Although some concordance (Stage 4) work was performed on this psalm, the results have not been presented here. By using a concordance, it is possible to search for the location of words like "Ziphites" to locate the source of the allusion made in the incipit.

are marked by relatively strict instances of synonymous parallelism, with each verse forming a distinct bicolon. These two verses set the tone for the remainder of the composition, introducing the psalmist's plea to God for deliverance. His plea is mirrored in the final two verses, the sixth stanza, where the psalmist expresses a deep assurance that God has heard and is responding to his supplication. Stanza six focuses on the theme of deliverance realized, as the psalmist vows to offer freewill sacrifices and offerings in gratitude for being delivered from all his distress. Linking the two outer sections is the word שֵׁם, "name." The psalmist invokes God's name in his plea for deliverance, and when salvation is realized, he pledges to offer thanks to that name. Repetition of שֵׁם, "name," underscores the connection between the plea and the expression of gratitude, framing the psalm's overarching theme of comfort amid persecution.

Stanza three (v. 5) corresponds with stanza five (v. 7), and together they form the second layer of the chiastic structure. Verse 5 provides a description of the psalmist's enemies, those from whom he seeks deliverance. A significant and crucial shift occurs in this second section with the change in verb forms—from the imperative verbs in the preceding verses to the three perfect forms in v. 5: קָמוּ, "[they] have risen up," בִּקְשׁוּ, "[they] seek," and שָׂמוּ, "they . . . put."[4] Together, these verbs reflect a transition from the psalmist's urgent pleas to a depiction of the threats he faces. The intensity of the psalmist's plight is conveyed through three cola in v. 5 that characterize the enemy rising up against him, and the primary reason for their hostility—they do not set God before them; they are godless. This rising up, self-ascension, of the enemies in v. 5 corresponds with their imagined downfall in v. 7. Connection between the two sections materializes through the terminology used for the enemies: זָרִים, "arrogant men," and עָרִיצִים, "ruthless ones," in v. 5, and שׁוֹרְרִים, "enemies," in v. 7. While these terms link the sections, the reversal of their fates cannot be ignored—the enemies who rise up in v. 5 are foreshadowed to fall in v. 7. In making this contrast, the psalmist emphasizes confidence in divine justice and the ultimate downfall of those who oppose God.

---

4. Verb forms can aid in the divisions of stanzas and strophes, so it is important to note them in the initial reading of the text.

At the center of the psalm lies v. 6, which serves as a profound declaration of the psalmist's trust and confidence in the Lord. The placement of this declaration at the heart of the psalm reflects not only the literary structure but also the psalmist's inner life. At the core of his being lies an unwavering hope and confidence in the Lord, who is his helper and sustainer of his soul. The shift in verb forms within this verse further distinguishes it from the surrounding verses, vv. 5 and 7. Uniquely in v. 6, the reader encounters two participles (the first singular and the second plural), עֹזֵר, "helper," and סֹמֵךְ, "sustainer," emphasizing the constancy and ever-present assistance that God provides to the supplicant. Through this grammatical choice the psalmist underscores the enduring nature of his reliance on God, marking v. 6 as the theological and emotional center of the psalm.

The overall chiastic structure of Ps 54 serves at least two purposes.[5] First, it generates a powerful sense of reversal in the psalmist's fortunes. The psalm begins with a desperate cry for help and deliverance, yet it concludes with an almost triumphant note of rejoicing, as the psalmist expresses confidence in offering sacrifices and proclaiming the goodness of God. Pivoting from distress to assurance is a well-known use of chiastic structures in Hebrew poetics. Second, the structure focuses the reader's attention on the central and most significant part of the psalm: the declaration in v. 6. This verse serves as the epicenter of the composition, emphasizing that everything in the psalmist's experience revolves around this profound declaration of trust. The transformation from despair to triumph is portrayed as being rooted in the psalmist's deep-seated conviction that, despite his circumstances, God is his constant helper. Underpinning the entire psalm is this central affirmation that reinforces the fact that the psalmist's confidence in God is the driving force behind the eventual reversal of his outlook.

Another related structural feature worth noting concerns the deliberate use of the name of the Lord throughout the psalm. From the beginning of the psalm proper, it is as if the psalmist guides the reader toward the epicenter of the chiasmus by invoking the word אֱלֹהִים, "God" in every verse leading up to v. 6. However, following the central declaration in v. 6, as a new sense

---

5. It is not enough to identify the poetic device used in the text. A comprehensive analysis must include a discussion of how it is used.

of hope and assurance is introduced, the references to God undergo a significant shift. The psalmist moves away from the more generic term אֱלֹהִים and adopts the more intimate term אֲדֹנָי, "my Lord."[6] This progression ultimately culminates in the invocation of the full divine name יְהוָה, YHWH (the Lord), the covenant name of Israel's God. Furthermore, this transition reflects the psalmist's deepening relationship with God, from a general plea to a personal and covenantal acknowledgment of the Lord's sovereignty.[7]

11.2 Poetic Analysis of Psalm 54

11.2.1 Superscription (vv. 1–2)

The opening verses of Ps 54, the superscription, establish the musical and proposed historical context for the composition. Musically, the song is addressed to a "choirmaster," indicating a supervisor responsible for the musical arrangement. In 2 Chr 2:2[1] the word מְנַצֵּחַ is used to describe overseers in charge of builders, making it logical that someone in a supervisory role over a musical arrangement would be described as a "choirmaster." The psalm is intended for performance on stringed instruments, referred to as a *neginot*. Because the term derives from the root נגן meaning "to play a stringed instrument," the noun form probably refers to a musical instrument, although its exact size, shape, and method of playing remains uncertain. The final detail provided in the superscription is that this composition is a Davidic *maskil*. Somewhat elusive, however, is the precise meaning or significance of the title *maskil*. The root שׂכל means "to be wise/prudent"[8] but it remains challenging to determine how, if at all, this meaning relates to the content of the psalm. Under the influence of the title, one might expect a wisdom psalm, a text offering instruction and guidance on how to live. Such a

---

6. This discovery resulted from Stage 2, reading the text and identifying common words and themes.

7. I am commenting here on the text that lies before us, notwithstanding any later revisions that may have occurred in this collection of psalms known as the Elohistic Psalter. For a thorough discussion of this psalter within a Psalter, see Hossfeld, "The Elohistic Psalter"; and Burnett, "The Elohistic Psalter."

8. It appears fourteen times in the psalms and links Ps 53 to Ps 55 in its immediate context. This observation serves as another example of the fruit yielded from Stage 4.

correspondence between the title and the contents is evident in Pss 32 and 78, where the content aligns with instructional themes. However, in other psalms bearing the title *maskil*, no immediately discernable correlation emerges.

Following the musical framework, the incipit advances to a proposed historical setting for the psalm. Regardless of the potential later date of this psalm segment, it is crucial to acknowledge that at some point in biblical history, an inspired author or redactor identified a connection between the psalm's contents and events in the life of David. The phrase בְּבוֹא הַזִּיפִים, "when the Ziphites came," establishes a direct literary correlation to events depicted in 1 Sam 26. In this narrative, the Ziphites, who were allied with Saul, betrayed David's whereabouts. They approached Saul, informing him that David was among them, concealing himself (מִסְתַּתֵּר) in the wilderness of Ziph, among the Ziphites.

11.2.2 Impassioned Plea[9] (vv. 3–4)

Verses 3 and 4 form the opening section of the psalm proper, as these verses begin to unveil the core sentiments of the psalmist. In these verses, the psalmist fervently implores God for deliverance. Both of these verses, which open the psalm, are set with internal half line parallelism, yielding two consecutive patterns of a—b // a′—b′.[10]

Structurally, the verses commence with an implicit vocative appeal to God. Although Hebrew lacks an explicit vocative form, the syntax and context clearly imply this interpretation. Following the vocative, the verses employ synonymous parallelism. The psalmist meticulously constructs the following sequence twice: prep.→n.→2ms suf.→impv.→1cs obj. suf. This pattern is mirrored in both cola, with the initial word invoking God omitted from the second colon. Furthermore, the precise parallelism creates a pronounced instance of repetition, as the essence of the plea is reiterated, underscoring the psalmist's desperation and urgency in seeking relief from his distressing predicament.

---

9. Attempting to summarize the contents of each stanza in this way can be useful for understanding the overall flow of the text. Such descriptions should remain short, and it is advisable to avoid using verbs to maintain a summary.

10. This observation resulted from Stage 6 of the process; however, I could also argue that it stemmed from Stage 8 because I only identified it after revising my work.

The psalmist seeks deliverance through two key concepts: God's name and his strength. In this context, the term שֵׁם, "name," signifies the power and authority inherent in the God of Israel. Parallel to this is the term גְּבוּרָה, "strength," which reinforces the notion of divine power at the disposal of an almighty God. It appears that the psalmist is drawing on a familiar word pair that also appears in Jer 16:21, "This time I will make them know / my power and my might; / and they shall know that my name is the LORD."[11] Here the psalmist evokes a similar sense of divine potency and authority, emphasizing the profound connection between God's name and his strength.

Two forms הוֹשִׁיעֵנִי, an imperative meaning "deliver me," followed by an imperfect carrying the same force, תְּדִינֵנִי, "vindicate me," convey a profound sense of urgency from the psalmist. Although these two expressions do not appear together elsewhere in biblical literature, their semantic overlap justifies their combined appearance here. The *hiphil* form of ישׁע frequently appears in personal laments, where it is used to request, beg, or plead for divine intervention (see Pss 22:22; 31:3; 44:17; and 59:3, for example). Complementing this is the *hiphil* imperfect of דִּין, "vindicate," which carries a dual nuance. The psalmist asks God to function as judge and adjudicate his case,[12] examining him both morally and legally to ascertain if there is any wrongdoing in his heart or actions. He believes that his righteousness will be recognized by God, leading to his deliverance from distress.[13] By invoking the term "vindicate," the psalmist further introduces a metaphorical legal framework for his plea, embedding his request within a context of divine judicial scrutiny.[14]

Overall, the opening plea establishes an emotive introduction to the psalmist's plight, reflecting both a personal request and a profound recognition that only divine assistance can provide relief. His plea implies that all

---

11. For this connection, see also Ps 106:8 and Jer 10:6.
12. To place a finer point on this idea, see the KJV, which reads, "Judge me by thy strength."
13. The possibility exists that the psalmist here is drawing upon an ancient understanding of God, recalling the words in Deuteronomy, "For the LORD will vindicate his people, / And will have compassion on his servants, / When he sees that their strength is gone" (Deut 32:36a). These words emphasize God's inherent nature to vindicate and subsequently deliver those in distress.
14. This verb frequently appears in contexts where the poor and oppressed seek justice, suggesting a legal setting (see Prov 31:9; Jer 5:28; 21:12; and 22:16). However, it may be overly presumptuous to assume a literal legal battle looms before the psalmist as Kraus suggests; see *Psalms 1–59*, 514.

human efforts have been exhausted, and it is now time for divine intervention to resolve the situation.

Verse 4 extends the plea with another direct address to God, employing a structure akin to the previous verse. It begins with a vocative invocation to God and demonstrates a relatively strict instance of both semantic and syntactic parallelism. In this verse, imperatives are used to amplify the sense of urgency. The parallelism follows a pattern of a—b // a′—b′ with elision of the vocative invocation and a ballast variant, "my mouth," inserted at the end of the verse. Additionally, the syntactic sequence follows an impv.→obj. sequencing. However, unlike the previous verse, the verb appears first in this bicolon.

The psalmist invokes the common word pair הַאֲזִין // שְׁמַע, "give ear // hear," to beseech God to listen to his words and his case. Joel further adopts this word pair to summon the attention of the elders and people of Judah, "Hear this, you elders; / give ear, all inhabitants of the land!" (Joel 1:2a ESV).[15] However, unlike Joel's address to the people, the psalmist directs this urgent call to God. The term הַאֲזִין, "give ear," is especially prominent in Hebrew poetry. Together these terms enhance the repetition and intensity of the psalmist's plea for divine attentiveness.

Complementing the verbs are the two terms that reflect the psalmist's posture before God. The word תְּפִלָּה denotes a request or prayer to God and is the more commonly used of the two, appearing in both prose and poetry. Within the context of laments, this word regularly represents a heartfelt plea of troubled soul, as attested by Ps 4:1, "Answer me when I call . . . be gracious to me and hear my prayer."[16] Its counterpart in the second colon, אִמְרֵי־פִי, "the words of my mouth," is a rarer form restricted to poetic contexts, and here it reflects the complaint the psalmist is about to speak.[17] Together, these terms delineate the content of the psalm, indicating that the psalmist's prayer and the utterances of his mouth are about to be presented.

The opening of the composition is unified through various poetic and

---

15. For further pairing see Ps 84:8; Jer 13:15; and Joel 1:2.
16. See also Pss 17:1 and 35:13.
17. Notice the detection of a poetic word here, which results from both Stages 4 and 7 of the analytical process. The concordance work reveals the locations of the expression, and then further investigation at the poetics level reveals that the form predominantly appears in poetry.

literary techniques. The repetition of the word "God" at the beginning of each verse creates cohesion within the stanza. Additionally, the consistent use of the first-person suffixes—"deliver *me*," "vindicate *me*," "*my* prayer," "the words of *my* mouth"—further ties the verses together. Each verse follows a similar structure, beginning with a vocative address and followed by a relatively strict form of synonymous parallelism. These elements collectively contribute to the structural and thematic unity of the opening section.

11.2.3 Complaint (v. 5)

Several features distinguish v. 5 from the previous verses. A notable change is the absence of the invocation of God; the term אֱלֹהִים, *'elohim*, no longer begins the verse. It appears that the shift indicates a change in focus or direction, as the psalmist transitions from calling for God's attention to detailing the nature of the complaint itself. Additionally, v. 5 exhibits a significant alteration in rhythm, with the number of words nearly doubling that of the previous verses. Increasing the word count may symbolize the disturbance and anxiety caused by the enemies confronting the petitioner. Furthermore, v. 5 departs from the imperative forms found in vv. 3–4, instead employing perfect forms to express its content, reflecting a shift in the psalmist's focus from God to the actions of the psalmist's antagonists.[18]

The verse is structured into three short cola, with the first two exhibiting synonymous parallelism in their syntax. With one exception, each of these cola follows a consistent sequence: pl. n.→pf. →(obj. + 1cs). Structuring the verse this way underscores the actions directed against the psalmist, highlighting how enemies rise up against him. In contrast, the third colon, 5c, diverges from this pattern by starting with a negative verb. Shifting the syntax in this way serves structurally and functionally, as it transitions from describing the enemies' actions to addressing their identity and the character flaw that drives their behavior.

The particle כִּי opens the second stanza[19] and serves a dual function. It can be interpreted causally, offering a reason for the heartfelt plea in the previous two verses, as in "give ear to the words of my mouth because. . . ."

---

18. Wherever possible, multiple factors should contribute toward an assessment of verse division.

19. This is by all estimations a small stanza; consequently, one may prefer to designate the division as a strophe, part of a larger stanza comprised of vv. 5–7.

However, its asseverative force should not be overlooked, where כִּי can convey the meaning of "truly" or "surely."[20] In this sense, it acts as an emphatic indicator, pointing toward the forthcoming words that express the psalmist's experience of oppression.

A parallel word pair: זָרִים "arrogant men" and עָרִיצִים "ruthless ones" portrays the psalmist's enemies. The first term, זָרִים, often suggests foreigners (as in Isa 1:7; 25:2; Jer 5:19) or those outside one's established community (as in Exod 30:33 and Lev 22:10) and is frequently associated with being an enemy or hostile force. Thus, translating זָרִים as "arrogant men" amplifies the sense of hostility and detachment, portraying them as a threatening, uncaring group.[21]

The second term עָרִיצִים, "ruthless ones," further intensifies this portrayal by emphasizing their lack of compassion and heartlessness. By adopting the parallel term, the poet reinforces the depiction of the psalmist's enemies as merciless oppressors. Elsewhere in Scripture, writers such as Isaiah adopt this word pair in similar contexts, see for example, Isa 29:5a, "But the multitude of your *enemies* will become like fine dust, / And the multitude of the *ruthless ones* like the chaff which blows away" (emphasis added).[22] This usage underscores the severity of the threat faced by the psalmist and the desperate nature of his plea.

Depicting a heightened state of anxiety, the psalmist claims the enemies קָמוּ עָלַי, "have risen up against me," indicating that they are preparing themselves to act against him. A similar expression appears in Deut 22:26b: "For just as a man *rises against* his neighbor and murders him, so is this case" (emphasis added).[23] Adopting this language underscores the severity of the threat,

---

20. For more on this less-cited use of the particle כִּי, see Muilenberg, "Linguistic and Rhetorical Usages of the Particle KI"; and Williams, *Williams' Hebrew Syntax*.

21. The interpretation of "arrogant men" additionally reflects an alternative reading of the word זָרִים to the morphologically similar form זֵדִים that appears in Ps 86:14, "arrogant ones have risen against me." According to the BHS apparatus, this same form is attested in Targums and some Hebrew manuscripts. Part of the initial translation work in Stage 3 involved establishing the text or determining the best reading of the text. A minor example of this need arises here because exegetes are forced to decide whether זָרִים is a better reading than the alternative זֵדִים. In this instance, there is no drastic difference the final interpretation, but in other cases, the variance in meaning may be significant and it falls on the exegete to decide which one is best.

22. See also Ezek 28:7 and 31:12 as a connected pair.

23. For this expression see also Deut 28:7; Josh 9:18; Judg 9:43; 20:5; and Ps 92:12. An implication of malicious intent often surfaces when the expression is used.

suggesting that the enemies' intent is to inflict serious harm on the psalmist. Specifically, they בִּקְשׁוּ נַפְשִׁי, "seek my life," a phrase conveying a direct and deadly threat. In prose, the definite direct object marker אֶת is typically used in this expression,[24] but in Hebrew poetry, lines are often contracted, leading to the omission of אֶת (as in Pss 40:15; 63:10; 86:14).[25] The word נֶפֶשׁ in the present context should be understood simply as "life," indicating the psalmist's enemies are seeking to kill him. However, due to the ambiguity inherent in the verse, and the literary style of Hebrew poetry, there is room to interpret this bicolon metaphorically, possibly as an instance of hyperbole. With this understanding, the threat could be understood more broadly, perhaps as coming from debt collectors or a disgruntled neighbor, where the outcome might not necessarily result in the psalmist's death. Adopting a more nuanced approach in this way allows for a broader understanding of the danger the psalmist faces, reflecting a situation that, while dire, might not be fatal.

The final part of the verse, 5c, diverges from the synonymous parallelism of the previous cola and pinpoints the core motivation of the psalmist's enemies: they do not put God before them. In essence, this means that they disregard the will and compassion of God, and as a result, they show no concern for the psalmist's life and well-being. Verse 5c reveals the third occurrence of the word אֱלֹהִים, "God," and its placement within the verse bears some significance. The psalmist appears to be drawing a contrast between his own attitude and that of his enemies. While the enemies' failure to put God before them drives their hostility, the psalmist's hope and reliance remains firmly rooted in God, keeping God always before him. This contrast is visually and thematically reinforced by the position of the word אֱלֹהִים at the beginning of vv. 3 and 4. Both verses open with an address to God, אֱלֹהִים, serving as a visual and rhetorical example of the psalmist putting God before him, in direct opposition to the attitude of his enemies. Therefore, the careful placement of אֱלֹהִים within these verses underscores the psalmist's devotion and reliance on God, contrasting starkly with the godlessness of those who seek his harm.

---

24. As in 1 Sam 20:1; 23:15; and 1Kgs 19:10.

25. This contraction of syntax is another feature mentioned in chapter 2. Uncovering anomalies such as this stem from concordance work, Stage 4, comparing the expression as it appears in a selected text to its usage elsewhere.

The second stanza advances the composition by providing the reader with more insight into the psalmist's predicament—enemies have risen against him, and these adversaries are described as people without regard for God. The terms used to describe the enemy are concrete, indicating that these foes are real and present, yet the wording is also deliberately vague. A later reader, looking back at the situation, remains without any clear understanding of the identity of these enemies or the specific actions they are taking to threaten the psalmist's life. While this ambiguity may be frustrating for a contemporary reader seeking a clearer glimpse into the historical realities of the psalmist's era, the psalmist's somewhat ambiguous description serves a purposeful function. Rather than focusing on the threat itself or on the motivations and attitudes of the enemies, the vague description of the adversaries allows the reader to concentrate on what lies within the psalmist—his hope and trust in God. By not dwelling on the details of the opposition, the psalmist shifts the emphasis away from the external dangers and instead highlights the inner spiritual strength and faith that sustains him. Adopting such an approach keeps the composition centered on the psalmist's relationship with God rather than on the particulars of his adversaries.[26]

11.2.4 Declaration of Faith (v. 6)

Verse 6 marks another palpable shift in topic, as the psalmist abruptly stops discussing his troubles and the threats posed by his enemies. The shift is further emphasized by a change in verb form, signaling the beginning of a new stanza. In this verse, the psalmist transitions from the perfect verbs used in the previous section to participles. Changing the verb forms at this juncture not only reflects the transition in subject matter but also introduces a new tone and focus to the composition, veering from the recounting of past events and threats to a different thematic emphasis, the source of his help.

---

26. The final word in v. 5 is *selah*, and its etymology, meaning, and poetic significance remains uncertain—despite its seventy-one appearances in the Psalter. It may serve as an interlude in the reciting of the psalm, a place where the congregation reciting it would prostrate themselves, or cymbals are sounded. Along these lines, it may also signify a short musical interlude, where the reciting of the psalm ceases and only instruments are heard. These usages imply that the word recognizes a logical pause in the composition's flow. Poetically, one could extrapolate that the appearance of *selah* in a poetic text signifies the logical end to a stanza or strophe. Although this possibility is real, it is advisable to seek further evidence when determining the boundaries of stanzas and strophes. For a further discussion on the potential meanings of *selah*, see Craigie and Tate, *Psalm 1–50*, 76; and Lyon, *Selah*.

Although v. 6 breaks from the previous section and introduces a new stanza, continuity is maintained through the repetition of אֱלֹהִים, "God," with the psalmist maintaining God at the forefront of his thoughts. This verse is also connected to the rest of the psalm through its use of synonymous parallelism. Semantically, אֱלֹהִים, "God," pairs with אֲדֹנָי, "my Lord," and the verbs עֹזֵר "helper" and סֹמֵךְ, "sustainer," correspond, creating an a—b // a′—b′ sequencing. The sequence is further mirrored in the syntax, where each line follows the structure n.—v. (participle) // n.—v. (participle). The parallelism here not only unifies the verse internally but also connects with the psalm's earlier parallel structures.[27]

The stanza begins with the interjection הִנֵּה, which, while often translated simply as "behold,"[28] serves as a crucial rhetorical device to shift the focus from the previous verse and redirect the reader's attention to what is truly important.[29] What follows is a powerful declaration of the psalmist's faith, altering the tone of the psalm. God is affirmed as the psalmist's helper, עֹזֵר לִי, the one who provides personal aid in times of need. This declaration resonates throughout the Psalter as a testament to God's personal and intimate care for those who call upon him. For instance, Ps 72:12 states, "For he will deliver the needy when he cries for help, / The afflicted also, and him who has no helper" (see also Pss 70:5; 86:17; and 118:7).

Colon B marks a significant transition in the psalm, particularly regarding the way God is addressed. Up until this point, including in the first colon, אֱלֹהִים, "God," has been the standard term used to represent the divine. However, in the second colon, God is addressed as אֲדֹנָי, "my Lord." Shifting the references to God not only emphasizes the transitional nature of the verse but also underscores a deepening or broadening of the psalmist's relationship with God. Changing the reference to the divine name marks a shift in tone and focus within the psalm, underscoring the verse's pivotal role

---

27. Another example highlighting the value of identifying the function of parallelism.

28. This is where the consultation of secondary sources comes into play early in the exegetical process. As I mentioned earlier, it is virtually impossible to perform all of the preliminary interpretive and translational work purely with a lexicon and concordance. Hebrew grammars, wordbooks, and even articles that specifically focus on individual words and their translation can make significant contributions to the initial work of translation.

29. Waltke and O'Connor, *Biblical Hebrew Syntax*, 330, suggest it draws special attention either to a certain statement as a whole or to a single word within a statement. In the present context, the former is undoubtedly true.

in advancing the psalmist's transition from despair to an expression of faith and trust in God.

God is further described as סֹמְכֵי נַפְשִׁי, "the sustainer[30] of my soul," complementing his role as "helper." The parallel between "sustainer" and "helper" is reminiscent of Isa 63:5a, where it is written, "I looked, and there was no one to *help*, / And I was astonished and there was no one to *uphold*" (emphasis added). The specific phrase "the sustainer of my soul" conveys the understanding that God is the one who preserves the psalmist's life. Interestingly, this particular expression does not appear elsewhere in biblical literature, suggesting that the psalmist may have coined it specifically to create a thematic link with v. 5. In that verse, the psalmist recalls how his enemies sought after his soul, נֶפֶשׁ, and in a powerful counterstatement, he now proclaims that God is the one who sustains his soul. Reinforcing the psalmist's confidence, this declaration asserts that he no longer needs to fear, knowing that the greater power—the one who truly holds his life—is on his side.

11.2.5 Imprecation Against Enemies (v. 7)

Verse 7 introduces a new section and thematically connects to v. 5. While verse 5 details how the psalmist's enemies seek his harm, v. 7 reflects a shift in perspective due to the psalmist's hope in God. Now, instead of focusing on his own plight, the psalmist turns the tables and seeks harm against his enemies. The phrase יָשׁוּב הָרַע ("may he [i.e., God] return evil") functions as an imprecation, expressing a desire for destruction to befall the psalmist's adversaries.[31] In a striking reversal of the earlier plea for deliverance, this

---

30. The Hebrew here is plural, thus it literally reads "the sustainers of my soul." Alternatively, with the *beth*, one could read the statement as "among the sustainers of my soul." The best understanding for this plural form here is that it serves as a corresponding plural of majesty (see Joüon, *A Grammar*, §136e). Thus, the plural form corresponds with the earlier plural of majesty אֲדֹנָי, "my Lord," in reference to God.

31. The *ketiv* form in this instance necessitates modification and may be interpreted in one of two ways. According to the *qere*, we can understand a reading of יָשִׁיב, which could represent "may evil return," but might also convey the sense of "may God return evil." Here I have chosen the latter interpretation, as it better captures the psalmist's profound longing for divine action against his adversaries. Rather than expressing a general hope that the consequences of the enemies' actions will naturally return against them, the psalmist appeals to God for a more direct and deliberate intervention. Regardless of the reading adopted, the meaning remains clear: The psalmist wishes ill upon his enemies, reciprocating the ill intent they devised against him. My final translation here resulted from the process of establishing the best reading of the text in Stage 3.

imprecation highlights the transformation in the psalmist's position from victim to one invoking retribution upon his enemies. The transition underscores the psalmist's confidence in God's justice and his belief that divine intervention will rectify the situation, ensuring that those who have sought his harm will face their own consequences.

Furthermore, v. 7 logically follows v. 6 as a potential consequence of God being the psalmist's helper. With God as his support, the psalmist feels empowered to request the destruction of his enemies. The relationship between the cola in this verse is less clearly defined compared to the synonymous parallelism observed earlier in the psalm. The verse presents a loose instance of syntactic chiasmus, with the structure v.—prep.phr. // prep. phr.—v. This somewhat ambiguous poetic structure introduces a degree of dissonance and incongruity with the more orderly elements of the psalm, possibly reflecting the inherent chaos and turmoil in the psalmist's request for retribution. Thus, the structural disarray reflects the tumultuous nature of the psalmist's desire for vengeance, contrasting with the otherwise orderly and focused nature of his earlier expressions of faith and hope.[32]

The request for evil to be returned upon an enemy, יָשִׁיב הָרַע, is a concept deeply rooted in biblical literature. A notable parallel surfaces with regard to Haman's punishment in Esth 9:25a, where it is written, "But when it came to the king's attention, he commanded by letter that his wicked [רָעָה] scheme, which he had devised against the Jews, should return [יָשׁוּב] on his own head." Haman's punishment reflects the principle of retributive justice, which in turn reflects the psalmist's desires that the harm intended by his enemies befall them instead. Such a sentiment hearkens back to v. 3, where the psalm begins in earnest by establishing a legal framework for the composition.[33] The psalmist's appeal for divine intervention against his enemies is framed within this judicial context, seeking a form of justice that mirrors the malicious intended actions of his adversaries.

The reference to the enemies in this verse undoubtedly connects to

---

32. It is impossible to know the psalmist's thought processes as he composed this composition. Consequently, what I propose here is admittedly laced with conjecture.

33. Corresponding with the legal framework, one can imagine the psalmist had Lev 24:19 in mind, "If a man injures his neighbor, just as he has done, so it shall be done to him." This idea of equal recompense sits at the heart of the psalmist's plea for retribution.

v. 5, where they are described as arrogant and ruthless. Encapsulating these descriptions in v. 5 is the simple yet potent term שׁוֹרְרִים, "enemies," summarizing the nature of those who oppose the psalmist. The desire for their wickedness to return upon them is a call for divine justice, ensuring that the evil they intended for the psalmist is visited upon them instead. This reinforces the legal and moral dimensions of the psalm, where the psalmist's plea for vindication is not merely personal but is rooted in a broader understanding of divine retribution and justice.

The phrase בַּאֲמִתֶּךָ, "in your faithfulness," serves as a vital interpretive key to understanding the psalmist's intentions. While he wishes for the destruction of those who persecute him and expresses a desire for retributive justice, he recognizes that the responsibility for such judgment lies beyond his reach. Instead, it is through God's faithfulness that any act of retribution is performed. The psalmist's invocation of God's faithfulness underscores his reliance on divine justice rather than human vengeance. Even amid his distress and suffering, he acknowledges that judgment—specifically the destruction of his enemies (הַצְמִיתָם)—must be executed by God, in accordance with his truth and faithfulness. This highlights the psalmist's understanding of divine justice as both righteous and inevitable, contrasting with any personal intent to seek revenge. It is crucial to recognize that the psalmist is not planning an attack against his enemies; rather, he is expressing his feelings, pain, and desires through prayer. By placing his trust in God's faithfulness, the psalmist relinquishes personal responsibility for retribution, entrusting the outcome to divine justice. His approach not only emphasizes his faith in God's moral order but also reflects a deep understanding of the nature of divine judgment—one that is carried out with righteousness and faithfulness rather than with human vindictiveness.

11.2.6 Assurance of Deliverance (vv. 8–9)

The final two verses, vv. 8–9, conclude the psalm with expressions of hope and restored order, despite the threats posed by the enemy. A stark contrast emerges between these final verses and the earlier portions of the psalm, which are marked by tones of urgency, pleas, and implied distress. From a position of desperation, the psalmist transitions to one of assurance, confidence, and profound gratitude. This transition highlights the transformative power of faith and trust in the divine. From fear to faith and from uncertainty to trust, the psalmist's journey illustrates the spiritual progression that leads to inner peace and confidence. The gratitude expressed in these final verses reflects the psalmist's conviction that God has heard his prayers and will respond favorably.

Verse 8 adopts a markedly different tone from the preceding verse. Shifting away from a focus on retribution and divine wrath against enemies, the psalmist instead announces what he will offer to God. Verse 8 serves as a pivotal moment in the psalm, introducing its final theme of gratitude. Structurally, the verse is organized with a syntactic terraced pattern, forming the sequence a—b // b'—c. The corresponding elements in this sequence are two cohortative verbs,[34] "I will sacrifice [אֶזְבְּחָה]" and "I will give thanks [אוֹדֶה]." The reintroduction of volitive verbs at this juncture effectively links the opening and concluding sections of the psalm. In the broader context of the Hebrew Bible, the roots of these two words are often connected in the expression "sacrifice of thanksgiving." Frequently, this phrase appears in Leviticus, where it describes the various sacrifices permitted for the Israelites. For instance, Lev 7:12a states, "If he offers it [a peace offering] by way of thanksgiving, then along with the sacrifice of thanksgiving [זֶבַח הַתּוֹדָה]."[35] Reinforcing the psalmist's intention to express gratitude through both word and deed, this connection highlights the shift from petition to praise.

As a result of his recognition in v. 6 of God as his helper, the psalmist vows to freely sacrifice, בִּנְדָבָה אֶזְבְּחָה, to the Lord. With these words, the psalmist signifies a rekindling of intimacy between himself and God, as reflected in the personal pronouns "I" and "you" used in the colon, underscoring the relational nature of the thanksgiving. Through his expression of hope, the psalmist anticipates a future moment of deliverance when he will be able to offer thanks for the salvation he expects to receive.

The second colon partially reiterates the sentiment of the first, deepening the psalmist's expression of gratitude that stems from his recognition of God as his helper. It specifies the type of sacrifice being offered, focusing on

---

34. Because the root ידה ends in *he*, we do not see an additional *he* added to indicate a cohortative. Cohortoative verbs may be either marked or unmarked with the additional of *he*. See Joüon, *A Grammar*, 790.

35. The expression also appears in Lev 22:29; Pss 50:14; and 107:22.

the expression אוֹדֶה, which conveys the idea of verbal thanksgiving. When paired with the corresponding verb אֲזַבְּחָה, it suggests that the psalmist intends to offer a thanksgiving sacrifice in response to his deliverance. This offering is made to שִׁמְךָ, "your name," honoring the Lord's name.[36] By invoking the term שֵׁם, "name," the psalmist creates a direct connection with v. 3, where the psalm's petition begins. The link emphasizes the relationship between divine deliverance and thanksgiving. The deliverance sought in v. 3 was accomplished "by your name," as the psalmist pleads, "O God, by your name deliver me." Correspondingly, the thanksgiving to be offered is directed to "your name," the very instrument of his salvation. Thematic repetition reinforces the psalmist's acknowledgment of the power of God's name in both delivering him from peril and receiving his gratitude.

Following the mention of "your name" comes the full revelation of the divine name יְהוָה, YHWH (the LORD), marking the first appearance of the Tetragrammaton in the psalm. Until this moment, the psalmist primarily relied on the term 'elohim to address God, with 'adonay appearing once in v. 6. It is only here, in v. 8, at a climactic point in the psalmist's experience, that the actual name of God is revealed. The gradual progression underscores the significance of the divine name, highlighting it as the ultimate source of the psalmist's salvation. By delaying the Tetragrammaton's revelation, the poet elevates a crucial moment, signifying that the psalmist's journey toward deliverance and thanksgiving reaches its peak in the recognition of the divine name, which holds the power to bring about his deliverance.

The final expression of the verse, כִּי טוֹב, "for it is good," in the immediate context modifies the name of the Lord, implying that his name is inherently good. His goodness serves as a fitting attribute to the first revelation of the divine name in the psalm. Furthermore, the clause can be interpreted as modifying the entire verse, encompassing both the act of thanksgiving and the psalmist's expression of gratitude. Anticipating deliverance, the psalmist thus affirms that it is good to give thanks to the name of the Lord. The phrases dual function underscores the psalmist's deep-seated

---

36. Normally, one expects to find a *lamed* prefixing the expression "your name," yielding the form לְשִׁמְךָ, as witnessed in Pss 92:9 and 115:1. However, its omission in the present psalm aligns the syntax with Isa 25:1 and Ps 99:3. Despite the preposition's omission, a feature common in poetry, it is still implied.

conviction that the divine name is both good in itself and worthy of praise and thanksgiving in response to anticipated salvation.

The particle כִּי serves as a crucial link between vv. 8 and 9, establishing a clear transition while offering further rationale for the psalmist's commitment to offering thanksgiving. This final verse of the psalm introduces a degree of dissonance in terms of verse structure, as it lacks a clear and discernible structural device that aligns with the previous verses. However, a loose reflection of syntactical parallelism can be detected, with the pattern of prep. phr.—v. // prep.phr.—v., followed by an additional noun at the end of the second colon. Subtle parallelism like this contributes to a sense of cohesion, even as the verse exhibits a less rigid structural form.

In summarizing the threats and dangers previously outlined in the psalm, the poet employs the expression כָּל־צָרָה, "all [my] distress." The term "distress" commonly appears in the Psalter as a broad depiction of various threats to the psalmists' lives.[37] In the present context, however, it seems to specifically refer to v. 5, where the psalmist's enemies rose up against him, seeking his life. Concerning the threats to his life, the perfect tense of the verb הִצִּילָנִי, "he has delivered me," suggests a past action,[38] implying that salvation has already been accomplished. However, the psalmist is not asserting that deliverance has already occurred in a literal sense; rather, by using the perfect tense, he expresses a profound assurance that his salvation is as certain as if it had already been realized.

The final expression of the psalm, due to its terse construction, presents no shortage of problems in its interpretation. A literal translation would read something like, "my eye has looked upon my enemies," but the precise meaning remains elusive. The phrase . . . רָאָה בְּ, "look upon," combined with the reference to enemies implies a nuance of triumph and victory over the adversary. This interpretation is supported by similar uses in other psalms, such as Ps 59:10[11], "My God in his lovingkindness will meet me; / God will let me look triumphantly upon my foes." Likewise, Ps 112:8 conveys this sense, declaring that the righteous man remains unshaken until he looks upon his

---

37. See for example Pss 22:12; 25:17; 31:8; 37:39; and 71:20.
38. Even though the EVs may differ regarding how they translate the tense of this word, either as a perfect or a simple past, they all reflect the action that has been completed in the past.

enemies in triumph (see also Ps 118:7).[39] These supporting texts suggest that the psalmist is expressing confidence in ultimate victory over his enemies, now he stands in a position to look down upon them, further emphasizing the theme of assurance that runs throughout the psalm.

In this verse the psalmist revisits the negative aspects of his experiences. His צָרָה, "distress," and his אֹיְבִים, "enemies," who were characterized as "arrogant men" and "ruthless ones" in v. 5, are recalled. However, these adversities no longer pose threats but are now elements over which the psalmist has achieved deliverance. Because the Lord has delivered him from all his enemies, the psalmist is granted a reprieve and potentially even a sense of satisfaction as he can now look down upon his enemies in triumph. The link between the cola in this verse reflects a cause-and-effect relationship: because the Lord has provided deliverance, the psalmist can now triumphantly gaze upon his enemies.

11.2.7 Summary

This brief discussion of poetics of Ps 54 is intended as an illustrative example rather than an exhaustive analysis, demonstrating the potential outcomes of applying the methodological guidelines outlined in the previous chapter. Psalm 54 appears to rely assiduously on structural features to communicate its message to the reader. The most prominent of these is the overall chiastic structure, a pivot pattern that enhances the sense of reversal within the composition. Regarding its progression, the composition guides the reader from an initial depiction of despair and hopelessness—where fear and uncertainty about the future overwhelm the psalmist—to a concluding state of peace and contentment. This transition is not due to the immediate defeat of the psalmist's enemies but rather flows from his confidence in God's ability to handle them. The chiastic structure effectively facilitates this shift from fear to contentment.

---

39. Translations of this colon across various English versions exhibit a notable degree of variance. For example, "and my eyes have looked in triumph on my foes" (NIV); "And my eye has looked with *satisfaction* upon my enemies" (NASB); "and helped me triumph over my enemies" (NLT); "and my eyes look down on my foes" (NABRE). Despite the differences, each translation conveys the sentiment of the psalmist overcoming his enemies with the Lord's help.

Another dominant structural feature of the psalm is synonymous parallelism, most clearly represented in vv. 3–5 and 8. These structural elements are the primary building blocks of the psalm's poetics, while other features such as anthropomorphism, metaphor, or simile remain absent. Hyperbole is perhaps the most notable, albeit subtle, poetic device present. In verse 7, the psalmist's imprecation against his enemies might be interpreted as a slight exaggeration, though it remains uncertain whether he literally wished for their destruction.

Overall, the discussion above serves as a prelude to further analysis and research of Ps 54. For example, engagement with scholarly books and articles forms a natural continuation of the analytical process. From a poetics standpoint, one could catalog all poetic features according to the list provided in this volume and apply a similar analysis to another psalm, laying the groundwork for a comparative study of the poetic intensity across psalms. Alternatively, further exploration of allusion might be fruitful, particularly in examining the psalm's incipit, which places the composition's words in the mouth of David when he was betrayed by the Ziphites. Additionally, a comparative study of Ps 54 with its neighboring psalms, focusing on thematic and content relationships, could be pursued. The potential stanza relationships discussed in the previous chapter offer a framework for analyzing such thematic connections. Ultimately, this initial poetic analysis positions exegetes at a crossroads, from which they may choose a direction for further study according to their specific needs.

11.3 Final Thoughts

As we approach the conclusion of our exploration of Hebrew poetry, it is appropriate to pause and offer some final reflections, thereby bringing our discussion full circle. Returning to the travel metaphor introduced at the outset, our journey has now reached its culmination. This juncture invites us to reflect on the significant insights and discoveries we have discussed along the way—key aspects that may have been overshadowed by the intricate analyses and myriad examples presented throughout this volume. Such reflection allows us to appreciate the broader landscape of Hebrew poetry and to understand how the present volume contributes to that expanse, ensuring that the essential points stand out amidst the richness of our detailed study.

The present volume was composed with the intent of encouraging and supporting students and laypeople who have long harbored a deep-seated desire to learn more about biblical poetry but have lacked either the courage or the resources to undertake such a study. In my numerous discussions with students, instructors, and laypeople, I have often witnessed a sense of apprehension, even dread, when I mention my investment in the field of biblical poetry. It appears to many as an impenetrable cloud, accessible only to the brave and the initiated. While this book may not grant the casual reader instant mastery over the topics covered, my hope is that it offers a window into that cloud, as well as a map to help them begin navigating this invigorating field of research.

Another motivation for writing this book is to dispel some of the prevalent myths surrounding biblical poetry. I recall advising a student several years ago who expressed surprise when I suggested a poetic analysis of a text they had chosen for exegesis. Their response revealed a limited understanding: they believed that biblical poetry was solely defined by the three types of parallelism—synonymous, antithetical, and synthetic—described by Robert Lowth's seminal work written over two hundred years ago. While Lowth's contributions were indeed groundbreaking, the field of biblical poetry has since seen substantial research and advancement. Unfortunately, many popular Bible dictionaries and textbooks continue to perpetuate these three broad categories as the entirety of poetic form in the Bible. This has been corroborated by frequent classroom discussions where students cite these three structures as the sum total of Hebrew poetry. My hope is that this volume will clearly demonstrate that biblical poetry is far more nuanced, dynamic, and complex than the model established by Lowth.

Furthermore, students and aspiring exegetes will likely find that many poetic features, despite being discussed individually, exhibit significant overlap, and the boundaries between various forms are not always as distinct as the discussions in this volume might suggest. For example, while a verse structured with chiasmus might also contain a merism, there are subtler overlaps that could complicate the identification of poetic features within a verse. Consider the metaphor, for example, which often serves as a vehicle for expressing hyperbole. In such instances, the exegete must be meticulous in identifying both poetic elements rather than simply defaulting to the first feature that comes to mind. This nuanced approach ensures a more accurate and comprehensive analysis of the poetry in question.

It is important to recognize that engaging with, appreciating, and analyzing biblical poetry is an ongoing process rather than a pursuit with a definitive endpoint. There is no final graduation point where one has exhausted every technique or applied it to every relevant passage in the Bible. As students progress in their studies, they will find that their methods of analyzing poetry evolve and deepen in ways they might not have anticipated. The more one learns, the more one's understanding and interpretation of the field will mature. From my own research experiences, I have found that the richness of biblical poetry is nearly inexhaustible. Revisiting a text several years after analyzing it and writing about it often reveals new insights and nuances. I might uncover deeper layers of meaning, observe different poetic features, or revisit images with a more refined perspective. The key takeaway is that students need not worry about exhausting all possibilities or interpretations of a given text. There is always more to discover and explore.

Finally, I wish to emphasize that this volume does not purport to be the definitive work on biblical poetry—indeed, no single volume could claim such a title. Rather, the aim of this book has been to serve as a window, a gateway, or a steppingstone into the rich and complex world of biblical poetry. Beyond the scope of this book, there remains a vast and intricate forest ripe for further exploration. There is much more to be said about various topics such as metaphor theory, the relationships between word pairs, diachronic developments in biblical poetry, classifications of hyperbole, and many other poetic attributes. My hope is that, after engaging with this volume, students and prospective exegetes will acquire a solid foundation for understanding the complexities of the poetic features discussed and how they fit into the broader landscape of Hebrew poetics. Although our journey has now come to an end, it is my sincere hope that it serves as the starting point for many further explorations and discoveries in the field of biblical Hebrew poetry.

APPENDIX

1

Meter

The astute reader of the present volume will have noticed my omission of what some might describe as an essential aspect of Hebrew poetry: the question of meter. Surely, if the ancient classical Greek poets wrote poetry under the framework of established metrical principles, it seems logical to assume that the Hebrew poets did the same. However, I believe that the transition from this reasonable assumption to a practical and definitive application is fraught with significant and insurmountable challenges.

One of the primary difficulties in studying Hebrew poetic meter is the absence of any ancient text that discusses a system of meter. Neither ancient Hebrew inscriptions nor texts from the library at Qumran provide any indication of how Hebrew poetry was systematically constructed from a metrical perspective.

Another challenge in establishing a metrical system relates to the chronological development of the Hebrew language and Hebrew poetry. Purely from a written perspective, the rules for writing poetry likely evolved from the earliest period, ca. 900 BCE to the later biblical period, 400 BCE.[1] During this time, the question of scribal developments—mistakes from repeated scribal copying, such as haplography, metathesis, and dittography—must be considered. Additionally, changes in spelling and vowel formation over five centuries further complicate the preservation of any consistent metrical system. This issue is compounded by systematic additions to biblical poetry, which include verbal explanations and updates to words that may have fallen out of use. Moreover, changes in pronunciation over time further

---

1. This is a conservative estimate, ignoring the possibility of oral composition. Hebrew poetry probably originated orally, well before it adopted a fixed written form.

complicate the task. The way a poetic text was pronounced at its inception likely differs from how it was pronounced five or six centuries later. Such changes can significantly impact a metrical system that relies on accents and syllable counts. This phenomenon is analogous to the shifts in pronunciation observed in the English language over the past four hundred years, which have similarly affected linguistic metrics and rhythm.

For the most part, contemporary scholars acknowledge the difficulties in establishing a metrical system for Hebrew poetry. Generally, there are two nuanced positions prevalent in modern scholarship. The first position argues that given the aforementioned issues, it is unlikely that a metrical system was used in Hebrew poetry. Ernst Wendland asserts, "For centuries biblical scholars have debated whether Hebrew poetry has meter or not. Most likely it did not, not in the strict sense of a predictable pattern of stresses."[2] Similarly, Matthew Patton contends, "Hebrew poetry does not use rhyme or meter as a structuring device."[3] Tremper Longman's critique of two proposed metrical systems for Hebrew poetry—Stuart, *Early Hebrew Meter*; and Kuryłowicz, *Semitic Grammar*—offers a thorough dismissal of the possibility of an accentual or syllabic system of meter. He identifies several insurmountable complications with these systems, leading him to conclude that no single system can reliably account for all Hebrew poetry.[4]

Other scholars, however, remain open to the idea of an ancient metrical system adopted by ancient Hebrew poets that has now been lost to us. Notable representatives of this view include The Word Biblical Commentary—all three volumes on the Psalms, Craigie and Tate, *Psalms 1–50*; Craigie, *Psalms 51–100*; and Allen, *Psalms 101–150*—and Hans-Joachim Kraus, *Psalm 1–59*. Although the volumes acknowledge the difficulties of reconstructing any ancient system of meter for poetry, they subsequently adopt two different systems of metrical analysis for the psalms, which they use throughout their commentaries. Additionally, the use of meter frequently appears in *BHS* to attempt the reconstruction of the original Hebrew text. However, many of

---

2. See Wendland, *Analyzing the Psalms*, 173

3. See Patton, *Basics of Hebrew Discourse*, 164.

4. See Longman, "A Critique of Two Recent Metrical Systems"; and in his later book he states more emphatically, "I believe it best ... to ignore any interpretation based on meter" (*How to Read the Psalms*, 108).

these meter-based alterations result in radical and conjectural changes to the MT without sufficient support from other textual witnesses.[5]

Finally, Samuel Goh, who analyzes major theories of meter, concludes his examination with the question of whether Hebrew poetry was indeed metrical and what such a system might have looked like. His ultimate assessment is: "Unfortunately, these seemingly simple questions have led to a protracted, complicated process of searching and inconclusive arguments. In sum, after centuries of searching, the Hebrew metrical system remains elusive."[6]

Given the uncertainty surrounding the existence of a metrical system in ancient Hebrew poetry, coupled with the lack of consensus on which metrical system to apply in contemporary analysis, I have chosen to exclude detailed discussions of meter from the main body of this volume. While an understanding of meter may be prevalent in scholarly commentaries, I do not consider it essential for the exegetical process. Therefore, I have addressed the topic briefly in this appendix. In doing so, my intention is to ensure that students are aware of the issue without allowing it to overshadow the primary exegetical focus.

---

[5]. Another problem with the assumption of a defined and strict metrical system is that it seduces scholars into "correcting" the MT according to their theoretical metrical system. In the words of Goh, "practitioners of the accentual system are at liberty to emend the MT for reasons they consider valid" (*Hebrew Poetry*, 65).

[6]. See Goh, *Hebrew Poetry*, 59–76. He provides an excellent overview of the struggles in determining a metrical system for ancient Hebrew.

APPENDIX 2

Wisdom Poetry

Throughout the present volume, I have for the most part treated all poetry uniformly, whether from the Psalms, Isaiah, Song of Songs, or other texts, including the short segments of poetry inserted within narrative texts. The reality is, however, that not all poetry in the Bible is identical, and subtle distinctions exist among different categories Ancient poetry—such as the poetry of Gen 49, Exod 5, and Judg 5—differs from later poetry like Pss 1, 105, and 107. Similarly, the poetry in prophetic texts such as Ezekiel, Joel, and Obadiah differs from much of the poetry in the Psalter. While an exhaustive discussion of all poetic forms is beyond the scope of this volume, one substratum of poetry deserves a little more attention: wisdom poetry. This category—encompassing Proverbs, Ecclesiastes, and Job[1]—presents various idiosyncratic features to which second-year students of Hebrew should be alerted. Typically, Hebrew grammars do not fully engage with wisdom poetry, so it is worthwhile to highlight a few key aspects here.

As second-year students begin to tackle wisdom literature, they should take note of the following traits and potential challenges that this genre presents. One challenge concerns the vocabulary that frequently arises in the wisdom corpus. The table below presents the distribution of words that are more closely related to sapiential texts:

---

1. The book of Job probably warrants categorization on its own. Furthermore, certain psalms could be included in this discussion, but I have omitted them for the sake of simplicity, and due to the likelihood that these psalms derive from wisdom traditions. For this corpus, see, Hurvitz, "Wisdom Vocabulary," esp. 43.

WORDS DESCRIBING FOOLS AND FOOLISHNESS

		Wisdom Corpus	Outside Wisdom Corpus
כְּסִיל	Stupid, insolent	67	3
אֱוִיל	Fool, foolish	21	5
פֶּתִי	A naive person	14	4
נָבָל	Foolish (intellectually and morally)	10	8

WORDS DESCRIBING THE WISE AND WISDOM

חָכְמָה	Wisdom, skill, shrewdness	85	54
בִּינָה	Understanding	23	15
מוּסָר	Discipline, instruction	34	16
דַּעַת	Knowledge	57	33
שֵׂכֶל/שֶׂכֶל	Insight, understanding, discernment	7[2]	9

Regarding the distribution of the words in the table above, it is important to note that these terms do not appear exclusively within the wisdom corpus. However, the authors of wisdom literature exhibit a distinct predilection for these words, more so than other biblical authors. In addition to the terms for the wise and wisdom mentioned above, other words also show a higher frequency in wisdom literature. For instance, הוֹן, meaning "wealth" or "property," appears eighteen times within the wisdom corpus—specifically in Proverbs—and only eight times outside of it.[3] Another expression worth

---

2. Here the percentage of times this word appears in wisdom literature is greater than the percentage of times it appears in other books. In its nine appearances outside of the wisdom corpus it is distributed among five other books: Samuel, Daniel, Ezra, Nehemiah, and Chronicles.

3. Ezekiel 4x, Psalms 3x, and Song of Songs 1x.

noting is סָר מֵרָע, meaning "to flee from evil," which occurs nine times in the wisdom corpus and only four times outside of it.[4]

Another challenge students may encounter when interpreting wisdom poetry is the terse nature of the cola, particularly the frequent omission of verbs. This characteristic can make the interpretation of certain passages more complex. Consider the following syntactically literal rendering from Prov 11:1:

מֹאזְנֵי	מִרְמָה	תּוֹעֲבַת	יְהוָה	וְאֶבֶן	שְׁלֵמָה	רְצוֹנוֹ
a balance	deceit	abomination	the Lord	but a weight	whole/just	his delight
n.	n.	n.	prop.n.	conj.+n.	adj.	n.+suf.

In essence, this verse is composed of five common nouns, a proper noun, and an adjective. The verse presents this list of substantives to the reader without explicitly stating the relationship between them, leaving the meaning to be discerned through careful reflection. A possibility exists that this arrangement reflects a deliberate strategy employed by the authors of wisdom literature. Such verses do not readily surrender their meaning; instead, they require the reader to actively seek out the wisdom contained within. Interpretation thus becomes the responsibility of those who possess understanding, echoing the sentiment found in Prov 14:33: "Wisdom rests in the heart of one who has understanding." This kind of verbless construction is not an isolated instance but rather a common feature throughout the book of Proverbs.[5] The absence of verbs in these terse statements invites readers to engage more deeply with the text, encouraging a process of contemplation and interpretation that is integral to the wisdom tradition.

---

4. It also appears once in Isaiah and three times in the Psalter, within wisdom psalms. See Hurvitz, "Wisdom Vocabulary," for this expression's distribution and its relevance for determining wisdom psalms.

5. See, for example, Prov 15:15, 16, 19; 16:1; 20:10; 26:1, 7; etc. In addition to the verbless clauses, one often finds individual proverbs ordered with consecutive nouns or nominal forms with a singular imperfect verb located at the end of the clause, as seen in Prov 16:15; 20:5; 21:27; 23:11, 18; 27:15. This sequencing demands a little more patience, and possibly wisdom, from to reader to figure out the correct reading and interpretation of the text.

Together with the clustering of verbless clauses, students should be aware of a persistent use of antithetical parallelism in wisdom literature. In these cases, the Hebrew *waw* frequently appears at the beginning of the second colon and is typically translated "but." While we have already discussed this specific type of colon relationship, one further example from Prov 12:4 may serve to reinforce the concept:

אֵשֶׁת־חַיִל עֲטֶרֶת בַּעְלָהּ	An excellent wife is the crown of her husband,
וּכְרָקָב בְּעַצְמוֹתָיו מְבִישָׁה׃	but she who shames him is like rottenness in his bones.

In this example the primary point of comparison concerns the "excellent wife" and the wife who brings shame on her husband. The two statements create an abrupt and memorable contrast, effectively highlighted by the *waw* conjunction, translated as "but."[6] This conjunction not only separates the two ideas but also intensifies the opposition between them, reinforcing the antithetical parallelism typical of wisdom literature.

Another expression that appears frequently in wisdom literature can be called a "better-than" saying, exemplified by Prov 12:9:

טוֹב נִקְלֶה וְעֶבֶד לוֹ	Better is he who is lowly and has a servant
מִמִּתְכַּבֵּד וַחֲסַר־לָחֶם	than he who honors himself and lacks bread.

These expressions are typically identified by the syntactic sequence of טוֹב ... מִן ..., translated as "better ... than ...," and they compare two situations, qualities, or choices to emphasize the superiority of one over the other. This form is used to convey practical wisdom, guiding the reader toward better moral or ethical decisions by illustrating the preferable option. Another example appears in Eccl 6:9a:

טוֹב מַרְאֵה עֵינַיִם מֵהֲלָךְ־נָפֶשׁ	What the eyes see is better than what the soul desires. (NASB)

---

6. Obviously, numerous examples in wisdom literature exist, including Prov 3:35; 10:1, 3, 4; 11:15; 12:6; Eccl 9:16, 18; 10:2, etc.

To be sure, the vocabulary and expressions mentioned in this brief appendix are not exclusive to the wisdom corpus.[7] However, they merit attention because of their frequent occurrence in wisdom literature.[8] Consequently, first-time exegetes approaching this genre should prepare themselves with the fundamental aspects outlined above. Doing so will facilitate the transition from studying introductory grammar to engaging with more sophisticated literary forms, ultimately enabling a more accurate understanding and ability to translate this body of literature.[9]

---

[7]. Number parallelism also belongs to this list, cf. Job 5:19; Prov 6:16; 30:15, 18, 21.

[8]. See also, for example, Prov 8:11; 16:8, 19, 32; 19:1, 22; 22:1; 27:5; Eccl 5:5; 6:9; 7:1, 5; and 9:4 (among other places).

[9]. For more details on the characteristics of wisdom literature, consult Driver's old but useful work, *An Introduction to the Literature of the Old Testament*, 392–407.

Bibliography

Allen, Leslie C. *Psalms 101–50*. WBC 21. Nashville: Thomas Nelson, 2002.
Alsene-Parker, Megan. "The ABCs of Hebrew Acrostic Poems." *Tyndale House's Ink Magazine* (2023): 34–35.
Alter, Robert. *The Art of Biblical Poetry*. New York: Basic Books, 1985.
———. *The Book of Psalms: A Translation with Commentary*. New York: Norton, 2007.
Assis, Elie. "The Alphabetic Acrostic in the Book of Lamentations." *CBQ* 69 (2007): 710–24.
Avishur, Yitsḥak. *Stylistic Studies of Word-Pairs in Biblical and Ancient Semitic Literatures*. AOAT. Neukirchen-Vluyn: Neukirchener Verlag, 1984.
Berlin, Adele. *The Dynamics of Biblical Paralellism*. Rev. and enl. ed. The Biblical Resource Series. Grand Rapids: Eerdmans, 2008.
———. "Parallelism." *ABD* 5:154–62.
———. "Motif and Creativity in Biblical Poetry." *Prooftexts* 3 (1983): 231–41.
Bloch, Yigal, "The Third-Person Masculine Plural Suffix Pronoun -mw and Its Implications for Dating of Biblical Hebrew." Pages 147–70 in *Diachrony in Biblical Hebrew*. Edited by Cynthia L. Miller-Naudé and Ziony Zevit. LSAWS 18. Winona Lake, IN: Eisenbrauns, 2012.
Brown, Francis, S. R. Driver, and Charles A. Briggs. *A Hebrew and English Lexicon of the Old Testament*. Peabody, MA. Hendrickson, 1994.
Brueggemann, Walter, and W. H. Bellinger, Jr. *Psalms*. New Cambridge Bible Commentary. New York: Cambridge University Press, 2014.
Buber, Martin M. "Keyword in the Pentateuchal Stories." Pages 284–99 in *The Method of the Bible*. Jerusalem: Mosad Bialik, 1978. [Hebrew]
Bullinger, E. W. *Figures of Speech Used in the Bible*. London: Eyre & Spottiswoode, 1898. Repr., Grand Rapids: Baker Books, 2004.
Burnett, Joel S. "The Elohistic Psalter: History and Theology." Pages 133–54 in

The Psalter as Witness: Theology, Poetry, and Genre: Proceedings from the Baylor University-University of Bonn Symposium on the Psalter. Edited by W. Dennis Tucker, Jr. and W. H. Bellinger, Jr. Waco, TX: Baylor University Press, 2017.

Carasik, Michael. "Janus Parallelism in Job 1:20." *VT* 66 (2016): 149–54.

Casanowicz, Immanuel M. "Paronomasia in the Old Testament." *JBL* 12 (1893): 105–67.

Ceresko, Anthony R. "The Function of Chiasmus in Hebrew Poetry." *CBQ* 40 (1978): 1–10.

———. "Janus Parallelism in Amos's 'Oracles against the Nations' (Amos 1:3–2:16)." *JBL* 113 (1994): 485–90.

———. "A Poetic Analysis of Ps 105, with Attention to Its Use of Irony." *Bib* 64 (1983): 20–46.

———. *Psalmists and Sages: Studies in Old Testament Poetry and Religion*. Indian Theological Studies Supplements 2. Bangalore: St. Peter's Pontifical Institute, 1994.

Chisholm, Robert B. *From Exegesis to Exposition: A Practical Guide to Using Biblical Hebrew*. Grand Rapids: Baker Academic, 1998.

Collins, C. John. "The Wayyiqtol as 'Pluperfect': When and Why." *TynBul* 46, (1995): 117–40.

Collins, Terence. *Line-Forms in Hebrew Poetry: A Grammatical Approach to the Stylistic Study of the Hebrew Prophets*. Studia Pohl. Series Maior. Rome: Biblical Institute Press, 1978.

Cook, John A., Robert D. Holmstedt, and Philip John Williams. *Intermediate Biblical Hebrew: An Illustrated Grammar*. Learning Biblical Hebrew. Grand Rapids: Baker Academic, 2020.

Craigie, Peter and Marvin E. Tate. *Psalms 1–50*. 2nd ed. WBC 19. Nashville: Thomas Nelson, 2004.

Cuddon, J. A. *A Dictionary of Literary Terms and Literary Theory*. 5th ed. Chichester: Wiley-Blackwell, 2013.

Dahood, Mitchell J. *Psalms*. The Anchor Bible. 3 vols. Garden City, NY: Doubleday, 1966.

Dell, Katharine J., and Tova L. Forti. "'Two Are Better Than One': The Conceptual and Thematic Use of Numbers in Ecclesiastes." *HUCA* 94 (2023): 1–20.

DeRouchie, Jason Shane. *How to Understand and Apply the Old Testament: Twelve Steps from Exegesis to Theology*. Phillipsburg, NJ: P&R, 2017.

Dobs-Allsopp, F. W. "The Enjambing Line in Lamentations: A Taxonomy (Part 1)." *ZAW* 113 (2001): 219–39.

Doron, Pinchas "Paronomasia in the Prophecies to the Nations." *HS* 20/21 (1979–1980): 36–43.

Driver, Samuel R. *An Introduction to the Literature of the Old Testament*. International Theological Library. 9th ed. Edinburgh: T&T Clark, 1891. Repr., Gloucester, Mass: Peter Smith, 1972.

Duvall, J. Scott, and J. Daniel Hays. *Grasping God's Word: A Hands-on Approach to Reading, Interpreting, and Applying the Bible*. 2nd ed. Grand Rapids: Zondervan Academic, 2005.

Eakins, J. Kenneth. "Anthropomorphisms in Isaiah 40–55." *HS* 20/21 (1979–1980): 47–50.

Elliger, K. and Rudolph W. eds. *Biblia Hebraica Stuttgartensia*. Stuttgart: Deutsche Bibelgesellschaft, 1997.

Emanuel, David. *From Bards to Biblical Exegetes: A Close Reading and Intertextual Analysis of Selected Exodus Psalms*. Eugene, OR: Pickwick, 2012.

———. *An Intertextual Commentary to the Psalter: Juxtaposition and Allusion in Book I*. Eugene, OR: Pickwick, 2022.

———. "An Unrecognized Voice: Intra-Textual and Intertextual Perspectives on Psalm 81." *HS* 50 (2009): 85–120.

———. "The Elevation of God in Psalm 105." Pages 49–64 in *Inner Biblical Allusion in the Poetry of Wisdom and Psalms*. Edited by Mark J. Boda, Kevin Chau, and Beth Laneel Tanner. LHBOTS 659. London: T&T Clark, 2019.

Floyd, Michael H. "The Chimerical Acrostic of Nahum 1:2–10." *JBL* 113 (1994): 421–37.

Fokkelman, J. P. *Reading Biblical Poetry: An Introductory Guide*. Louisville: Westminster John Knox, 2001.

Freedman, David Noel. "Acrostic Poems in the Hebrew Bible: Alphabetic and Otherwise." *CBQ* 48 (1986): 408–31.

Freedman, David Noel, ed. *The Yale Anchor Bible Dictionary*. 6 vols. New York: Doubleday, 1992.

Freedman, David N. "Pottery, Poetry, and Prophecy: An Essay on Biblical Poetry." *JBL* 96/1 (1977): 5–26.

Futato, Mark David. *Basics of Hebrew Accents*. Grand Rapids: Zondervan Academic, 2020.

Gaines, Jason M. H. *The Poetic Priestly Source*. Minneapolis: Fortress, 2015.

Gesenius, Wilhelm. *Gesenius' Hebrew Grammar*. Edited by Emil Kautzsch. Translated by A. E. Cowley. 2nd ed. Oxford: Clarendon, 1910.

Giffone, Benjamin D. "A 'Perfect' Poem: The Use of the Qatal Verbal Form in the Biblical Acrostics." *HSS* 51 (2010): 49–72.

Goh, Samuel T. S. *The Basics of Hebrew Poetry: Theory and Practice*. Eugene, OR: Cascade, 2017.

Gordis, Robert. "Rhetorical Use of Interrogative Questions in Biblical Hebrew." *AJSL* 49 (1932–33): 221–127.

Greenstein, Edward L. "How Does Parallelism Mean?" Pages 41–70 in *A Sense of Text: The Art of Language in the Study of Biblical Literature*. Edited by Stephen A. Geller, Edward L. Greenstein, and Adele Berlin. JQRSup. Winona Lake, IN: Eisenbrauns, 1983.

Grossberg, Daniel, and Ronald J. Williams. "Noun/Verb Parallelism: Syntactic or Asyntactic." *JBL* 99/4 (1980): 481–88.

Henry, Matthew and Martin H. Manser. *The New Matthew Henry Commentary: The Classic Work with Updated Language*. Abridged ed. Grand Rapids: Zondervan, 2010.

Hernández, Dominick S. "Metaphor and the Study of Job." *HS* 61 (2020): 391–415

Holladay, William L. "Form and Word-Play in David's Lament over Saul." Pages 53–89 in *Poetry in the Hebrew Bible: Selected Studies from Vetus Testamentum*. Edited by David E. Orton. Brill's Readers in Biblical Studies. Leiden: Brill, 2000.

Holmstedt, Robert D. "Hebrew Poetry and the Appositive Style: Parallelsim, Requiescat in pace." *VT* 69 (2019): 617–48.

Honeyman, A. M. "Merismus in Biblical Hebrew." *JBL* 71 (1952): 11–18.

Hornkohl, Aaron D., and Geoffrey Khan, eds. *New Perspectives in Biblical and Rabbinic Hebrew*. Cambridge: Open Book, 2021.

Hossfeld, Frank-Lothar. "The Elohistic Psalter: Formation and Purpose." Pages 117–32 in *The Psalter as Witness: Theology, Poetry, and Genre: Proceedings from the Baylor University-University of Bonn Symposium on the Psalter*. Edited by W. Dennis Tucker and W. H. Bellinger. Waco, TX: Baylor University Press, 2017.

Hurvitz, Avi. "Wisdom Vocabulary in the Hebrew Psalter: A Contribution to the Study of 'Wisdom Psalms.'" *VT* 38 (1988): 41–51.

James, Elaine T. "The Aesthetics of Biblical Acrostics." *JSOT* 46 (2022): 319–38.

———. *An Invitation to Biblical Poetry*. Edited by Patricia K. Tull. Essentials of Biblical Studies. Oxford: Oxford University Press, 2022.

Jastrow, Marcus. *A Dictionary of the Targumim, the Talmud Babli and Yerushalmi, and the Midrashic Literature*. London: Luzac, 1903. Repr., Jerusalem: Horeb 1984.

Joüon, Paul. *A Grammar of Biblical Hebrew*. Translated and revised by T. Muraoka. 2 vols. Subsidia Biblica. Rome: Pontifical Biblical Institute, 1996.

Justiss, Joseph L. "Identifying Alphabetic Compositions in the Hebrew Bible." *VT* 74 (2024): 331–51.

Kaiser, Walter C. *Toward an Exegetical Theology: Biblical Exegesis for Preaching and Teaching*. Grand Rapids: Baker Academic, 1998.

Kalimi, Isaac. *The Reshaping of Ancient Israelite History in Chronicles*. Winona Lake, IN: Eisenbrauns, 2005.

Keil, Karl Friedrich, and Franz Delitzsch. *Psalms*. Vol. 5 of *Commentary on the Old Testament*. Edited by Karl Friedrich Keil and Franz Delitzsch. Translated by James Martin. Grand Rapids: Eerdmans, 1982.

Kennedy, Charles A. "Isaiah 57:5–6: Tombs in the Rocks." *BASOR* 275 (1989): 47–52.

Kirk, Alexander. "Agur's Beastly Ethics: The Numerical Saying, Animal Imagery, Humor, and Coherance in Proverbs 30:11–33." Pages 147–200 in *Agur's Wisdom and the Coherance of Proverbs 30*. Ancient Israel and Its Literature 30. Atlanta: SBL Press, 2024.

Klaus, Natan. *Pivot Patterns in the Former Prophets*. Sheffield: Sheffield Academic, 1999.

Koehler, Ludwig, Walter Baumgartner, and Johann J. Stamm. *The Hebrew and Aramaic Lexicon of the Old Testament*. Translated and edited under the supervision of Mervyn E. J. Richardson. 4 vols. Leiden, Brill, 1994–1999.

Kraus, Hans-Joachim. *Psalms 1–59: A Commentary*. Translated by Hilton C. Oswold. Minneapolis: Augsburg, 1988.

Kugel, James L. *The Idea of Biblical Poetry: Parallelism and Its History*. New Haven: Yale University Press, 1981.

Kuntz, Kenneth J. "Hendiadys As an Agent of Rhetorical Enrichment in Biblical Poetry, With Special Reference to Prophetic Discourse." Pages 114–34 in Vol. 1 of *God's Word for Our World: Biblical Studies in Honor of John De Vries*. Edited by Deborah L. Ellens, J. Harold Ellens, Isaac Kalimi, and Rolf Knierim. 2 vols. London: Bloomsbury, 2009.

Kuryłowicz, Jerzy. *Studies in Semitic Grammar and Metrics*. Wroclaw: Polsk. Akad. Nauk, 1972.

Lambdin, Thomas Oden. *Introduction to Biblical Hebrew*. London: Darton, Longman & Todd, 1973.

Law, Helen H. "Hyperbole in the Mythological Comparisons." *The American Journal of Philology* 47/4 (1926): 361–72.

Leonard, Jeffery M. "Identifying Inner-Biblical Allusions: Psalm 78 as a Test Case." *JBL* 127 (2008): 241–65.

———. "Inner-Biblical Interpretation and Intertextuality." Pages 97–142 in *Literary Approaches to the Bible*. Edited by Douglas Magnum and Douglas Estes. Bellingham, WA: Lexham, 2017.

Lillas, Rosmari. "Hendiadys in the Hebrew Bible: An Investigation in the Application of the Term." PhD diss., University of Gothenburg, 2012.

Loewenstamm, Samuel E. "The Expanded Colon Reconstructed." *UF* 7 (1975): 261–64.

Longman, Tremper, III. "A Critique of Two Recent Metrical Systems." *Bib* 63 (1982): 230–54.

———. *How to Read the Psalms*. 2nd ed. How to Read Series. Downers Grove, IL: InterVarsity Press Academic, 2024.

Lowth, Robert. *Isaiah. A New Translation: With a Preliminary Dissertation, and Notes, Critical, Philological, and Explanatory*. London: Nichols, 1778.

Lund, Nils Wilhelm. "The Presence of Chiasmus in the Old Testament." *AJSL* 46 (1930): 104–26.

———. *Chiasmus in the New Testament: A Study in the Form and Function of Chiastic Structures*. Peabody, MA: Hendrickson, 2013.

Lunn, Nicholas P. *Word-Order Variation in Biblical Hebrew Prose: Differentiating Pragmatics and Poetics*. Paternoster Biblical Monographs. Eugene, OR: Wipf & Stock, 2006.

Lyon, Ashley E. *Reassessing Selah*. Georgia: College & Clayton Press, 2021

McClish, Dub. "Recognizing and Interpreting Synecdoches." The Scripture Cache. https://thescripturecache.com/?p=15581. Accessed January 15, 2025

McComiskey, Thomas Edward. *The Minor Prophets: An Exegetical and Expository Commentary*. 3 vols. Grand Rapids: Baker, 1992.

Meek, Theophile J. "The Structure of Hebrew Poetry." *JR* 9/4 (1929): 523–50.

Meek, Russell L. "Intertextuality, Inner-Biblical Exegesis, and Inner-Biblical Allusion: The Ethics of Methodology" *Bib* 95/2 (2014): 280–91.

Meir, Amira. "On the Study of Pentateuchal Poetry." Pages 96–113 in Vol. 1 of *God's Word for Our World: Biblical Studies in Honor of John De Vries*. Edited by Deborah L. Ellens, J. Harold Ellens, Isaac Kalimi, and Rolf Knierim. 2 vols. London: Bloomsbury, 2009.

Melamed, E. Z. "Break-up of Stereotype Phrases as an Artistic Device in Biblical Poetry." *ScrHier* 8 (1961): 115–53.

Meshel, Naphtali "Whose Job Is This? Dramatic Irony and *Double Entendre* in the Book of Job." Pages 47–76 in *The Book of Job: Aesthetics, Ethics, Hermeneutics*. Edited by Leora Batnitzky and Ilana Pardes. Perspectives on Jewish Texts and Contexts. Berlin: de Gruyter, 2017.

Miller, Cynthia L., and Ziony Zevit, eds. *Diachrony in Biblical Hebrew*. LSAWS 18. Winona Lake, IN: Eisenbrauns, 2012.

Montefiore, C. G. "A Tentative Catalogue of Biblical Metaphors." *JQR* 3/4 (1891): 623–81.

Moshavi, Adina Mosak. "Can a Positive Rhetorical Question Have a Positive Answer in the Bible?" *JSS* 56 (2011): 253–73.

Muilenburg, James. "The Linguistic and Rhetorical Usages of the Particle Ki in the Old Testament." *HUCA* 32 (1961): 135–60.

———. "Form Criticism and Beyond." *JBL* 88/1 (1969): 1–18.

Muraoka, T. *Emphatic Words and Structures in Biblical Hebrew.* Jerusalem: Magnes, 1985.

Noegel, Scott B. "Janus Parallelism in Job and Its Literary Significance." *JBL* 115 (1996): 313–20.

Noonan, Benjamin J. *Advances in the Study of Biblical Hebrew and Aramaic.* Grand Rapids: Zondervan Academic, 2020.

O'Connell, Robert H. "Telescoping N + 1 Patterns in the Book of Amos." *VT* 46 (1996): 56–73.

O'Connor, Michael Patrick. *Hebrew Verse Structure.* Winona Lake, IN: Eisenbrauns, 1980.

Olley, John W. "'No Peace' in a Book of Consolation. A Framework for the Book of Isaiah?" *VT* 49 (1999): 351–70.

Patton, Matthew H., Frederic C. Putnam, and Miles V. Van Pelt. *Basics of Hebrew Discourse: A Guide to Working with Biblical Hebrew Prose and Poetry.* Grand Rapids: Zondervan Academic, 2019.

Paul, Shalom M. "Polysemous Pivotal Punctuation: More Janus Double Entendres." Pages 369–74 in *Texts, Temples and Traditions: A Tribute to Menahem Haran.* Edited by Michael V. Fox. Winona Lake, IN: Eisenbrauns, 1996.

Pinker, Aron. "Nahum 1: Acrostic and Authorship." *JBQ* 34 (2006). https://jbqnew.jewishbible.org/assets/Uploads/342/342_Acrostic.pdf

Preminger, Alex, and T. V. F. Brogan, eds. *The New Princeton Encyclopedia of Poetry and Poetics.* Princeton: Princeton University Press, 1993.

Rendsburg, Gary. "A Comprehensive Guide to Israelian Hebrew." *Orient* 33 (2003): 5–35.

———. "Janus Parallelism in Gen 49:26." *JBL* 99 (1980): 291–93.

———. "Israelian Hebrew in the Book of Amos." Pages 717–40 in *New Perspectives in Biblical and Rabbinic Hebrew.* Edited by Aaron D. Hornkohl and Geoffrey Khan. Semitic Languages and Cultures 7. Cambridge: Open Book Publishers, 2021.

Revell, E. J. "Pausal Forms and the Structure of Biblical Poetry." *VT* 31 (1981): 186–99.

Reymond, Eric D. *Intermediate Biblical Hebrew Grammar: A Student's Guide to Phonology and Morphology*. Resources for Biblical Study. Atlanta: SBL Press, 2018.

Roth, Wolfgang M. W. "The Numerical Sequence X/X+1 in the Old Testament." *VT* 12 (1962): 300–11.

Ruiz, Javier Herrero. "Paradox and Oxymoron Revisited." *Procedia—Social and Behavioral Sciences* 173 (2015): 199–206.

Ryken, Leland. *A Complete Handbook of Literary Forms in the Bible*. Wheaton, IL: Crossway, 2014.

Ryken, Leland, Jim Wilhoit, Tremper Longman III, Colin Duriez, Douglas Penney, and Daniel G. Reid. *Dictionary of Biblical Imagery*. Downers Grove, IL: IVP Academic, 1998.

Sakenfeld, Katharine Doob, ed. *New Interpreter's Dictionary of the Bible*. 5 vols. Nashville: Abingdon, 2006–2009.

Samet, Nili. "The Gilgamesh Epic and the Book of Qohelet: A New Look." *Bib* 96 (2015): 375–90.

Sanders, Paul, and Raymond de Hoop. "The System of Masoretic Accentuation: Some Introductory Issues." *JHS* 22 (2022): 37–45. https://jhsonline.org/index.php/jhs/article/view/29622.

Schniedewind, William, and Daniel Sivan. "The Elijah-Elisha Narratives: A Test Case for the Northern Dialect of Hebrew." *JQR* 87 (1997): 303–37.

Schnittjer, Gary Edward, and Matthew S. Harmon. *How to Study the Bible's Use of the Bible: Seven Hermeneutical Choices to Study the Old and New Testaments*. Grand Rapids: Zondervan Academic, 2024.

Schökel, Luis Alonso. *A Manual of Hebrew Poetics*. Subsidia Biblica 11. Rome: Pontifical Biblical Institute, 1988.

Segert, Stanislav. "Parallelism in Ugaritic Poetry." *JAOS* 103/1 (1983): 295–306.

Seidel, Moshe. "Maqbillot Ben Sefer Yeshaya Lesefer Tehillim." *Sinai* 38 (1956): 142–79.

Seidler, Ayelet. "Literary Devices in the Psalms: The Commentary of Ibn Ezra Revisited." *JSQ* 22/4 (2015): 377–402.

Seow, C. L. *A Grammar for Biblical Hebrew*. Rev. ed. Nashville: Abingdon, 1995.

Shemesh, Y. "Measure for Measure in the David Stories." *SJOT* 17 (2003): 89–109.

Sommer, Benjamin. *A Prophet Reads Scripture*. Stanford, CA: Stanford University Press, 1998.

Speiser, E. A. *Genesis: A New Translation with Introduction and Commentary*. The Anchor Bible. Garden City, NY: Doubleday, 1964.

Strauss, Mark L., and Tremper Longman III. *The Baker Expository Dictionary of Biblical Words*. Grand Rapids: Baker Academic, 2023.

Stuart, Douglas K. *Old Testament Exegesis: A Handbook for Students and Pastors*. 5th ed. Louisville: Westminster John Knox, 2022.

———. *Studies in Early Hebrew Meter*. Harvard Semetic Monographs 13. Lieden: Brill, 1976.

Tate, Marvin E. *Psalms 51–100*. WBC 20. Nashville: Thomas Nelson, 2000.

Tov, Emanuel. *Textual Criticism of the Hebrew Bible*. Rev. and enl. ed. Minneapolis: Fortress, 2012.

Tsumura, David Toshio. "Literary Insertion (AXB Pattern) in Biblical Hebrew." *VT* 33 (1983): 468–82.

———. *Vertical Grammar of Parallelism in Biblical Hebrew*. Ancient Israel and Its Literature Series 47. Atlanta: SBL Press, 2023.

———. "Janus Parallelism in Hab. III 4." *VT* (2013): 113–116.

Waltke, Bruce K., and M. O'Connor. *An Introduction to Biblical Hebrew Syntax*. Winona Lake, IN: Eisenbrauns, 1990.

Wansbrough, John. "Hebrew Verse: Apostrophe and Epanalepsis." *BSOAS* 45 (1982): 425–33.

Watson, Rebecca S. "הֲ: A Rhetorical Question Anticipating a Negative Answer." *JSOT* 44 (2020): 437–55.

Watson, Wilfred G. E. *Classical Hebrew Poetry: A Guide to Its Techniques*. JSOTSup 26. Sheffield: JSOT Press, 2001.

———. "Internal Parallelism in Classical Hebrew Verse." *Bib* 66 (1985): 365–84.

———. *Traditional Techniques in Classical Hebrew Verse*. JSOTSup 170. Sheffield: JSOT Press, 1994.

Weber, Beat. "Mockery and Irony in the Psalms." Pages 163–80 in *Irony in the Bible: Between Subversion and Innovation*. Edited by Tobias Häner, Virginia Miller, and Carolyn J. Sharp. Biblical Interpretation 209. Leiden: Brill, 2023.

Weiss, Meir. *The Bible from Within: The Method of Total Interpretation*. Jerusalem: Magnes, 1984.

———. "The Pattern of Numerical Sequence in Amos 1–2: A Re-Examination." *JBL* 86 (1967): 416–23.

Wendland, Ernst R. *Analyzing the Psalms: With Exercises for Bible Students and Translators*. 2nd ed. Dallas: SIL International, 2002.

Williams, Ronald J. *Williams' Hebrew Syntax*. 3rd ed. Toronto: University of Toronto Press, 2012.

Williamson, H. G. M. "Isaiah 62:4 and the Problem of Inner-Biblical Allusions." *JBL* 119 (2000): 734–39.

Yoder, Perry B. "A-B Pairs and Oral Composition in Hebrew Poetry." *VT* 21 (1971): 470–89.

Scripture Index

Genesis
1:2 167
1:26b 26
4:10 130
4:23 . . . . 13, 29, 51
9:6a 75
11:9 76
12:16 . . . . .10, 11
14:19 43
18:27 146
25:23 13
27:28 43
32:32 76
37 189
41:49 118
41:52 151
43:31 129
49 . . . . 12, 30, 120, 236
49:22 34

Exodus
5 236
5:7 33
9:14b 26
14–15 185
15 . . . . 12, 29
15:1 185
15:4 . . . . 42, 185
15:6 179
15:6 . . . . 92, 185
15:7b 32
15:8 52
15:9 185

15:11 . . . . 32, 92, 185
15:16 92
15:21 185
15:22 185
17:7 76
28:30 147
30:33 219

Leviticus
7:12a 226
8:31 129
11:42b 32
22:10 219
22:29 226
24:19 224

Numbers
21:27–30 13
22–24 12
23 . . . . .29, 43
23:18 . . . . 42, 51
23:19a 49
23:19b 50
24:3b–4a 84
24:16 31

Deuteronomy
12:24b 26
22:26b 219
28:7 219
32–33 . . . . 12, 29
32:1 177
32–33:30a 44

32:36a 216
32:37–38 155

Joshua
6:26 13
9:18 219
10:12–13 13

Judges
5 . . . . .12, 29, 30, 236
5:3a 51
5:4 146
5:4a 26
5:12 84
5:23 83
5:23b 81
5:27a 47
5:27b 48
5:28–30 155
5:28b 60
9:43 219
20:5 219

1 Samuel
2 .12
13:1 199
19:25, 27 92
20:1 220
23:15 220
26 215

2 Samuel
1:19–27 . . . . 13, 177

1:21....................177	20:9....................132	9–10..................111
5:20b..................10	21:7......................5	10..............111, 197
7:7a....................29	22:2.....................33	10:1............171, 197
12:2....................26	22:6....................175	10:9....................125
22............12, 29, 188	23:17.....................5	11:1....................125
22:31..................122	28:7....................132	12:3–4 [12:4–5]........70
	29:6....................142	13:1–2..................173
1 Kings	29:19....................34	14......................188
1–20..................27, 28	30:19..................146	14:2....................113
17:6....................129	30:22a..................34	15......................141
19:10..................220	31:23....................73	15:1.....................59
22:19..................133	33:14.....................5	15:3a..................141
	34:2....................41	15:5a..................160
2 Kings	35:7....................160	16......................110
17:40....................29	35:8.....................50	16:6....................149
	38–41..................173	17:1..............41, 217
1 Chronicles	38:33....................43	17:12..................125
20:5....................10	40:10..................146	18......................188
	42:6....................146	18:8....................147
2 Chronicles	42:11..................129	18:13..................142
2:2 [2:1]..............214		18:31 [18:30]..........29
	Psalms	19.......................72
Esther	1............16, 196, 236	19:1 [19:2].............71
9:25a..................224	1–101..............27, 28	21:6....................146
	1:2b............160, 161	22:1–11................56
Job	1:3.....................24	22:12..................228
1:3....................139	1:6...........72, 76, 77	22:16a [22:17a]...126, 127
1:21....................160	2:1..............41, 173	22:22............56, 216
5:8....................145	2:2.....................51	22:25...................56
5:12............103, 104	2:3.....................32	23..........119, 123, 196
5:19............44, 240	2:4.....................73	23:1....................22
6:16....................33	2:11...................177	23:2a..................119
7:4....................34	3:4.....................60	25.............109, 111
8:11....................62	4:1....................217	25:4....................30
8:12a....................5	4:3.....................60	25:16..................106
9:25–35...............110	5:9....................128	25:17..................228
10:14....................74	6:8 [6:9]..............177	27:2....................68
10:19..................159	7:3 [7:4]..............127	27:14....................73
10:21..................167	8................54, 89	28:5....................141
12......................154	8:1a [8:2a]........54, 89	29.................89, 110
12:1–2..................153	8:3 [8:4]..............103	29:1....................179
13:1....................46	8:7–8..................163	29:1–2..................84
14:16.....................5	8:9 [8:10]........54, 89	29:1b....................90
16:7.....................5	9..............111, 197	29:11a....................90

Scripture Index

31 187	44:17–19 16	57:7–11. 188
31:3. 216	44:18–23. 16	58:12. 5
31:8. 228	44:20–26. 16	59:3. 216
31:13 [31:14] 186, 187	44:24–27. 16	59:8. 73
32 . . . . 110, 215	45:4. 146	59:10 [59:11] 228
32:4. 130	49:2. 41	60:5–12 188
32:6. 146	50:14. 226	60:6 [60:8]. 201
33 110	51 196	62:2. 5
33:18. 134	51:1–8 [51:3–10] 74	62:12 44
34 . . . . . . 107, 108, 110, 111	51:2 [51:4] 74	63:10. 220
34:1–5 [34:2–6] 107	51:5 [51:7] 46	67 . . . . 90, 91
34:8 [34:9]. 25	51:9. 74	67:3 [67:4] 91
34:8–9 110	53 . . . . 188, 214	67:5 [67:6] 91
34:9. 106	54 . . . . 209, 211, 213,	68:22 5
34:19 [34:20] 100, 101	214, 229	69:2a [69:3a] 120
35:13. 217	54:1–2 214	69:4 [69:5] 120
37 109	54:1a. 211	69:4a [69:5a] 138
37:36. 50	54:1a–6b. 210	69:13. 62
37:39. 228	54:2. 211	69:34 43
38 110	54:3. . . . 215, 220, 224, 227	70:5. 222
38:2 [38:3]. 135	54:3–4 . . . . . . 211, 215, 218	71 187
38:4. 125	54:3–5 230	71:20 228
38:13 [38:14] 124	54:4. . . . . 215, 217, 220	72:12 222
39:5. 122	54:4 [54:6]. 201	72:15. 130
39:10. 135	54:5. . . . 212, 213, 218, 221,	73:1. 5
39:12. . . . . .51, 106	223, 225, 228, 229	73:16. 105
39:12a [39:13a] 41	54:5 [54:7] 199	73:19. 168
40:15 220	54:5–7 218	74:1. 173
42 .63	54:5c. 218, 220	76 123
42:1 [42:2]. 63	54:6 . . .213, 221, 222, 224,	77 161
42:3. 168	226, 227	77:2a [77:3a] 161, 162
42:4 [42:5]. 169	54:7. . . . . 212, 213, 223,	77:7–9 [77:8–10] 173
42:5 [42:6]. 177	224, 230	77:16 [77:17] 177
42:5b [42:6b] 167	54:7–9 211	77:16a. 83
43:1. 167	54:7a–9b 211	78 . . . . .29, 67, 76, 80,
43:1b 167	54:8. . . . 226, 227, 228, 230	93, 215
44 .16	54:8–9 225	78:9. . . . . 80, 81
44:1–3 16	54:9. 228	78:10–11 56
44:1–9 16	55 214	78:14. . . . . .79, 162
44:4–8 16	55:5 [55:6] 166, 169	78:17. 93
44:6 [44:7]. 129	55:5a. 169	78:18. 103
44:9–16 16	55:10. 161	78:32 . . . . 56, 93
44:10–17 16	57:1 [57:2] 14	78:33. 61
44:17 216	57:6. 43	78:40 . . . . 56, 93

78:43 . . . . 66, 67	94:9. . . . . 171, 173	105:38 . . . . 95, 96
78:46 128	94:22 122	105:42 . . . . .55, 56
78:56. . . . . 56, 93	95 . . . . .76, 96, 135, 137	105:42a 55
78:57. . . . . 80, 81	95:1. . . . . 122, 127	105:44 42
80 .92	95:4. 135	105:45 . . . . .67, 75
80:3 [80:4]. 92, 93	95:4–5 97	106 . . . . 106, 184, 186
80:7 [80:8]. 92, 93	95:5. . . . . .161, 162	106:8 216
80:14. 69	95:7. 97	106:9–12 185
80:18. 50	95:11. 136	106:13 168
80:19 [80:20] 92, 93	96 .98	106:13–15. 157
81:5–6 [81:6–7] 201	96:1–2a 84	106:22 47
82 196	96:2. 84	106:29–30. 104
82:2. 173	96:3. 48	106:30 28
83:2. 94	96:7–9 84	106:33 106
84:8. 217	96:12 69	106:45 136
84:11a [84:12a]. 121	98:4–5 . . . . 82, 83	106:47 79
85 24	98:7–8 162	107 236
85:3 [85:4]. 24	99 91	107:5. 5
85:5–6 173	99:3. . . . . 91, 92, 227	107:8, 15, 21 91
85:8 [85:9] 14	99:5. 92	107:22 226
85:10. 5	99:9. 92	107:31. 91
85:11 [85:12]. 43	103 54	108:1–6 188
86:14. . . . . 219, 220	103:1. 48	108:6–13 188
86:17. 222	103:1–2 89	108:9 [108:10]. 34
88:6 [88:7]. 22	103:1a. 55	111 108
88:6a [88:7a] 23	103:2. 177	111:1b–5 108
88:6b [88:7b] 23	103:10. 57	111:3. 146
88:8 [88:9] 23	103:15. 31	112 109
88:10–12 [88:11–13]. . .172	103:22 89	112:6 166
90 181	103:22b 55, 89	112:8 228
90:2 181	104 135	112:9. 168
90:4 181	104:1 146	114 165
90:5. 181	104:23 35	114:1–2 165
90:6 181	105 . . . . 56, 95, 96, 157,	114:2. 166
90:9. 181	184, 189, 236	114:3–4 166
90:10 181	105:6. 46	114:3–5 166
90:12 181	105:8–9 . . . . .55, 56	114:5–6 165
90:14. 181	105:15. . . . . 76, 77	114:7. 166
90:15 181	105:17. . . . . . . 164, 165, 188	115 82
92 71	105:18–19 156	115:1. 227
92:2. 179	105:23 . . . . 95, 96	115:2. 173
92:2 [92:3]. 71	105:23–38. . . . . 95, 96, 199	115:12a 82
92:9. 227	105:30, 32, 35. 96	115:15. 43
92:12 219	105:36 199	116:1. . . . . 83, 113

118:7 . . . . 222, 229	145:10b 45	16:8. 240
118:9. 102	145:16. 135	16:15. 238
118:15b–16 69	146:45b 136	16:19. 240
119 . . . . 108, 110	148 181	16:25. . . . . 178, 179
119:1–6 108	148:3. 177	16:32. 240
119:1–24 109	148:11. 178	17:12. 101
119:7–24 109	148:12 163	19:1, 22 240
119:9–11 109		20:5. 238
119:65–66a. 94	**Proverbs**	20:10 238
119:105 121	1:16. 129	21:27 238
119:105a 121	1:20–33 73	22:1. 240
119:106 121	1:26. 73	23:9. 31
119:164 138	3:35. 239	23:11, 18 238
121 . . . . .79, 80	5:15. . . . . 62, 147, 148	24:10 142
121:1–8 179	6:15. 62	25:11, 13 64
121:3, 4, 5 180	6:16. . . . . 44, 240	25:15. 176
121:6 79	6:23. 121	26:1, 7 238
121:7. 180	7:12. 68	27:5. 240
122:6 145	8:1. 132	27:15. 238
122:6–7 146	8:4. 50	28:19 176
122:7 145	8:11. 240	28:24 141
123:2 125	8:15. 51	30:1. 83
126:1, 4 92	10:1, 3, 4 239	30:15, 18, 21 240
129:5 166	10:9. 51	31:2. 84
129:5–6 142	10:9a. 51	31:4. . . . . 51, 179
132:2, 11 56	10:13. 75	31:9. 216
132:15 129	10:26 64	31:10–30 109
132:18 150	11:1. 238	
135 82	11:2. 101	**Ecclesiastes**
135:6. 163	11:15. 239	3:18. 150
135:12 82	11:22 63	5:5. 240
135:16–17a 53	11:24 176	6:6. 138
136 93	12:4. 239	6:9. 240
136:6 93	12:6. 239	6:9a. 239
136:18 93	12:9. 239	7:1, 5 240
136:25 129	12:20 75	9:4. 240
137:1. 5	13:12a. xviii	9:16, 18 239
139:2 161	13:24 75	10:2. 239
139:9. . . . . .55, 56	13:25a. 74	10:4. 143
139:16 . . . . .55, 56	13:34 42	
140:14 5	14:18. 128	**Song of Songs**
141:8. 31	14:33. . . . . 57, 58, 238	1:6. 132
145 109	15:15, 16, 19 238	1:6a. 131
145:10. 45	16:1. 238	2:7. 92

2:12...................85
2:15...................83
3:5....................92
4:8...................179
5:8....................92
6:9....................84
6:10...................14
8:4....................92

Isaiah
1:2....................51
1:7...................219
2:4a...................58
3:8a...................68
5:2....................60
5:15..................138
6:1...................133
8:16, 20...............80
11:1...................68
13:5..................164
15:8...................27
15:8c..................27
16:10.................142
21:14..................31
22:22..................66
22:22b.................66
24:4..................147
24:6..................146
24:19-20a..............53
25:1..................227
25:2..................219
28:26.................166
29:5...................92
29:5a.................219
29:9b..................94
29:16..................92
30:23.................129
31:3...................68
32-33:9................51
38:11..................83
40............105, 196
40:4...................69
40:6..................104
42:22b.................26

44:15.................129
44:22..................46
48:9...................27
51:17, 22..............80
55:12.................130
56:9...................69
58:10..........142, 176
59:1..................134
59:12a................132
61:3...................69
62:3a.................146
62:63a................147
63:1-2................152
63:2..................142
63:5a.................223

Jeremiah
2:12..................177
2:14-15................85
4:2b...................14
4:7...................127
5:4-5.................110
5:19..................219
5:21..............94, 97
5:28..................216
5:30-31...............166
6:7...................167
10:6..................216
13:15.................217
13:20b.................25
15:8..................137
15:10.................177
16:21.................216
20:10.........186, 187
20:15.................187
21:12.................216
22:16.................216
22:19.................176
31:13a................161
34:17.................143
41:1..................129
46:12..................68
47:6..................177
48:2..................152

49:1c.................149

Lamentations
1-4...................109
1:19b..................33
1:21-26................78
2-4...................111
3:22...................68
5.....................110
5:7....................74

Ezekiel
1:1...................133
8:12...................80
9:9....................80
16:6-7, 22.............80
23:32.................123
23:32-34..............122
24:6..................139
28:7..................219
29:3-5................123
31:12.................219
39:11.................152

Daniel
1-6....................31
2:10, 38...............31
3:10...................31
4:13...................31
4:34...................30
5:23...................30

Hosea
1:20..................126
2:3...................126
4:13...................60
4:16..................126
5:10, 12, 14..........126
6:2....................44
6:3...................126
7:4, 6, 7, 11, 16.....126
8:1...................126
8:7...................147
9:4...................126

9:16 151
11:10 126
12:3–6 110
12:4 152
13:7–8 125
13:11 160

Joel
1:2 .... 41, 217
1:2a 217
1:10 131
2 97
2:1b 98
2:11b 98
2:13 136
2:21–22 178
2:22 177
3:16 169

Amos
1:3 44
4 91
4:1a 126
4:4–5 154
4:6, 8, 9, 10, 11 91

6:9 138
6:12a 170
7:3 136
9:1 133

Micah
1:10–16 152
3:2–3 123
4:6 79
5:10b [5:9b] 61
6:2 177
6:9 128
7:18–20 76

Nahum
1 .... 110, 112
1:2–8 110
1:3b–7a 110
1:8 110
3:15 138

Habakkuk
1:6–11 139
1:10 51
2 71

3:8 179

Zephaniah
1:13 62
2:4 150
3:14–20 76
3:19 78

Haggai
2:20–23 76

Malachi
3:24 78
4:6 [3:24] 77

Luke
10:30–37 76
10:37 76
20:9–17 76

John
1:18 133

1 Timothy
6:16 133

Subject Index

acrostics
  definition, 107
  examples of, 107–9, 109n. 7
  function of, 110–12, 111n. 10, 111n. 11, 112n. 12, 112n. 13
  partial, 109–11, 112
  quasi, 110n. 8, 112
alliteration, 51, 144–46, 144n. 4, 146n. 5, 146n. 6, 146n. 7, 147n. 10, 152
allusion
  analyzing, 183–88
  biblical, 182–88, 183n. 32
  definition, 182
  functions of, 184, 186, 188–89
  inner-biblical, 56, 56–57n. 26
  markers in, 183, 185, 187, 188, 200–201
  necessary conditions for success of, 182–84, 183n. 32, 183n. 33
  poetry vs. prose, 182–83n. 30
  vs. textual duplication, 188
anadiplosis, 149–50, 149n. 17
analyzing Hebrew poetry
  identifying poetic features, 203, 213n. 5
  identifying structural features, 202–3, 211–14
  initial translation, 198–200, 210n. 1, 219n. 21
  looking at the big picture, 204–6
  purpose of, 195
  reading the text, 197–98, 198n. 6
  revision in, 195–96, 203–4
  stanza division, 201–2, 212n. 4
  text selection, 196–97, 210n. 1
  textual associations in, 206–7
  use of commentaries in, 194–95, 207–8, 209
  use of concordance in, 200–201, 200n. 13, 209, 211n. 3, 220n. 25, 222n. 28
  worked example of, 209–30
animation, 131n. 22
anthropomorphism, 133–35, 136, 136n. 27
anthropopathism, 136–37, 136n. 27
antithetical parallelism, 100–102, 239, 239n. 6
aperture, 57n. 26
apostrophe, 176–78, 177n. 26
Aramaic words, in Hebrew poetry, 30–31
assonance, 144n. 4, 148–49, 152
atnakh, 6, 12n. 10, 22–24, 24n. 5, 39, 113
augmented pairs, 42

ballast variants, 58, 59–60, 60n. 34
"behold," use of in poetry, 222, 222n. 29
"better-than" sayings, 239
bicolon (pl. bicola), 14, 27n. 13

cantillation marks, 21–24
  atnakh, 6, 12n. 10, 22–24, 24n. 5, 39, 113
  conjunctive, 22
  disjunctive, 22–24, 24n. 5
  origins of use of, 21–22n. 1, 24n. 6
  oleh veyored, 23–24, 24n. 5, 39, 113
  purpose of, 21–22
  silluq, 22, 24n. 5
  sof pasuq, 22

causal relationship between cola, 105–7
cause and effect relationship between cola, 103–4, 141, 229
chiasmus
   closing poetic units, 72–73, 75–76
   creating midpoint, 73–74
   definition of, 10, 65–66, 68–69
   distant, 80–81
   enhancing merismus, 79–81, 117n. 1
   expressive functions of, 74–81
   for contrast, 74–75
   for emphasis, 75–77
   four-cola, 70
   loss of in English translations, 66–68, 71n. 8
   mirror, 66, 66n. 1
   opening poetic units, 71–72
   phonological, 69, 69n. 6
   reversal of state, 77–79
   split-member, 68, 68n. 3
   structural functions of, 70–74, 203
   tricola, 69–70, 73
   within a single colon, 68
chorus, 93
closure, 57n. 26
cohortative verbs, 226, 226n. 34
colon (pl. cola)
   definition of, 14, 39
   See also bicolon, monocolon, tricolon
conjunctive cantillation marks, 22
continuous relationship between cola, 107n. 6
couplet. *See* bicolon

delayed explication. *See* delayed identification
delayed identification, 164–66, 166n. 9
discontinuous relationship between cola, 107n. 6
disjunctive cantillation marks, 22–24, 24n. 5
distant parallelism, 40, 54–56
double-stepped terrace, 83
duplication, textual, 188

"ear," use of in poetry, 29
eisegesis, 196
ellipsis, 27n. 13, 48–50, 53
emblematic parallelism, 63–64
emeth books, 23, 113
emphatic structures, 4–5, 4n. 3, 5n. 3
enclosure, 57n. 26
end rhyme, 146–48, 147n. 11
end-stopping, 113, 113n. 14
enjambment, 112–14, 114n. 17
enveloping structures
   chorus, 93
   envelope figure, 54n. 23, 69n. 5, 73, 88–90, 88n. 1, 94n. 9
   inclusion, 54n. 23, 94–99, 94n. 9
   refrain. *See* refrain
epanalepsis, 94, 178–79, 179n. 27
epanastrophe, 149n. 17

figurative language, as identifier for poetic text, 11n. 8
final words, biblical importance of, 76n. 13

general to specific relationship between cola, 103
grammatical parallelism, 45, 57–58, 57n. 27, 58n. 31

hendiadys, 166–70, 167n. 10, 168n. 12
hinge, literary, 65
hyperbole, 137–39, 137n. 30, 139n. 37, 175, 186n. 36, 231–32
hypocatastasis, 123–24, 126–27, 127n. 15

imagery
   anthropomorphism, 133–35, 136, 136n. 27
   anthropopathism, 136–37, 136n. 27
   hyperbole, 137–39, 137n. 30, 139n. 37, 231–32
   hypocatastasis, 123–24, 126–27, 127n. 15
   as identifier for poetic text, 11n. 8, 117, 118

Subject Index

interaction of with poetic structure, 117, 118
metaphor. *See* metaphor
metonymy, 127–28, 128n. 17, 129, 159, 159n. 2
personification, 130–33, 130n. 20, 131n. 21, 131n. 22
purpose of use of, 117–18
simile. *See* simile
synecdoche, 129–30, 129n. 18, 130n. 19, 159n. 2, 163
use of in prose, 118
imprecation, 223–24, 230
inclusio. *See* inclusion
inclusion
  assonance and, 93n. 6
  definition of, 94
  examples of, 54n. 23, 94n. 12
  identifying, 95–98, 179n. 27
  primary function of, 94, 98–99
  increasing numbers, law of, 59n. 32, 60
  internal half-line parallelism, 50–52
intertextuality, 183n. 33
irony, 153–58
isocolic principle, 59n. 32

Janus parallelism, 85–86, 86n. 26, 143n. 2
juncture, 57n. 26

lleitwörter, 179, 179n. 28
lexical features
  Aramaic words in, 30–31
  vocabulary, 29–30
  wayyiqtol frequency, 11, 28–29
lines. *See* colon (pl. cola)

markers, 183, 185, 187, 188, 200–201
maskil, 211, 214–15
Masoretes, 21
Masoretic divisions, 21–24, 113
measure for measure principle, 144n. 3, 153
merismic list, 162–63, 163n. 8
merismus, 79, 159–64, 159n. 1, 159n. 2, 169n. 13, 178

metaphor
  definition, 119
  elements of, 119, 120n. 3
  extended, 120, 122–24, 123n. 10
  hypocatastasis, 123–24, 126–27, 127n. 15
  hyperbole, 137–39, 137n. 30, 139n. 37, 231–32
  as identifier for poetic text, 11n. 8
  interpreting, 119–20, 120n. 3
  personification, 130–33, 130n. 20, 131n. 21, 131n. 22
  in series, 120n. 4
  simile as, 124
  simple, 120–22, 122n. 8
meter, 233–35
metonymy, 127–28, 128n. 17, 129, 159, 159n. 2
monocolon, 14, 14n. 15
morphological features
  poetic prepositions, 33–35
  rare suffixes, 31–33

oley veyored, 23–24, 24n. 5, 39, 113
oxymorons, 175–76, 175n. 22, 176n. 23

parallelism
  antithethical, 100–102, 239, 239n. 6
  Aramaic words in, 30–31
  ballast variants, 58, 59–60, 60n. 34
  definition of, 39–40, 39–40n. 1
  distant, 40, 54–56, 57n. 27
  emblematic, 63–64
  formal, 205n. 16
  grammatical, 45, 57–58, 57n. 27, 58n. 31
  as identifier for poetic text, 11n. 8
  internal half-line, 50–52, 215
  Janus, 85–86, 86n. 26, 143n. 2
  numerical, 43–44, 240n. 7
  pacing, 205
  phonological, 58–59n. 31, 61–63, 62n. 35
  quatrain, 40, 53–54
  staircase, 83–84, 179n. 27
  strict, 47, 51, 54, 67, 205, 212, 217, 218

synonymous. *See* synonymous parallelism
synthetic, 205
tricola, 40, 52–54
types of, 39–40n. 1, 40
word pairs, 41–44
parataxis, 28n. 14
paronomasia, 140–44, 142n. 1
personification, 130–33, 130n. 20, 131n. 21, 131n. 22
phonological parallelism, 58–59n. 31, 61–63, 62n. 35
pivot patterns
  chiasmus. *See* chiasmus
  Janus parallelism, 85–86
  terraced pattern, 81–83, 83n. 19, 150, 205, 226
  staircase parallelism, 83–84, 84n. 22
poetry, Hebrew
  analysis of. *See* analyzing Hebrew poetry
  Aramaic words in, 30–31
  common poetic words in, 29–30
  development of rules for writing, 233, 233n. 1
  identifying, 10–12, 11n. 8, 21, 30, 117, 118
  imagery in. *See* imagery
  lexical features of, 28–31
  location of in the Hebrew Bible, 12–13
  Masoretic divisions of, 21–24
  morphological features of, 31–35
  parallelism in. *See* parallelism
  substrata of, 12, 12n. 10
  syntactic features of, 25–28
  units of, 13–16
  word order in, 28n. 15
poetry, wisdom, 12, 236–40
prepositions, poetic, 33–35
proper noun wordplays, 150–52, 152n. 20
prosopopoeia, 130n. 20
pseudo-acrostics. *See* quasi-acrostics
pun. *See* paronomasia

qere-ketiv readings, 198, 199, 199n. 10
quasi-acrostics, 110n. 8, 112

refrain
  chorus, 93
  distinguishing, 92n. 4
  strict, 90–91
  thematic, 93n. 6
  variant, 90, 91–93
repetition, 179–82, 179n. 28, 198, 227
rhetorical questions
  audience involvement in, 174
  closing poetic units, 173–74, 174n. 19
  clustered, 172–73, 173n. 16
  definition of, 170–72
  for emphasis, 174
  opening poetic units, 173, 173n. 18
  syntax of, 170
rhyme
  assonance, 144n. 4, 148–49, 152
  end rhyme, 146–48, 147n. 11

selah, 221n. 26
silluq, 22, 24n. 5
simile
  "as" or "like" with, 124–26, 125n. 12
  definition of, 10
  examples of, 124, 125, 125n. 12, 126n. 13
  extended, 125
  function of, 124–25
  predominance of in Hebrew poetry, 10
sof pasuq, 22
sound pairs, 148
staircase parallelism, 83–84, 84n. 22, 179n. 27
stanza, 15
strict refrain, 90–91, 92n. 4
strophe, 14n. 15, 15
suffixes, rare, 31–33
synecdoche, 129–30, 129n. 18, 130n. 19, 159n. 2, 163
synonymous parallelism
  ellipsis in, 48–50, 53
  grammatical, 45, 57–58, 57n. 27, 58n. 31
  internal half-line, 50–52
  linguistic, 57

and pacing, 205
phonological, 57, 58–59n. 31, 61–63
quatrain, 53–54
semantic, 45–50, 51, 53, 57, 58n. 31
strict, 47, 51, 54, 67, 205, 212, 217, 218
syntactic, 45
tricola examples, 52–54
types of, 44–45
typical sequencing of, 45, 66
syntax, terse, 11n. 8, 25–28, 27n. 13, 28n. 14

temporal relationship between cola, 104–5
terraced pattern, 81–83, 83n. 19, 150, 205, 226
terse syntax, 11n. 8, 25–28, 27n. 13, 28n. 14
text presentation, 6–7, 13n. 12
tricolon (pl. tricola), 14, 23, 52–54

variant refrain, 90, 91–93, 92n. 4
verses, 14, 15
verset. *See* stanza
vocabulary, in Hebrew poetry, 29–30

wayyiqtol sequences
 frequency of use of, 28–29
 use of in poetry, 11, 28, 104

wisdom literature, 175n. 22
wisdom poetry, 12, 236–40
"word," use of in poetry, 29
word pairs
 augmented, 42
 criteria for, 41–42, 41n. 6
 definition, 41
 intensification in, 45–46
 lack of synonymity in, 43, 45
 numerical, 43–44
 origins of, 41, 41n. 4, 43n. 8
 other names for, 41n. 3
 reasons for use of, 44
 sound pairs, 148
wordplay
 alliteration, 51, 144–46, 144n. 4, 146n. 5, 146n. 6, 146n. 7, 147n. 10, 152
 anadiplosis, 149–50, 149n. 17
 function of, 152–53
 identifying, 140, 144–45, 150, 151, 152, 153
 irony. *See* irony
 paronomasia, 140–44
 proper noun, 150–52, 152n. 20
 rhyme. *See* rhyme
words, as component of Hebrew poetry, 13–14

Author Index

Allen, Leslie C., 234
Alsene-Parker, Megan, 111
Alter, Robert, 12, 179, 197
Assis, Elie, 111
Avishur, Yitsa, 51

Bellinger, W. H., Jr., 197
Berlin, Adele, 62, 63, 148, 208
Bloch, Yigal, 32
Brogan, T. V. F., 137
Brueggemann, Walter, 197
Buber, Martin, 179
Bullinger, E. W., 119, 128, 130, 131, 133, 176, 177, 179
Burnett, Joel S., 214

Carasik, Michael, 86
Casonowicz, Immanuel M., 146, 147, 148, 150
Ceresko, Anthony R., 77, 80, 86, 157, 162
Chisholm, Robert B., 199
Collins, C. John, 104
Craigie, Peter, 221, 234
Cuddon, J. A., 14, 15, 179

Dahood, Mitchell J., 208
de Hoop, Raymond, 22, 24
Delitzsch, Franz, 208
DeRouchie, Jason Shane, 206
Dobs-Allsopp, F. W., 113
Doron, Pinchas, 153
Driver, Samuel R., 240
Duriez, Colin, 121, 122, 123, 130, 139

Duvall, J. Scott, 206

Eakins, J. Kenneth, 136
Emanuel, David, 187, 188, 197, 207

Floyd, Michael H., 110
Fokkelman, J. P., 193, 208
Freedman, David Noel, 4, 110, 199
Futato, Mark David, 21, 24

Gaines, Jason M. H., 78, 149
Giffone, Benjamin D., 110, 111, 112
Goh, Samuel T. S., 11, 12, 16, 235
Gordis, Robert, 174
Greenstein, Edward L., 63

Hays, J. Daniel, 206
Henry, Matthew, 208
Holladay, William L., 148
Holmstedt, Robert D., 40, 102
Honeyman, A. M., 159
Hossfeld, Frank-Lothar, 214
Hurvitz, Avi, 236, 238

James, Elaine T., 110
Jastrow, Marcus, 31
Joüon, Paul, 25, 31, 223, 226
Justiss, Joseph L., 110

Kaiser, Walter C., 206
Kalimi, Isaac, 80, 88, 179
Keil, Karl Friedrich, 208
Klaus, Natan, 10

Kraus, Hans-Joachim, 197, 216, 234
Kugel, James L., 45, 46
Kurylowicz, Jerzy, 234

Leonard, Jeffery M., 185, 188
Lillas, Rosmari, 167
Loewenstamm, Samuel E., 63, 179
Longman, Tremper, III, 121, 122, 123, 130, 139, 199, 234
Lowth, Robert, 39, 40, 44, 63, 102
Lund, Nils Wilhelm, 10
Lunn, Nicholas P., 12, 28
Lyon, Ashley E., 221

Manser, Martin H., 208
McComiskey, Thomas Edward, 126
Melamed, E. Z., 43
Meshel, Naphtali, 154
Moshavi, Adina Mosak, 174
Muilenburg, James, 219
Muraoka, T., 5

Noegel, Scott B., 86
Noonan, Benjamin J., 198

O'Connell, Robert H., 44
O'Connor, M., 198, 222
O'Connor, Michael Patrick, 40
Olley, John W., 98

Patton, Matthew H., 104, 107, 198, 234
Paul, Shalom M., 143
Penney, Douglas, 121, 122, 123, 130, 139
Pinker, Aron, 110
Preminger, Alex, 137
Putnam, Frederic C., 104, 107

Reid, Daniel G., 121, 122, 123, 130, 139
Rendsburg, Gary, 86, 148
Roth, Wolfgang M. W., 44

Ruiz, Javier Herrero, 175
Ryken, Leland, 121, 122, 123, 128, 130, 137, 139, 158, 179

Samet, Nili, 183
Sanders, Paul, 22, 24
Schniedwind, William, 148
Schökel, Luis Alonso, 43, 69, 131, 146, 173, 208
Segert, Stanislav, 41
Seidel, Moshe, 80
Shemesh, Y., 144, 153
Sivan, Daniel, 148
Sommer, Benjamin, 183, 188
Speiser, E. A., 167
Strauss, Mark L., 199
Stuart, Douglas K., 206, 234

Tate, Marvin E., 221, 234
Tov, Emanuel, 21, 24, 199
Tsumura, David Toshio, 43, 86

Van Pelt, Miles V., 104, 107

Waltke, Bruce K., 198, 222
Wansbrough, John, 179
Watson, Rebecca S., 174
Watson, Wilfred G. E., 12, 14, 35, 41, 51, 52, 59, 60, 63, 66, 68, 74, 85, 89, 90, 93, 110, 112, 113, 114, 120, 139, 144, 146, 162, 169, 173, 174, 208
Weber, Beat, 153
Weiss, Meir, 11, 44, 80, 193
Wendland, Ernst R., 56, 57, 193, 201, 208, 234
Wilhoit, Jim, 121, 122, 123, 130, 139
Williams, Ronald J., 167, 219
Williamson, H. G. M., 188

Yoder, Perry B., 41

www.ingramcontent.com/pod-product-compliance
Lightning Source LLC
Chambersburg PA
CBHW060726201225
36978CB00017B/163